THE LAWYER'S GUIDE TO
Collaboration Tools and Technologies

Smart Ways to Work Together

Dennis Kennedy

Tom Mighell

LAW PRACTICE MANAGEMENT SECTION
MARKETING • MANAGEMENT • TECHNOLOGY • FINANCE

Commitment to Quality: The Law Practice Management Section is committed to quality in our publications. Our authors are experienced practitioners in their fields. Prior to publication, the contents of all our books are rigorously reviewed by experts to ensure the highest quality product and presentation. Because we are committed to serving our readers' needs, we welcome your feedback on how we can improve future editions of this book.

Screen shots reprinted with permission from their respective owners. All rights reserved.

Cover design by Jim Colao.

Nothing contained in this book is to be considered as the rendering of legal advice for specific cases, and readers are responsible for obtaining such advice from their own legal counsel. This book and any forms and agreements herein are intended for educational and informational purposes only.

The products and services mentioned in this publication are under or may be under trademark or service mark protection. Product and service names and terms are used throughout only in an editorial fashion, to the benefit of the product manufacturer or service provider, with no intention of infringement. Use of a product or service name or term in this publication should not be regarded as affecting the validity of any trademark or service mark.

The Law Practice Management Section, American Bar Association, offers an educational program for lawyers in practice. Books and other materials are published in furtherance of that program. Authors and editors of publications may express their own legal interpretations and opinions, which are not necessarily those of either the American Bar Association or the Law Practice Management Section unless adopted pursuant to the bylaws of the Association. The opinions expressed do not reflect in any way a position of the Section or the American Bar Association.

Printed in the United States of America.

10 09 08   5 4 3 2 1

Library of Congress Cataloging-in-Publication Data

Mighell, Thomas L.
  The lawyer's guide to collaboration tools and technologies / by Thomas L. Mighell and Dennis M. Kennedy.—1st ed.
      p. cm.
  Includes index.
  ISBN-13: 978-1-59031-979-6
  ISBN-10: 1-59031-979-6
  1. Law offices—United States—Automation. 2. Trial practice—United States—Technological innovations. I. Kennedy, Dennis M., 1958– II. Title.

  KF320.A9M54 2008
  340.068—dc22

                                                                            2008002931

Discounts are available for books ordered in bulk. Special consideration is given to state bars, CLE programs, and other bar-related organizations. Inquire at Book Publishing, ABA Publishing, American Bar Association, 321 North Clark Street, Chicago, Illinois 60610-4714.

www.ababooks.org

Contents at a Glance

Contents

Chapter 10
Hidden Dangers, Security, and Metadata   73

PART IV
COLLABORATION ON CASES, TRANSACTIONS,
AND PROJECTS   79

Chapter 11
Benefits of Collaboration in Lawsuits and Transactions   81

Chapter 12
Instant Collaboration—from Conference Calls
to Instant Messaging   87

Chapter 24
Collaboration Tools: Free vs. Pay   185

Chapter 25
Involving Clients in Your Decisions and Choices   191

Chapter 26
Determining Which Factors Will Drive Your Strategic Planning   197

PART VII
PRACTICAL ISSUES, TIPS, AND TECHNIQUES   203

Chapter 33
Creating a Culture of Collaboration   245

Chapter 34
The Future of Collaboration in the Practice of Law   253

Appendix 1: Glossary   257

Appendix 2: Collaboration Resources   263

Appendix 3: Tools by Category   275

About the Authors

Dennis Kennedy is an information technology lawyer and legal technologist based in St. Louis, Missouri. A frequent speaker and an award-winning author with hundreds of publications to his credit, Dennis writes the legal technology column for the *ABA Journal* and his articles on legal technology and electronic discovery topics can be found in many print and Internet publications. His blog, DennisKennedy.Blog (http://www.denniskennedy .com/blog/), is a highly regarded resource on legal technology topics.

Dennis was named a Top 100 global legal technology leader in 2006 by London's *CityTech* magazine, and received awards as the 2001 TechnoLawyer of the Year, and 2003 Contributor of the Year from TechnoLawyer.com for his role in promoting the use of technology in the practice of law. He is a member of the ABA Law Practice Management Section's Council and is an editor and board member of the *Law Practice Today* webzine (http://www.lawpracticetoday.org). Dennis received his J.D., cum laude, from the Georgetown University Law Center in 1983 and B.A., magna cum laude, from Wabash College in 1980.

Tom Mighell is Senior Counsel and Litigation Technology Support Coordinator at Cowles & Thompson in Dallas, Texas. Tom is a frequent speaker and writer on the Internet and legal technology issues. Tom has published the *Internet Legal Research Weekly* newsletter since 2000, and the Internet research and legal technology weblog Inter Alia (www.inter-alia.net) since 2002. Tom's blog was named one of the "ABA Blawg 100," as one of the Top 100 law-related weblogs on the Internet. Tom is a regular contributor to *Law Practice* magazine, the webzines *Law Practice Today* and *Law Technology Today*, and his articles have appeared in many national and Texas-based legal publications.

Tom served on the ABA TECHSHOW® planning board from 2003 through 2008, and served as Chair of ABA TECHSHOW® 2008. He is a member of the ABA's Law Practice Management Section and serves on the Section's Council. Tom received both his B.A. (1987) and J.D. (1990) degrees from the University of Texas at Austin.

Acknowledgments

Any book, but especially a book about collaboration, is the result of the work, influence, and, indeed, collaboration of many people. We want to acknowledge the many people who have taught us, mentored us, worked with us, and written with us over the years. Each played a part in helping us reach a point where we could give this book life. We want to single out for special thanks our friends and colleagues in the legal technology and legal blogging communities.

This book arose from the persistence and confidence of Bev Loder that we had a book inside us that needed to be written, and we are grateful to her for pushing us toward this project. We also want to thank the ABA Law Practice Management Section's Publishing Board and publishing team for all their efforts, especially Sharon Nelson and Tim Johnson. Annie Beck and her team at Lachina Publishing Services made the copyediting and production process easy and painless.

A big thank you to Bruce Olson for all his great work as a first-time project manager on our first-ever book and for turning around his review of our first draft in record time.

Dennis wants to acknowledge his parents, Dale and Evelyn Kennedy, for their constant example of how to work together with others and how helping others brings its own rewards. The book would not be possible without his wife, Colleen, and daughter and future author, Grace, who not only helped with page proofs, but whose love and inspiration make all things possible. Dennis appreciates their patience and tolerance with the time and energy that he had to take from them to put into this book.

Tom likewise acknowledges the people who collaborated to become his parents, Ken and Judy Mighell, and thanks them for their love, support, and for showing him that cooperation and working together leads to the best, longest-lasting relationships. Tom also wants to thank Kenny Coupel for his infinite patience, love, and encouragement not only during the writing of this book, but also in all of Tom's extracurricular legal technology activities.

Introduction

Introduction 1

We trace the birth of the idea for this book to a column we wrote called "The Strongest Links: Instant Messaging Resources" in September 2005 for the ABA's *Law Practice Today* webzine. We had been cowriting the regular monthly column on the best Internet resources for lawyers on a variety of law practice management topics for some time. For fun, and to find a different way to work together, we wrote the column in real time as an instant messaging session using Skype's instant messaging tools—including emoticons and acronyms like IMHO and FWIW.

Although we were intrigued by how well our column on instant messaging turned out—it's one of our favorite columns—we did not return to Skype or instant messaging as a writing tool. Our writing practices seemed to lend themselves more to asynchronous (not occurring at the same time) rather than real-time collaboration. However, it's also important to note that we never returned to our previous practice of one of us writing the first draft in Microsoft Word and sending it to the other as an email attachment, then the other making revisions and additions and emailing it back as an attachment, and so on until we were done.

In large part, the reason was that in August 2005, the Writely online word processing tool arrived on the Internet. Both of us began using Writely in September 2005, and we began to use it for articles we cowrote with others. Google later purchased Writely in 2006 and renamed it Google Docs, and we have consistently written our columns and articles using this online tool.

As time passed, we started each column in Google Docs. Each of us would add to and edit the column over the course of a few days or a week, working on it whenever we had a little time or a new idea. And an interesting thing happened. The columns started to have a voice that was a combination of the two of us. Dennis recalls a time when he read a paragraph in a column and realized that he could not tell which of us had written or revised it, and that it was better than what either of us would have written alone.

As we looked at the methods we used to collaborate and started to look at all of the other tools that might be available, we began to realize that technology was evolving toward the development of "social networking" and different collaborative tools. We also saw how the tools we were using, especially Google Docs, had practical implications for the practice of law, not just our writing.

Both of us also maintain blogs that cover legal technology and Internet topics. As bloggers, we saw how we and other bloggers were starting to use wikis and other collaboration tools on a regular basis. The "Web 2.0" era of Internet applications was in full swing, and our blogging friends seemed to be trying and recommending Web 2.0 tools on a daily basis. When we wrote about Web 2.0 resources for lawyers in our "Strongest Links" column in January 2006, we were struck by the way innovative solo and small firm lawyers had already experimented with these tools. With low-cost services like Basecamp, these lawyers had done things for themselves and their clients that many large law firms hadn't even tried with the high-end applications they already owned.

Another step in the evolution of collaboration technologies involved Microsoft Office 2007, which became a great example of the way software vendors started to incorporate collaboration features into the standard programs lawyers use on a daily basis. Adobe Acrobat 8 also included significant improvements in its collaboration features. In fact, everywhere we looked we found standard legal technology tools with new collaboration capabilities.

At the same time, Wikipedia captured everyone's attention as a new form of collaborative encyclopedia. Several legal wikis followed the Wikipedia model. We saw Microsoft SharePoint, a collaboration tool, becoming the hot topic at legal technology conferences we attended. The explosion of electronic discovery in litigation also required the use of collaborative tools for review, case management, document storage, and other legal tasks.

As we worked with our friends and colleagues on various projects, we saw the value of these tools. We also saw conference calls, webinars, document sharing, and other methods of collaboration becoming more routine in the practice of law. At the same time, we saw lawyers struggling to learn how to use redlining tools and Track Changes and to deal with the whole issue of metadata in documents. Collaboration tools brought both a new promise and a new layer of challenges to the legal profession. In his annual article on legal technology trends, Dennis highlighted collaboration technologies as one of his top legal trends to watch for in 2007.

Collaboration has always been part of the development of legal technology. Developments in electronic discovery have clearly begun to drive lawyers, clients, and vendors to work together in new ways. Outsourcing and working from remote locations have also grown in popularity in the legal profession.

We concluded that collaboration technologies and tools are the most important current development in legal technology and are likely to remain so for the foreseeable future. *Legal technology has reached a turning point; it is less about personal productivity and more about using technology to make it easier for people to work together.* This book grew out of that realization. We hope to give you a guidebook to our collaborative future and help you select the tools and strategies that will serve you well now and for years to come.

We chose to write this book using the collaboration tools we discuss in this book. In the computer business, that is often referred to as "eating your own dog food." In other words, it means having the courage to use your own products. This book reflects our own practical experience using these tools.

Each of the chapters was written as a separate document on Google Docs. One of us started each chapter, and then both of us revised and finished the chapters on Google Docs. We stored and shared research by sharing bookmarks through Yahoo's MyWeb. We used email much less than you might expect, although it was our primary channel to work with our editors and publishers. We often used Skype instant messaging to discuss new ideas and directions for the book and to divide work assignments. An outline and a couple of simple spreadsheets in Google Docs turned into our project management tools. When we spoke to each other, we used Skype, especially if we wanted to record our conversation about the book for later use. We used plain old telephone calls when we needed to talk through the division of work, deadlines, and how we planned to write chapters—what to leave out, and more often, what to include. We also spent some time experimenting with the tools we discuss in the book. Our hands-on experience using these collaboration tools provides many of the practical insights and tips you will learn in this book.

Who Should Read This Book?

- Practicing lawyers
- Paralegals, secretaries, librarians, and other legal professionals who work with lawyers
- Executive directors and office managers of law firms and law departments

- CIOs, IT directors, and technology committees of firms making decisions about implementing collaborative technologies
- Clients of lawyers
- Software vendors and others who work with lawyers

What You Will Learn

- Collaboration technologies now available to lawyers
- Practical tips for using collaboration tools in common settings
- How to select the right tools and understand the issues involved in using collaboration technologies
- Trends and developments in collaboration tools
- How to make decisions about what collaboration tools to use in a variety of settings

What We Will Cover

Part II: Getting Started

In this part, you will learn the basics of collaboration and collaboration tools and be introduced to some of the underlying themes of this book. In Chapter 2, we describe how lawyers have reached a crossroads in the use of collaboration tools. We believe these tools are evolutionary rather than revolutionary, but the benefits of using them well might be revolutionary indeed. What lawyers traditionally have used for collaboration has served them well in many cases, but we have reached a point where lawyers and those who work with lawyers must consider new directions, or have those directions chosen for them by others. Chapters 3 and 4 discuss the important distinctions between collaborating within the organization and outside the organization. Chapter 5 ends Part II with a road map of steps to consider when you are beginning to use collaboration tools.

Part III: Collaborating on Documents, Online and Off

It's easy to take the simplest form of collaboration—working together on a legal document—for granted. In this part, you will learn about the wide range of ways you can now collaborate on electronic documents and get some practical lessons on how to improve your work processes on this most common of all legal tasks. Chapter 6 explores the many benefits of improving your ability to collaborate on documents. Chapter 7 delivers practical tips and lessons for basic document collaboration, including "track changes" and redlining tools. Chapters 8 and 9 introduce you to the new world of online document sharing and demonstrate how these services can help improve your ability to collaborate on documents with others. Chapter 10 takes a hard look at the potential difficulties and dangers of document collaboration, including backup and security issues.

Part IV: Collaboration on Cases, Transactions, and Projects

While collaboration on documents is useful, it's even more interesting and beneficial in the broader context of cases and transactions. In this part, you will learn practical ways to use collaboration tools to manage your cases and transactions like projects. Chapter 11 looks at the many benefits of using online collaboration tools in both litigation and transactional matters. Chapter 12 looks at real-time collaboration—from the standard conference call to instant messaging and beyond. In Chapter 13, we move to a basic building block of online collaboration—holding a meeting on the Internet. Chapter 14 discusses simple project management tools and how legal professionals can use them. Part IV ends with Chapter 15's discussion of a great example of advanced online collaboration—extranets and deal rooms.

Part V: Commonly Used Collaboration Platforms

Increasingly, collaboration takes place by means of the Internet, and many of the tools we discuss in this part make use of the online medium. Here we move from the different ways that you might use collaboration tools to the main platforms people use to collaborate. There's no question that email is the dominant platform on which collaboration occurs today, and Chapter 16 takes a look at whether email should remain the primary medium of collaboration and how to use it better. Chapter 17 focuses on Microsoft's SharePoint, perhaps the most-discussed collaboration platform in the legal profession. Chapter 18 expands on Chapter 15 and takes a closer look at the extranet platform. Chapter 19 looks at Adobe Acrobat, an increasingly ubiquitous tool in the legal profession, and some of the opportunities it offers as a collaboration platform. Chapters 20 and 21 introduce you to the new species of Internet collaboration tools often referred to as Web 2.0, including wikis, which are important enough to rate a whole chapter. Part V ends with Chapter 22's survey of a wide range of specialty collaboration platforms.

Part VI: Developing a Collaboration Strategy

In this part, we discuss different ways of thinking about collaboration tools, as well as formulating strategies and making decisions for you, your firm, or your organization. In Chapter 23, we cover the features of collaboration tools we consider to be must-haves. Chapter 24 guides you through one of the most interesting aspects of collaboration technologies—many of the worthy tools we discuss in this book are free. Chapter 25 offers important advice for involving clients in your collaboration decisions. Finally, in Chapter 26 we'll provide you with a practical guide to help you formulate your collaboration strategy.

Part VII: Practical Issues, Tips, and Techniques

In this part, we get practical and offer some of our best tips on several key topics. Chapter 27 focuses on the importance of communication within collaboration tools and how to deal with the thorny problem of "silos of information." Chapter 28 addresses ethical, security, and other concerns you should consider carefully before diving into the use of collaboration technologies. Chapter 29 surveys the complex world of ownership, control, and other legal issues involved in using these tools. Although we have a very positive view of collaboration tools, we also recognize it's vital to understand the risks and concerns involved in using them; Chapter 30 addresses the potential pitfalls of using collaboration technologies. And Chapter 31 lists some of our best practical tips for implementing collaboration tools, no matter the size of your firm or organization.

Part VIII: Conclusion

In this part, we pull all of the topics together and offer guidance in three important areas. Chapter 32 presents recommendations for choices of collaboration tools to consider in a wide variety of settings. Chapter 33 recognizes that it's people, not technology, who make collaboration tools work best, and it offers advice for creating the necessary culture of collaboration within your organization. Chapter 34 ends with a look into the crystal ball and the future of collaboration in the practice of law.

The book's appendices include a helpful glossary of terms (words that appear in **boldface** in the text are defined in the glossary), lists of useful resources, and a first-of-its-kind list of legal collaboration tools by category.

In the end, as we discuss in Chapter 33, we found that the particular tools you use are less important than establishing the right culture of collaboration. Having written articles, produced podcasts, and prepared presentations together for several years, we felt this book was a natural step in the evolution of our own collaborative process. We could have used several different tools rather than the ones we chose to write this book; there are many good choices out there. When you choose your collaboration tools, you will want the ones that best fit your style of collaboration. The tools that evolve out of and mesh with the ways that you already work with others give you the greatest chance for successful projects. Let's get started down that road.

Getting Started

Collaboration at the Crossroads 2

Collaboration has never been optional for lawyers. The image of the solitary lawyer fighting for justice against overwhelming odds may be the attraction that leads many individuals to law school. But practicing lawyers know better. The practice of law is, has been, and will continue to be a collaborative process. Lawyers collaborate with clients, colleagues, and others every day and in many ways.

The idea of the solitary lawyer battling the forces of injustice is also a classic theme seen in movies and television, but it breaks apart quickly under close examination. Even the most solo of solo practitioners routinely works in collaboration with a wide range of people. Lawyers work with a significant number and variety of categories of people and service providers in firms or organizations. Many of these categories—clients, partners, associates, paralegals, and secretaries—are familiar to us. Many others—IT staff, litigation support managers, marketing directors, third-party service providers—represent relatively new developments in the profession.

Let's think about who the average lawyer might work with during an average day in an average practice:

- Attorneys and paralegals within the firm—Partners (equity and non-equity), senior counsel, associates (partner-track and non-partner track), part-time lawyers, contract lawyers, law clerks, and paralegals (generalists and specialists)
- Staff—Secretaries, administrative assistants, office managers, bookkeepers and accountants, receptionists,

- messengers, mail and copy room workers, IT directors, IT staff, librarians, litigation and practice support personnel, and a growing variety of personnel that depends upon the size and practice areas of the firm or organization
- In-house counsel, "C-level" executives and their respective staffs, including the chief executive officer, chief financial officer, human resources director, and others
- Opposing counsel and their staffs
- Court personnel, judges, and professionals in regulatory agencies
- Experts and specialists (medical, accounting, forensics, et al.)
- Vendors—providers of various products and services
- Other lawyers—through member associations, networks, or mailing lists
- Clients—the most important collaborators of all, often with several points of contact

If you check your notes and time sheets for the past few weeks, you probably will be surprised by the number and variety of people with whom you have collaborated, even if you are a solo working alone out of a home office. Just take a few minutes to identify your collaborators using the bullet list above, and you'll appreciate that a law practice is, at its root, a collaborative proposition.

Although lawyers have been collaborating with each other since the beginning of the practice of law, the methods of collaboration have evolved significantly over time. Nowhere is this more evident than in the evolution of the modern law office. Twenty years ago, the classic lawyer's office had a massive and authoritative desk with a large, imposing leather chair. The bookshelves that were full of treatises and other legal books have become a cliché. We chuckle when we see shelves of old law books behind a lawyer interviewed on television today. The desk was covered with legal pads and file folders, and often more paper than most nonlawyers would see in a lifetime. Filing cabinets and two chairs set in front of the desk completed the arrangement. As a lawyer rose through the partner ranks, a small conference table might be added, in part to hold meetings but more often to hold more file folders and legal pads. The lawyer's technology consisted of a telephone and, in many cases, some form of dictation equipment. Tax and deal lawyers sometimes had calculators out on their desks. Legal work was largely done with pen, pencil, and paper, much as it had been done for decades—if not centuries.

In contrast, the focal point of today's law office is typically a computer. The computer monitor is often the most imposing and impressive part of the office, at times obscuring a visitor's view of the lawyer behind it. The file folders and legal pads remain, but the working parts of the files reside on the computer system more so than on the papers. As the traditional lawyer's desk proved to be ergonomically unsuitable for working at a computer all day, lawyers have moved either to separate computer workstations beside their desks, or to desks no different than those you would find in any other business setting. The books on the shelves are often untouched, as are the filing cabinets. Office technology has changed dramatically; many lawyers now use notebook computers, would be lost without BlackBerrys and cell phones, and have at their disposal scanners, printers, and other electronic accessories.

The evolution of the law office is but one indicator of the great changes that have taken place in the legal profession over the last twenty years. The practice of law is more electronic, digital, and reliant on technology than ever before. While technology has no doubt changed the way lawyers provide legal services and the documents that are its primary deliverables, the greatest change brought about by technology is the way lawyers use it to collaborate with others in their practices.

There's a well-worn adage that the only lawyer in a town starves until a second lawyer opens a practice, and then they both thrive. The adage contains an important truth about the legal profession as well as the subject of this book; it emphasizes that in the legal profession, collaboration can take many forms.

"Collaborate" originates from the Latin "collaborare," meaning simply "to work with." For our purposes, we define collaboration broadly to mean working together with others in a cooperative or joint effort. Collaboration can occur when everyone is on the same side and working at the same purpose. It can also occur when opposing sides are forced, often grudgingly, to work together to accomplish a goal or project.

As we have discussed, a lawyer's typical day requires a wide range of collaborative efforts, from negotiations to putting agreements in final form to trying cases to filing patents. Day after day, there are exchanges of information, agreements, approvals, delegation of projects, and other work requiring the involvement and cooperation of other people. Lawyers take much of this collaboration for granted, as an assumed part of the practice.

A recurring theme of this book will be that the movement to electronic and digital tools for collaboration is evolutionary, not revolutionary. Lawyers consistently adapt the same fundamental collaborative acts to different technologies as those technologies have evolved. The greatest difference today is that the rise of the Internet has increased dramatically the pace of technological change, resulting in an explosion of the number and variety of collaborative tools.

A few examples will illustrate the role technology plays in the evolution of the ways lawyers work with others. Consider the movement from wax seals to ink signatures to electronic signatures. The fundamental legal process—obtaining legally valid confirmation of the agreement of a specific individual or entity—has remained the same. The process and the technology, however, have evolved. Similarly, lawyers who once attended meetings by walking, riding a horse, driving a car, or flying in a plane now do so by telephone or video conference.

Has this easily understood evolutionary process itself changed in the last few years? Are we now moving toward a time of revolutionary change? That is a possibility, and we will note in this book where we see potentially revolutionary changes occurring. When it comes to collaboration technologies, we believe the changes are more evolutionary than revolutionary. However, the legal profession is experiencing a rapid increase in the *pace* of evolution. The fundamental legal processes, tasks, and activities have not, and likely will not, change drastically. Legal services are based on a traditional core or set of time-honored practices. At the same time, the tools that lawyers use to provide those services *are* changing rapidly. It is the increased pace of that change, more than the actual changes, that will put the greatest pressure on lawyers.

Our advice to you is not to think of lawyer collaboration tools as evolutionary, or even revolutionary, but as *coevolutionary*. The tools enable and shape what lawyers do; at the same time, lawyers define, shape, and change the tools at their disposal. This is a symbiotic process that lawyers who take advantage of and successfully use collaboration tools will understand.

As you read this book, you will be struck by the wide range of tools now available to lawyers. In particular, the Internet-based tools seem to grow in number and variety every day. You can be certain that this book discusses more tools than you will have time to evaluate, understand, or use. To get the most out of this book, take the time to gain a basic understanding of how collaborative technologies work and then choose those tools that work best for you in your practice.

The choice of collaboration tools does not occur in a vacuum. You may be forced to use some collaboration tools by the requirements and mandates of others. Think about how you and your firm first began to use fax machines, email, conference calls, FedEx, or any number of the collaborative technologies we now take for granted. It's a surprisingly small step from where you may be now to the world of instant messaging, videoconferencing, extranets, deal rooms, and wikis.

Every practicing lawyer, including you, will inevitably arrive at a crossroads in connection with the collaboration tools he or she uses. Until now, the tools you use have probably worked well for you. However, you may be feeling the pressure of things to come, with the push coming from clients, opposing counsel, the courts, young lawyers, and others. How do you move confidently and successfully forward into the rapidly changing world of collaboration tools for lawyers? The following chapters will show you the way.

Collaboration Inside the Office | **3**

One of the simplest and yet most effective ways to begin our discussion on collaboration and collaboration tools is to visualize two different types of collaboration—inside and outside the office. Technologists often refer to these two "zones" of collaboration as "inside the firewall" and "outside the firewall." Lawyers who can imagine collaboration tools existing both inside and outside the office will find it much easier to understand and address key issues like security, confidentiality, ethics, and even feature choices.

In this chapter, we look at collaboration inside the office—how people work together inside your firm, law department, government agency, or other organization. In the next chapter, we turn to external collaboration.

To get an idea of how collaboration works within the firewall, it is useful to take a closer look at an average day of an average lawyer—perhaps someone like you—with an eye toward the processes that lead you to work with others. Once we illustrate these processes, we will discuss the best way to determine the types of tools you will use to collaborate. We then will suggest that you begin looking at your own work processes to understand how you can put these tools to work for you as you collaborate with others in your practice.

Let's consider a partner in a law firm. This law firm partner will work with other partners, associates, paralegals, and a secretary on a daily basis. To a lesser extent, but still on a regular basis, the partner will work with other staff—from the receptionist to the librarian. All of this interaction typically involves some type of client work, but it all takes place inside the walls of the firm, as long as everyone happens to be in the office that day. As we look more closely at that client work, we can start to break it down into a number of common collaborative processes:

1. Routinely communicating with coworkers
2. Delegating work
3. Managing workflow (including status and deadlines)
4. Reviewing and approving work
5. Producing documents
6. Scheduling
7. Receiving internal news and updates (including "watercooler talk")

These processes can occur in both formal (structured) and informal (much less structured) ways. Even where formal systems have been implemented, the bulk of the activities involved in these processes happen on an informal basis.

A lawyer arriving at her firm in the morning might pick up a message from the receptionist and hear some bit of firm news or that another lawyer wants to speak to her. While walking down the hall to her office, she might get an update on a matter from a paralegal, or stick her head into an associate's office to ask him to stop by later. At her secretary's desk, she may receive messages, calendar updates, and new documents or files to review. Upon entering her office, she may find a new file, a memo, or even a sticky note with a new assignment, question, or reminder. And all of this activity occurs before she even checks for phone or email messages.

Lawyers may look back with fondness on the early days of their practices and think about the many strategies they developed to get into a busy partner's office to talk about a matter or get a question answered. In many firms, leaving completed assignments for review on a partner's chair or with a secretary was the accepted practice. These were the tools of collaboration because they fit the reality of the workplace.

We've listed the seven basic processes used by lawyers to collaborate with others inside the office. Let's further consider each in turn, both in terms of the "tools" lawyers have long used and how electronic tools are now entering into the equation.

Routinely Communicating

With busy lawyers, routine communication usually takes the path of least resistance, and is in whatever form that works at that particular moment. Face-to-face communication is always possible in law firms, but sometimes not as often as people might like. Phone calls, voice mail messages, written notes of all forms, sticky notes that say "sign" or "review," messages left with secretaries, and many other forms of routine communication have been used for years. Nowadays, email, instant messaging, pagers, and other technological tools may be more successful at getting the attention of and communicating with busy lawyers. If a partner religiously checks her email on a BlackBerry, a lawyer two offices away who is trying to communicate with her may well email her rather than walk down the hall. Collaboration tools include the telephone, phone message pads, pens and pencils, sticky notes, and almost anything else that can communicate a message effectively.

Delegating Work

Projects are assigned in several different ways. In the ideal world, communication of delegation is clear and direct. A partner calls an associate into his or her office and talks about the background of the project, the file, the expectations, and the expected work product. More often than not, however, work gets delegated by leaving the file on an associate's chair with a sticky note that says "see me" or "cover hearing on motion this morning." While the assignment of projects tends to be an informal and personal process, some firms make use of an assignment binder, especially in summer clerk programs and for some associate projects. Email and voice mail have also become standard tools of delegation in recent years. In some firms, case management and workflow tools are used to make and keep track of work assignments. The most important development in this area may be the changing notion of what constitutes a "file," as we move away from standard paper file folders passed from lawyer to lawyer to an "electronic file" accessible to many lawyers at the same time.

Managing Workflow

Once a project is assigned, lawyers manage the progress of the project in various ways. Most of them are interpersonal, and many involve management techniques that will never be praised in any management course or manual. Legal projects tend to take the form of one lawyer or paralegal preparing a draft of a document that will be reviewed and moved forward by the assigning lawyer. Some lawyers have "dockets" that list all of their projects and their expected deadlines. "Management" most often occurs by contacting the lawyer or paralegal working on the project when the assigning lawyer starts to get nervous about an upcoming deadline. To a limited extent, case management software, use of Microsoft Outlook features (including tasks, calendars, and shared folders), and workflow tools are being used to manage the progress of legal work, but typical project and workflow management tools used in other businesses and industries are not common in the legal profession.

Reviewing and Approving Work

A cherished rite of passage for young lawyers is the turning in of a memorandum or document to a partner, and receiving it back covered in red ink with corrections and comments. The term "bleeding memo" is often used to describe this phenomenon. The process of a lawyer preparing a draft for another occurs more often in large firms; in smaller firms, lawyers may ask their colleagues for comments and proofreading. In any firm, this process generally involves giving the reviewing lawyer a typed draft of the document. That lawyer reads it, makes revisions and comments on the paper draft, and then returns it either to the preparing lawyer or to a secretary for generation of a new or final draft. The process is one that can be made completely digital, limited to a transmittal and revision of documents in electronic form. Some tools, including the Track Changes function in Microsoft Office, are increasingly used in the everyday practice of law for these purposes. Other document review, transmittal, and content management software tools offer lawyers a growing number of options to improve this process. However, many lawyers still prefer to read and mark up the actual paper document.

Producing Documents

The primary deliverable for many legal services engagements will be some form of document. The drafting and preparing of documents has long been one of the most collaborative areas in the practice of law. Handwritten and dictated drafts move from lawyers to secretaries, word processor operators, and transcriptionists for preparation of drafts or final documents. And although the creation of many documents now takes place more regularly on a lawyer's computer, they are still often passed on to a secretary or assistant for polishing and then distribution. As document management and assembly tools have appeared in firms and law departments, lawyers have a greater ability to locate and repurpose documents prepared by others in their firm and take advantage of the experience and expertise of those who have prepared similar documents.

Scheduling

Lawyers *live* off their calendars. In the not so distant past, the desks of many lawyers featured both a large desk calendar with a monthly view as well as a daily calendar. Their secretaries kept an identical calendar (or so everyone hoped). Lawyers shared their calendars by having others physically look at it, or having others ask their secretary. Lawyers would change appointments by crossing out the entry on one day and writing it in on the new day, or even by talking a secretary into scheduling time on the other lawyer's calendar. Today, lawyers tend to use either an Outlook-type calendar or a case management tool with an electronic calendar. Appointments can be easily added, changed, or removed on electronic calendars. Lawyers are also able to share their calendars with others, who can then set appointments by finding open times on the lawyer's schedule.

Receiving Internal News and Updates

Traditionally, lawyers learned firm or company information through stopping by a colleague's office for a chat, engaging in hallway conversations, or receiving paper memos distributed to employees. Technology makes dissemination of firm news much more efficient and economical. Telephone conversations became common as firms claimed whole floors of buildings as well as multiple floors. Email offers savings in paper costs as well as easy and timely distribution. Instant messaging is also a new tool for quick conversations and status updates. Knowledge management and similar tools can be used as a way to capture and distribute the information formerly transferred through daily conversation, watercooler talk, or similar impromptu consultations. While we do not expect to see the wiki replace the watercooler in the near future, routine internal news, updates, and even gossip can be distributed within the firm using technology.

Even within the law office, collaboration tools, especially email, have made significant inroads in only the past few years. These tools are even more valuable to lawyers who work from home or on the road, and they are *vital* to firms with multiple offices.

Collaboration within the law office has always been a naturally occurring, relatively easy phenomenon, whether or not technology is used. The concerns that may arise in external collaboration simply are not present in an internal setting, or they can be satisfactorily addressed by IT staff.

Collaboration and transfer of information within the firm can generally be handled safely and securely; confidentiality, ethics, and privacy issues typically do not arise until the information passes outside the office firewall.

The underlying processes of collaboration within the law office often do, and in reality should, drive the selection of tools. In the internal setting, you can often improve your collaboration by making use of existing features in programs that you already own but are not currently using. Implementing "shared folders" in Outlook is just one of many examples we'll discuss in this book. Formal processes lend themselves better than informal processes to the implementation of internal collaboration tools.

From the simplest (Track Changes) to the more complex (intranets and sophisticated knowledge management tools), lawyers can benefit in many ways from the use of internal collaboration tools. Furthermore, lessons learned internally can later be applied to the more complex world of external collaboration. We'll take a closer look at specific internal collaboration platforms in Part V.

Collaboration Outside the Office 4

When collaboration moves outside the office, the potential benefits as well as the risks substantially increase. As a result, we must change both the way we think about collaboration and the tools we use to work with others outside the firm. While processes similar to those we discussed in Chapter 3 are at play, the motivation for using collaboration tools to further those processes changes, depending on the people with whom we work and the channels we use for this collaboration. In simplest terms, external collaboration takes us out onto the Internet, which can be a dangerous place.

Regarding the technology used, the essence of the change from collaboration inside to outside the office can be captured in the movement from the **intranet**—an internal website used by and accessible to members of a firm or organization—to the **extranet**, a private, secure website available over the Internet to anyone with permission to use it. Security and access rights are a greater concern with extranets because of their availability over the Internet, and because decisions must be made concerning the access to and use of firm information made available to outside parties.

As we'll discuss later in the book, large law firms (as well as some small firms and solos using tools like Basecamp) routinely set up extranets for many of their clients. These extranets allow the firm to share with its clients the documents and other information about their cases and matters. Extranets may take the form of litigation repositories or as deal rooms for transactions. They are a well-accepted and reasonably common form of external collaboration for lawyers, and they represent a sophisticated and advanced approach to the idea of external collaboration.

Let's step back and take a closer look at the basic ways lawyers collaborate externally and the tools they have used and might use in the future. In many ways, the processes for external collaboration echo those of internal collaboration, except that the parties with whom we collaborate are quite different and not always on the same side. As a result, we must consider new and additional issues.

As much as technology has changed the typical law office over time, so has it affected a lawyer's average day of dealing and working with people outside the office. A surprisingly large amount of any lawyer's time is now spent handling email and participating in conference calls. Even internal meetings routinely have a speakerphone in the center of the table for people who cannot attend in person.

Consider the people with whom a lawyer might work during an average day, who are not present in the office. The lawyer might email, call, or exchange documents with opposing counsel or even other lawyers in his firm who are on the road or working from home. He might contact court or regulatory personnel, judges, experts, vendors, witnesses, other professionals, and perhaps most importantly, clients in the same manner. The telephone and email are the most commonly used tools for outside collaboration, but other means of communication are also entering the picture.

The result is that lawyers are effectively "on call" and available more than ever before. BlackBerrys and cell phones make lawyers accessible to clients and others on an around-the-clock basis. Clients and other lawyers now expect you to be more responsive and able to handle work from wherever you happen to be. However, phone calls and email get you only part of the way there. The frantic pace of technological change often leaves lawyers pining for the old days when the day or two it took for mail to arrive gave them time to think. The word "instant" in instant messaging gives an unsettling insight to how the pace of a lawyer's practice can increase with technology.

Let's revisit the seven processes we considered for internal collaboration in the previous chapter and modify them slightly to fit what happens when working with others outside the office:

1. Routinely communicating with those outside the office
2. Delegating work/Initiating new projects
3. Managing workflow (including status and deadlines)
4. Reviewing and approving work/obtaining signatures on originals
5. Producing documents

6. Scheduling
7. Receiving news and updates

Routinely Communicating with Those Outside the Office

The days of the twelve-page, single-spaced, perfectly typed letter from a lawyer to his or her client are fading fast. The telephone is now the lawyer's primary channel for communication, and many lawyers work with a headset similar to those worn by telemarketers for ease of use and to prevent neck strain. As clients grew weary of being charged at regular hourly rates for chatty phone calls with their lawyers, email became an alternative form of communication. With email, it is conceivable that a lawyer could handle an entire project for a client without ever speaking to that client in person or on the phone. Another common channel of communication is the conference call, which allows many people in different places to come together easily without leaving their desks. In certain industries, instant messaging and other forms of rapid Internet communication are starting to make some inroads. A lawyer's use of the once-popular fax is on the decline, while attaching documents to email gains in popularity.

Delegating Work/Initiating Projects

The face-to-face meeting to kick off a project is becoming a rare event. Clients now initiate new projects by phone calls or email. Lawyers also commence projects with vendors, experts, or other lawyers in much the same way. Firms or companies that are already using extranets or instant messaging may begin projects using those tools instead.

Managing Workflow

Clients tend to use email or the phone to learn about the status of their projects. Lawyers also use email and telephone communications to manage workflow with opposing counsel, vendors, and other professionals. Extranets might be employed to manage a project—and to a lesser extent, clients or other professionals may work with an outline, a spreadsheet, or even a dedicated project management tool like Microsoft Project to map out timelines and manage responsibilities and deadlines.

Reviewing and Approving Work/Obtaining Signatures on Originals

Today, lawyers routinely send drafts of legal documents for review and approval as email attachments, usually in the form of editable Microsoft Office documents. Original documents might be couriered overnight to obtain original signatures, faxed, or scanned and emailed as attachments. The Track Changes feature in Microsoft Office is a commonly used tool to make and track revisions to documents. Many lawyers also use stand-alone redlining software programs to manage document revisions.

Producing Documents

In a transactional practice, two key questions are which form will be used, and who will produce the first or next draft of the document? Producing document drafts has become a highly collaborative process; the use of email and email attachments dominates this area of practice, and phone and conference calls are also being used to drive the process forward.

Scheduling

When it comes to scheduling meetings or conference calls, an astonishing amount of time is spent trying to coordinate calendars to find the best time to meet. Where secretaries once coordinated paper calendars, lawyers now email possible times back and forth using their electronic calendars in Outlook or in other software programs. Further, the ability to carry a calendar on a BlackBerry or smart phone is a huge convenience, enabling lawyers in court or in other settings to make appointments that can be synchronized with their calendars back at the office. We are now beginning to see tools that provide limited access via the Internet to calendars that facilitate the scheduling of calls and appointments.

Receiving News and Updates

Phone calls and email have become the primary channel for news and updates from outside the office, while periodicals and paper newsletters gradually have receded in importance and popularity. Extranets also offer a location where clients and others can visit to find news and updates at their convenience. **Blogs** and **Really Simple Syndication (RSS)** feeds provide other promising channels for pushing news out to clients and others.

Today, the telephone and email are clearly the lawyer's primary external collaboration tools. They have their benefits—familiarity, ubiquity, and suitability for many tasks. They also have limitations—spam filters, email overload, and it's not called "voice mail hell" without good reason. In the following chapters, we'll show you some of the advanced tools starting to take the place of phone calls and email.

Collaborating outside the office raises new concerns that are not present to the same extent in internal collaboration. These concerns deal primarily with the need to balance collaboration with security and control. For example, the Track Changes feature in Microsoft Word can be a great benefit when working on multiple drafts of a document, but the metadata that remains in the document might become a source of public embarrassment or subject a lawyer to potential liability. (**Metadata** is "data about data," including hidden data about documents that can range from creation dates and author names to revisions and comments.) Although password-protecting or converting documents to Portable Document Format (PDF) will prevent changes to agreed-upon language, it is difficult and cumbersome to make simple changes to a locked document.

The constant process of balancing the concerns of each party when collaborating externally can make the whole process of working with others outside the office quite complicated. For this reason, we find it useful to split the idea of external collaboration into two "territories." The first we call friendly territory, where lawyers collaborate with clients and others who are on the same side of the matter. The second is obviously called unfriendly territory, where the collaboration is between people on opposite sides—opposing counsel and others.

In friendly territory, the concerns about security and confidentiality still exist, but you'll also want a certain degree of openness that makes working together easier. The use of collaboration tools in this territory may require education and training, and some form of agreement for its use. You will not have quite the same degree of openness that you have in the internal office setting; with external collaboration, documents and other work products are put into the collaborative flow in a more or less "finished" form, after internal review and approval have taken place.

In unfriendly territory, collaboration occurs with perhaps the same overall goal in mind—executing a contract or resolving a dispute—but the parties to the collaboration will have very different priorities. To the extent there is openness in the process or in the exchange of documents, it is limited in scope and tightly controlled. An excellent example occurs in the area of electronic discovery, where the "meet and confer" rules require parties to cooperate and reach agreement on the processes and tools with which they will collaborate. A word sometimes used in this context is "coopetition," which refers to how parties cooperate in putting together the process and platform with which they will compete. Collaboration can help make the overall process of the lawsuit or transaction smoother, but it is still within the context of competing parties who want to win.

Given the context in which external collaboration occurs, it should be no surprise that the selection of the tools you will use is itself many times a collaborative process. The choice of collaboration tools is sometimes the result of compromise, often unspoken or implied. If you receive a document draft as an email attachment for a particular matter, you reasonably can expect that email attachments will be the collaboration tool for exchanging drafts until the matter is concluded. Collaboration tools can also be dictated; if a draft is returned to you with the Track Changes function turned on and instructions to make your revisions to that document, you probably have had your collaboration tool selected for you. Clients are one source of the dictation of collaboration technologies, increasingly requiring their lawyers to use tools like extranets to work on matters.

The choice is yours: you can take a passive approach to collaboration, or you can have your say in the process by knowing what collaboration tools are available to you and those with whom you work. In the next chapter, we'll show you how to get started down that path.

First Steps 5

Choosing collaboration tools is surprisingly easy. In fact, you probably are already using many of them every day. Consciously choosing collaboration tools that will work for you in your law practice is a different story.

The simple fact is that most of us collaborate by using tools chosen for us by others or those we simply use by default. Today, most drafts of legal documents are exchanged as unlocked Microsoft Word files. These files are attached to unencrypted emails sent out over the open Internet to email systems whose security may be questionable. Spam filters may well delete the email before it is delivered to its intended recipient. If you were designing an effective document collaboration system from scratch, this is not likely the system you would choose.

Before you can begin to select collaboration tools or move to new ones, you'll need to rethink some of the ways you currently work with others. This chapter will provide you with practical, easy-to-accomplish steps that can help you get started with collaboration tools.

Let's start with a few basic principles:

1. **For better or worse, you already have a system (or systems) for collaboration.** You may not fully understand them, and you might not have chosen them for yourself, but they do exist and you do use them.

2. **Your technology decisions must be made in the context of and in consideration for the systems you already have in place.** For example, you may decide to buy some scanners and implement a paperless office, but until you fully understand the flow and life

cycle of paper in your office, your odds of implementing the right system are roughly the same as simply throwing darts at the latest Dell catalog.

3. **When you select any collaboration tool, it must either (a) improve an existing system or (b) implement a new system that is measurably better than the system it replaces.** This is a relatively simple idea, but if you understand it your chances for success will markedly increase.

4. **Choices about collaboration tools will be made collaboratively.** You will need to address the needs of various constituencies, including clients and coworkers. The people with whom you work will have different concerns, wants, options, budgets, and other constraints. Compromise often is a necessary element in the selecting of collaboration tools.

5. **Technology choices are always more about culture than they are about technology.** The tools you choose to collaborate with others will always involve finding the technology that best fits the way you work.

With these five principles in mind, you'll be off to a good start in finding the right tools for implementing a collaboration platform that will work well for you and those with whom you work.

As with most decisions, your mission in selecting collaboration technology tools is to get from point A—where you are—to point B—where you want to be—by finding the right path. Unfortunately, too many of us jump right to figuring out the path without first figuring out where we currently stand. With collaboration tools, the more effort you put into determining where you are—point A—the easier it will be to determine where you realistically need to be—point B. The path from point A to point B will become straighter and clearer.

Here is our twelve-step process for developing a plan to take your first steps with collaboration tools. You will learn more details about these steps in subsequent chapters.

Step 1: The Collaboration Audit—The Processes

The term "audit" carries a lot of negative implications, especially around tax time. When it comes to understanding your current situation, a collaboration audit is absolutely vital. Finding your point A requires a thorough knowledge of your current processes. You simply must understand how you currently collaborate in your day-to-day practice.

We suggest you start by taking a closer look at each of the seven standard processes we discuss in Chapters 3 and 4. These processes will be familiar to lawyers in nearly every type of practice or firm. At this point, you want to collect information, not make judgments or reach conclusions. You should, however, take note of bottlenecks, sources of frustration, inefficiencies, and just plain silliness in the ways you work with others.

Step 2: The Collaboration Audit—The Tools

As we've discussed, most lawyers use the telephone and email to collaborate. But lawyers use more than just these tools to work with others. Make a list of all the tools you currently use. Be as complete as possible—mail, messengers, and conference calls definitely count and should be included on the list.

Step 3: The Collaboration Audit— Painting a Picture of Where You Are

We suggest taking the information you gathered in the first two steps and analyzing it in two ways. First, prepare a simple chart that lists your processes and the tools you actually use in each process. Leave space for notes.

Collaboration Audit—Processes

Process Description (e.g., sharing comments on drafts)	Tools Currently Used in Process	Other Tools Under Consideration for This Process	Notes

Next, prepare another chart that reverses the first one. List each of the tools you use for collaboration and then set out the processes for which each tool is used, again with room for notes.

Collaboration Audit—Tools

Tools or Software Used (e.g., Track Changes in Microsoft Word)	Collaboration Process	Other Tools Under Consideration for This Process	Notes

You can go into more or less detail, but with these two charts you now should have a good sense of point A and be ready to define point B.

Step 4: Brainstorming Where You Want to Be

We believe that classic brainstorming should be part of the next step—determining the point B that you want to reach. There are many different brainstorming techniques. We believe that group brainstorming makes the most sense when considering collaboration tools. No matter the technique you use (and we have listed some resources in Appendix 2), you must adhere to the basic brainstorming principle that no idea should be ruled out. The main purpose is to generate ideas; you will sort them out and consider their practicality later.

Step 5: The Client Survey

Here we use the term "client" in the broadest sense. You'll need to consider the people with whom you collaborate on a regular basis, especially those with whom you would like to improve your collaboration. It might startle your clients to hear their lawyer asking them for input on making the working relationship easier, but once they recover from the shock they'll probably be happy and all too willing to make some helpful suggestions. We suggest a simple survey with a few basic questions designed to get some overview information, an indication of the collaboration tools they use and like, and other details that will give you an idea of their collaboration style. The survey should be followed up with a phone call.

Step 6: Define Your Point B

Take your own ideas and the survey input from your clients, and see if any themes emerge. Next, work on defining how these themes will take you to the next point. You should see your journey to point B as a series of destinations, not one big step. Now that you have an idea of what point B looks like, you can break your goals down into internal and external collaboration categories.

Step 7: Determine What Your Existing Tools Can Do

Lawyers, like most people, use only a small fraction of the capabilities available in the programs they have on their computers. Collaboration functionality is increasingly built into software, especially in recent years. We all know it's easier to get more business from an existing client than it is to find a brand-new client. Likewise, it is easier to get more out of software you already own than it is to buy new software and train your people how to use it. Manuals, reviews, websites, and the vendors themselves are good resources for learning how to maximize the use of your current software. The more you can use the tools you already have, the cheaper, easier, and less disruptive your collaboration efforts will be.

Step 8: Research and Become Familiar with the Current Landscape for Collaboration Tools

We are consistently surprised by lawyers who are not aware of common collaboration tools that will suit the needs of their practice. If you think there may be one or two products in a particular category of collaboration tool, think again; there may well be dozens of them. Here's where the client survey in step 5 can really help you out and let you take advantage of the knowledge and experience of others. Throughout this book and in the appendices, we'll cover many categories of collaboration tools and suggest further resources in this area for you to review. If you become familiar with the available tools, you'll be able to make more informed choices. Attending vendor **webinars** (live meetings over the Internet or by conference call), getting demos, and evaluating trial versions of software or services also can be a tremendous help in researching collaboration software.

Step 9: Set Some Priorities

The Chinese philosopher Lao-tzu said, "The journey of a thousand miles begins with a single step." With collaboration tools, we will modify the philosophy slightly. The journey to working more efficiently with others begins with a number of steps, and likely several tools. As you reach point B, you may well decide to use a bundle of tools rather than a single, multipurpose, one-size-fits-all tool. That is the reality of collaboration. As with most technology initiatives, it's best to start with small steps that address common concerns and frustrations and deliver good "bang for the buck." You can then build on those small successes. The simple fact is that despite the best intentions, many large-scale knowledge management and collaboration systems projects instituted by law firms have never been completed. Our approach is to have you focus on what you use on a daily basis and start from there, rather than set out to build the Taj Mahal of collaboration systems right out of the gate.

Step 10: Get Buy-in for the Project

Technology projects succeed when people want them to succeed, and where there is solid support from the top, with all constituencies represented. If your firm or organization's management is not behind the effort, your chances for success are diminished.

Step 11: Consider Your Culture

Your collaboration project will see the best results when you work within your firm or company culture and do not significantly change the way your coworkers go about their business. Solicit feedback, be receptive to suggestions, and be the first to admit that you do not have all the answers. Observe and listen.

Step 12: Treat This as a Process

Some collaboration initiatives will work well and some will not. Fortunately, you can learn lessons from both. Go back to step 1 from time to time and rework the steps. To get started on developing a collaboration strategy, just ask this question to the people with whom you work: "How can I make it easier for you to work with me?" If you ask this question, and then follow our twelve-step program to create a collaboration plan, you'll be well on your way to enhancing your working relationships with clients, colleagues, and everyone else you encounter in your practice.

But enough of strategy. Let's talk about some specific tools, and see how you can use them to increase collaboration both inside and outside your office.

Sample Client Collaboration Technology Survey

We are always working on ways to improve how you interact with our lawyers and staff and make your dealing with us easier.

We especially want to make better use of technology. We value your opinions and want to make good use of the experience that you may already have to help us design and implement tools and systems that will help us work together.

Your completion of this short survey will help us gather information, set priorities, and make selections that best fit the needs and wishes of our clients. We would appreciate it if you would help us out by taking a few minutes to complete the survey and return it to us. If you would like to talk to us in more detail about any of the topics raised in this survey, we would be happy to talk further with you. Simply give your contact attorney at the firm a call.

Survey Questions

Part 1: Help Us Work with Your Technology—General

1. What word processing program do you use (name and version)?

2. What email program do you use (name and version)?

3. Do you have a preference for whether we communicate with you by email or other means?

4. In what format do you prefer to receive documents? (Microsoft Word, PDF, etc.)?

5. Do you have existing systems that we might make better use of (extranets, electronic billing, etc.)?

6. Do you currently have any compatibility or other technology problems when working with us (please describe)?

Part 2: Help Us Work with Your Technology—Collaboration

1. Do you routinely use instant messaging or other forms of communication in addition to email? If so, what software do you use?

2. Do you use Microsoft Word's Track Changes or a redlining software program to show revisions in draft documents?

3. Do you use or readily have available Adobe Acrobat?

4. Do you have any preferences or expect any problems in receiving (or sending) PDF files?

5. Do you use a conference call service, or would you prefer that we set up conference calls with our lawyers for you?

6. Do you already use extranets with customers, partners, or other service providers?

7. Would you like to learn more about using an extranet for your legal work with the firm?

8. Our clients have found the following benefits of extranets valuable. Please indicate which of the following benefits would be valuable to you:
    _____ a. Access electronic copies of filings and final versions of documents.
    _____ b. Access an electronic copy of your "file" in one place on the Internet.
    _____ c. Check on status of filings, due dates, and calendar information.
    _____ d. Track various matters in one place.
    _____ e. Review and comment on drafts in progress.
    _____ f. Send direct messages to attorneys working on a specific matter.
    _____ g. Allow all your team members to access legal documents and files.
    _____ h. Obtain information about billing and administrative information.

9. Do you have any special security or firewall issues that we will need to address in working with you?

Part 3: Help Us Work with Your Technology—Moving Forward

1. Do you have questions about the technology we use and ways that you might be able to work more efficiently with us?

2. Have you noticed ways that we might make better use of technology to save you money (e.g., reducing copying or postage costs)?

3. Who is the best person for us to talk with about technology issues when working with you?

Thank you for your help. Please fill in the blanks below with your contact information and return the form to _____.

Name: _____

Company: _____

Telephone: _____

Email: _____

Collaborating on Documents, Online and Off

Benefits of Improving Document Collaboration and Using Document Collaboration Tools

6

The legal document, in its many forms, is the primary tangible "deliverable" of a lawyer's services. From the opinion letter to the appellate brief, from the summary judgment motion to the memorandum, from the contract to the revocable trust, the legal profession produces documents—so many, in fact, that a special size of paper was named for them—legal size. As lawyers moved from quill and ink to typewriter to word processor, however, the basic structure and content of legal documents evolved slowly and changed little.

Paper documents are solid. Lawyers often feel more comfortable with something they can hold in their hands. They can control the document and point to its original. They can mark on documents, edit them, and put proofreading marks on them. They can sign them with fancy pens, stamp them with notary seals, and make endless paper copies of them to place in manila file folders or stack in large piles on their desks.

The world of the comfortable and familiar has begun to change, and fast. Most documents today are born in electronic form, and some suggest that 90 percent of the documents created today will never be printed. Litigators facing an increase in electronic discovery requests now must determine what is and is not a document.

The days of placing a draft on the partner's chair or mailing out paper drafts to clients are fading fast. We now send documents to the partner or client by email, or we post them on the Internet. We less frequently write comments and revisions directly on the page. Instead, we use Track Changes and add "comments" directly to the electronic documents. Some of us can remember preparing redlines to show changes in documents, using a red ink pen or marker and a ruler. Now, software instantly generates document comparisons with our choice of redlining features.

The world of legal documents is evolving rapidly. The rise of electronic documents brings up new questions about the documents themselves. What is an original? What is a signature? What is the working version? Who has control of the draft? What format should be used? How do I edit a "locked" document? How do we best place comments and revisions into an electronic document?

Regardless of the answers to these questions, the same principles of collaboration still apply to documents; we still move them from one set of eyes to another. We still communicate comments, questions, and revisions. Someone still makes the changes to originals. Final versions of documents still must be signed. Documents still must be kept in some kind of file or archive for future retrieval. It is the processes by which these actions occur that are changing, as technology evolves and affects the way we deal with electronic documents.

In this part, we discuss methods for collaborating on documents with others. Of all the tools mentioned in this book, these perhaps affect lawyers and other legal professionals most in their day-to-day affairs. In the electronic evolution that is growing out of our traditional paper world, we can expect our documents to become increasingly electronic and less paper oriented. The trend toward working with documents in electronic format is unlikely to diminish, let alone reverse itself.

Lawyers often find themselves thrown into the world of electronic document collaboration. For example, a client or opposing counsel sends a draft to you with Track Changes turned on and asks you to reply with your "markup." Or perhaps a colleague asks you to make a document available on the Internet so others are able to work simultaneously on it. What do you do? Will you be active or passive, a leader or a follower, when it comes to implementing collaboration tools?

Here's the good news: if you can appreciate that using technology to collaborate on documents is an evolutionary process that builds on how you already work, and not a mystical and radical new process (even though redlining and Track Changes can certainly be mystifying at times), you will see that document collaboration technologies address many of the problems inherent in working with paper documents. They also offer some important benefits.

In the last few years, lawyers have seen a great transformation in the standard processes they use to move documents, especially drafts, from one place to another. Need to get a document to someone? You send an email, often to more than one recipient, with the word processing file attached. Overnight shipping and faxes are now the exception rather than the rule. And when was the last time you sent a draft of any document by postal mail? Law offices today run on email.

The shift to using email for transmitting documents has certainly picked up the pace of document exchange. It has also changed how files are kept. In the not too distant past, a lawyer would send a cover letter with a document through the mail. A secretary would make a copy (or two, if the file had a "correspondence folder") and file all of the copies in the client's file. Everything was kept together in one place. Now, documents might never be printed. An email might never make it into a paper file, and the document management system might not integrate the email. Today, the "complete" client file might just be a fantasy. Unfortunately, this is the new reality in the modern law practice.

Document collaboration tools can help with this issue, and many more. Here are a few benefits document collaboration tools bring to lawyers, legal professionals, clients, and others with whom lawyers work.

Document Integrity

Collaboration tools can identify the current version and show exactly who made what changes to the document, and when. Documents can be "locked" to prevent changes. "Control of the draft" can take on a completely new meaning when a file is password protected, especially when you do not have the password.

Meaningful Asynchronous and Synchronous Review

When we move paper around, the only person who can review or work on a document is the person actually holding it. Further, if you circulate multiple copies of the document, you would need to integrate any revisions from all reviewers into a single master document, and by hand. Document collaboration tools create a workflow so the appropriate person reviews the document at the appropriate time. Efficiency is increased, because several people can review and revise a document at the same time. Comments, markups, and other modifications can then be brought together automatically in a final draft.

Increase the Number of Eyes Reviewing Documents

Centrally located or easily accessible electronic versions make it simple for clients, co-counsel, supervising lawyers, and others to review documents, even on short notice. More eyes generally means fewer mistakes and better ideas incorporated into the documents.

Tracking the Negotiation and Drafting Trail

If you had worked on a paper document over the course of several months, and someone later asked you why a particular change was made, you might not remember why—or even be able to track down the reason—the change was made. Document collaboration tools let you track versions and revisions, and they provide you with an audit trail of changes to a document. Details about why a change was made, negotiation notes, or other explanatory material can be added to the document as comments.

Metadata and Other Electronic Document Management Issues

Later we discuss the difficult problem of hidden data (often called **metadata**) in electronic documents. Collaboration tools can help you manage and remove this metadata. They can also track versions and clearly identify which electronic document is the original. Electronic or digital signatures can also be managed with these tools.

Bringing New People Up to Speed

Suppose someone new is added to the team or needs to quickly catch up on a deal or document. Having the ability to track the history of the document using collaboration tools makes this process easier and faster.

Training, Quality, and Knowledge Improvement

The tools we discuss can be used inside a law firm or organization to help train new people, show best practices, track processes, ensure quality control, and capture knowledge.

You probably didn't realize it, but the evolution of electronic documents in the legal practice has been moving you gradually toward the use of document collaboration tools. Not only are the trends in electronic documents and the legal practice moving you toward document collaboration tools, but these benefits and more that you will discover throughout this book are driving you toward improving the way you collaborate on documents. You need to understand your options and learn to choose the best tools for your practice, needs, and clients. That journey begins in the next chapter.

Basic Collaboration on Documents

7

Document collaboration has been part of the practice of law since the first partner used a red stone to scratch up the stone tablet drafted by the first associate. Well, maybe it didn't happen quite that way, but the idea of "marking up" paper drafts has been integral to the practice of law for many, many years. In this chapter, we'll discuss the evolution of paper document collaboration to the electronic world, and the tools available to improve that most basic of legal functions—producing legal documents where several authors are involved.

Conceptually, collaboration on electronic documents is no different than working together on paper documents. We read, review, revise, compare versions, and get input from the relevant people working on the document. However, because we do not ship the paper around, the process can happen faster in the digital world. With electronic documents, you can do almost everything you could do with a pen and paper, especially if you happen to be using a Tablet PC with a stylus. Digital documents also free us from some of the limitations of pen and paper. For example, because our comments and revisions are typed, they are going to be legible—often not the case, given the handwriting of lawyers we all know. Electronic pages automatically resize and renumber. We can mark a document with an unlimited number of revisions, without writing on the back of pages or attaching new pages from a legal pad with extensive edits. We can also use different fonts, effects, colors, highlighter tools, brackets, and other techniques to embed questions, make comments, suggest changes and improvements, and even indicate who made the changes and comments. In effect, electronic documents greatly enlarge the collaboration "palette."

Although we'll discuss new document collaboration options in upcoming chapters, it most often occurs today within word processing programs, with delivery by email. Word processing tools have evolved to reflect the importance of review and collaboration. Indeed, with Word 2007 Microsoft devotes an entire "ribbon" to collaboration, under the always visible "Review" button. The Review ribbon offers in one convenient place the tools for proofing, commenting, tracking, accepting and rejecting changes, and comparing and protecting documents.

Microsoft Product screenshots reprinted with permission from Microsoft Corporation.

FIGURE 7.1 Word 2007 Review Ribbon

If you combine these tools with inventive uses of fonts, highlighting, and bold or underline formatting, you can convert the current generation of word processors into powerful collaboration platforms. By using these simple word processing tools, you can accomplish quite a lot before you even get to the dedicated review and collaboration features. We have utilized and seen a wide variety of simple document collaboration techniques using a basic word processing program. It's well worth the time to consider the benefits of even the simplest tools before you jump into more advanced collaboration features. Here are a few examples:

- Inserting bracketed comments with bold and/or italics to raise questions, make comments, or suggest changes.
- Highlighting text that needs to be reviewed.
- Using different font colors for different reviewers.
- Using larger font sizes to highlight text under review.
- Drawing boxes or circles to highlight items.
- Setting larger margins to allow more room for comments and revisions.

It's surprising how even the simplest techniques can help others work more effectively with you on a document.

As we have mentioned elsewhere in this book, the most common collaboration channel is an email message with an attached document. For some collaborators, that email contains a lengthy, numbered list explaining each of the changes and raising questions to be considered in the next draft, much like a lengthy cover letter summarizing the key points of a paper legal document. These emails are often as long as the actual document. It is striking how often these messages simply are not read, at least not with the care that the author would expect.

The Table Method of Document Collaboration— Tried and True

There's a simple but effective method for document collaboration we call the table method, and we'd like to show you how it works. It uses the basic table function in a word processing document to create an easy and intuitive structure to share comments, questions, and suggested revisions. The table structure aids document reviewers in subsequent discussions about the document, and it also helps lawyers and others who enter the process at a later time understand the document's status and its outstanding issues.

Let's use a standard contract as our example and Microsoft Word 2007 as our tool, although you can use the table method in any version of Word or other word processor. Open the draft you plan to send out for review. Use your mouse to select the entire document other than the title and the signature blocks. Using the Insert tab, simply insert a single-column table. Word will move each of your paragraphs into a separate box in the column. Move your mouse inside one of the boxes, right-click, and choose to insert a column to the right. You then have a two-column table with each paragraph in the first column, and a blank column beside it.

The right-hand column is intended as a place to type notes, questions, comments, or suggested revisions. You can resize the columns and the document margins for a look and feel that works best for you. You can even change the document to landscape (rather than the standard portrait) view to provide more room for comments. You'll be surprised how the table approach makes document review more convenient, and others working with you will no doubt feel the same.

When you are ready to finalize the document, you can revert to the original "untabled" version of the document and make your changes there, or you can simply remove the table. To do this, make your revisions in the left-hand column, then delete all the comments and notes in the right column. Right-click in the right column to delete it, and now you're left with the original single-column document.

To finish, you need to convert the table back to text. In Word 2007, select the Convert to Text option under Data in the Layout tab. Under "separator characters," you can change back to the original paragraph form, and

|INDEPENDENT CONTRACTOR AGREEMENT

Independent Contractor Agreement

THIS INDEPENDENT CONTRACT AGREEMENT ("Agreement") is made and entered into as of the later signature date set forth below ("Effective Date"), by and between ABC Corp., a Missouri corporation ("ABC"), and DEF Corp., a _____ corporation ("Contractor").	
The parties hereto do hereby covenant and agree as follows:	
1. **Definitions**. As used in this Agreement, the following terms shall have the following:	
1.1 **"Agreement"** shall have the meaning ascribed to that term above.	
1.2 **"Competitor"** means any individual or entity that (a) is in the business of providing, or (b) otherwise provides, directly or indirectly, collaboration technology services.	
1.3 **"Contractor"** shall have the meaning ascribed to that term above.	
1.4 **"Contractor's Work"** means and includes any and all work product relating to, and/or resulting from, the services performed by Contractor hereunder including, without limitation, any and all items made, designed, developed, conceived and/or reduced to practice by Contractor pursuant to this Agreement.	
1.5 **"Deliverables"** means (a) Contractor's Work, and (b) Pre-existing Deliverables, collectively.	

Microsoft Product screenshots reprinted with permission from Microsoft Corporation.

FIGURE 7.2   Two-Column Table

voila! Your document is ready to finalize. If you like this method, you can create a macro or two to automate the process.

Be careful with documents that have auto-numbering enabled, because the table method sometimes treats the rows of the right-hand column as new paragraphs for numbering purposes. Not to fear—simply delete the numbers in the right column and the left column will return to its regular numbering scheme.

The table method is a great collaboration technique that colleagues, clients, opposing counsel, and even the clients of opposing counsel will like. People see this technique as a good way to streamline the negotiation and revision process, focus the discussion, and keep track of key issues. It's easy to skip over sections that are finalized and focus on those with outstanding questions. Meetings and conference calls go much faster if this technique is used when documents are the subject of the discussion.

THIS INDEPENDENT CONTRACTOR AGREEMENT ("Agreement") is made and entered into as of the later signature date set forth below ("Effective Date"), by and between ABC Corp., a Missouri corporation ("ABC"), and DEF Corp., a _____ corporation ("Contractor").	Confirm DEF name and state of incorporation.
The parties hereto do hereby covenant and agree as follows:	Note: Should we add a recitals section?
1. **Definitions**. As used in this Agreement, the following terms shall have the following:	OK
1.1 **"Agreement"** shall have the meaning ascribed to that term above.	OK
1.2 **"Competitor"** means any individual or entity that (a) is in the business of providing, or (b) otherwise provides, directly or indirectly, collaboration technology services.	ABC: Will want to develop better description of "collaboration technology services."
1.3 **"Contractor"** shall have the meaning ascribed to that term above.	OK
1.4 **"Contractor's Work"** means and includes any and all work product relating to, and/or resulting from, the services performed by Contractor hereunder including, without limitation, any and all items made, designed, developed, conceived and/or reduced to practice by Contractor pursuant to this Agreement.	DEF: Does this include jointly developed work?
1.5 **"Deliverables"** means (a) Contractor's Work, and (b) Pre-existing Deliverables, collectively.	DEF: Make sure pre-existing deliverables includes DEF software products.

Microsoft Product screenshots reprinted with permission from Microsoft Corporation.

FIGURE 7.3   Table Method with Comments

Track Changes and Comments in Word— Another Collaboration Standby

There are two traditional approaches to document review by multiple individuals: mailing a copy of the document to everyone at once, or passing it from one reviewer to the next. With either method, the document author's objective is the same—to receive edits, revisions, comments, and feedback from the others and then incorporate them into the next (or even final) draft of the document.

To keep track of the revisions made by various reviewers, Microsoft Word's Track Changes feature is now the default standard used by legal professionals and other businesspeople. When activated in Word, Track Changes literally monitors every change made to a document and lets you easily manage, accept, or reject those changes once the document is ready to be finalized. In Word 2003, you can see your Track Changes options by selecting View, then Toolbars, then Reviewing. The Reviewing toolbar contains all of the commands you need to enable and work with Track Changes. Word 2007 has all of the same features, but in a slightly different place. To find Track Changes in Word 2007, click on the Review ribbon, and all of the options are laid out at the top of your document.

Microsoft Product screenshots reprinted with permission from Microsoft Corporation.

FIGURE 7.4   Word 2003 Reviewing Toolbar

Microsoft Product screenshots reprinted with permission from Microsoft Corporation.

FIGURE 7.5   Word 2007 Review Ribbon

To activate Track Changes, simply click the Track Changes button. In Word 2007, you'll find it in the handy Review ribbon. In Word 2003, it's the second button from the right on the toolbar. This button is a toggle switch, so when you turn it off, Word will no longer track the changes you make to a document. Once this button is switched on, each change—inserted or deleted text, punctuation, and so on—is identified with a colored font and underline color. You can assign a different color to each reviewer, which makes it easy to see their individual changes. Users have the option of having the changes appear within the body of the document, or displaying them in balloons in the right-hand margin. To turn off the balloons, click the Show button, then Balloons, then Never (in Word 2007, select Balloons from the Review ribbon and click "Show all revisions inline"). From the Show menu, you can also choose the items you want to view in the document—Comments, Ink Annotations, Insertions and Deletions, and Formatting. You also have the option of deciding which reviewer's changes appear in a particular viewing of the document. Regardless of the method used to display changes, a vertical line always appears in the left margin beside any line that contains changes.

Another feature of the Track Changes toolbar is Comments, which reviewers can use to ask questions, reply to other reviewers, or make other types of statements that aren't appropriate as actual changes in the document. Adding a comment is easy. In Word 2003, simply click the Insert Comment button, which looks like a yellow sticky note. In Word 2007, you'll see the Comment button on the Review ribbon. A balloon will appear in the right margin with the comment, including the name or initials of the reviewer making the comment.

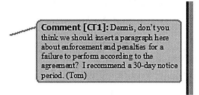

Comment [CT1]: Dennis, don't you think we should insert a paragraph here about enforcement and penalties for a failure to perform according to the agreement? I recommend a 30-day notice period. (Tom)

Microsoft Product screenshots reprinted with permission from Microsoft Corporation.

FIGURE 7.6   Example of a Comment

Before sending a Word document out for review, it is important to make sure the document is configured so that all reviewers are forced to use Track Changes. Otherwise, changes made to the document might not be apparent when the revisions are combined at the end of the review. Locking a document for Track Changes is simple. Here's what to do in Word 2003:

1. Select Tools from the main menu, then Protect Document. The Protect Document task pane opens at the right of your screen.
2. Under 2 (Editing restrictions), check the box next to "Allow only this type of editing in the document," then choose "Tracked changes" from the pull-down menu.
3. Under 3 (Start enforcement), click "Yes, Start Enforcing Protection."
4. Enter a password here, which you'll have to remember when you're ready to accept or reject the tracked changes.

In Word 2007, click the Protect Document button on the Review ribbon, and follow the same directions as above.

What if you send one document out, but your reviewers send back their changes in multiple documents? Word makes it easy to consolidate these documents into a single file, for comparison and further review. Just make a copy of the original document, and then select Compare and Merge Documents from the Tools menu. Select a document from one of your reviewers, and then click the Merge button at the bottom right. You'll have to follow the same process for each separate reviewed document that you receive, but once they are all merged into the copy of the original, you can see everyone's changes in the same document.

Track Changes and Metadata

The rise of e-discovery in the practice of law has brought to the forefront a feature found in all electronic documents: metadata. The technical, unhelpful definition of **metadata** is "data about data," but a better description is "data associated with a document that is not apparent from the face of that document." In fact, "hidden data" might be a better term than "metadata" for lawyers to use. Metadata is information about the file that is embedded within the file, and it can contain such information as the author(s) name; the date the file was created, revised, and printed; and the names of everyone who edited the document.

Track Changes and Comments are another form of metadata found in Word (and other Microsoft Office) documents. They can be hidden from view with just a few mouse clicks; but they still remain with the file, and if handled improperly they can be easily revealed. Having someone else view comments or changes you or your client make to a document is not only potentially embarrassing, it can also be a breach of confidentiality. To learn more about Track Changes and metadata, see our *Strongest Links* article, "Staying on Track with Track Changes" (http://www.abanet.org/lpm/lpt/articles/slc03071.shtml).

The good news is that you can remove metadata with a minimum of effort. There are several ways to make sure metadata does not exist in the electronic documents you share with others:

1. Convert to PDF—probably the easiest method, converting your Word document to PDF removes most of the original document's metadata. A disadvantage to this approach is that the person receiving the document will not be able to edit it; but if you do not want your collaborator to do any editing, this is a good solution.

2. Use a metadata remover—several commercially available products do a remarkable job of removing metadata from your electronic documents. Payne's Metadata Assistant (http://www.payneconsulting.com), iScrub (http://esqinc.com), and WorkShare Protect (http://www.workshare.com) are some well-known tools for lawyers. A metadata remover is probably your best bet for completely eradicating the embedded information from your documents.

3. Convert your Word file to Rich Text Format (RTF)—this will remove most but not all of the metadata in the document.

4. Manual removal—there are several ways you can tweak Word's settings to remove the metadata yourself, including the steps we describe below.

5. Use Word alternatives, like WordPerfect, OpenOffice, or even the free, limited-feature WordPad built into Windows—as long as you understand that metadata will also exist to some extent in these alternative programs.

It's fairly simple to rid a document of tracked changes or comments. On the Reviewing toolbar, just click the pull-down arrow next to the Accept

Change or Reject Change buttons. If you intend to accept all of the changes in the document, just select Accept All Changes. That's all there is to it; the tracked changes are wiped from your document, and no one else can view them. If you want to keep some changes and reject others, it's a bit more time-consuming. You'll need to work on a change-by-change basis and separately click Accept or Reject for each change. One way to move quickly through the document is to press the Shift key while accepting or rejecting changes. This will automatically advance your cursor to the next change in the document.

Deleting comments is equally easy. Click on the pull-down menu next to the Reject Change button, and select Delete All Comments Shown or Delete All Comments in Document, depending on your preference. Instantly, the comments vanish from your document, never to return.

For those who prefer the belt-and-suspenders approach, you can save your document as a new file after you accept or reject all changes, and make sure that Track Changes is not turned on in the new document. Of course, it's possible to combine several of the above methods, and convert to RTF or PDF as well, depending on your level of concern about metadata in a given document.

Redlining Tools—Benefits and Limitations

Another way lawyers collaborate on documents is through the use of redlining software. Again, let's look first at how it was done in the world of paper. An associate, paralegal, or secretary took a red pen and a ruler and carefully marked the differences between the current draft and the prior draft, creating a "redlined" version. This approach was time-consuming and cumbersome.

Electronic redlining tools are incredibly fast—and unlike humans, they don't miss changes. They have revolutionized the ways lawyers negotiate and work on documents. We increasingly hear clients as well as lawyers say that it is "unprofessional" to send a revised document without redlining it. Keep that in mind as you consider whether you should use redlining tools.

A redlining product will take your original document, compare it to a revised version of the same document, and highlight all of the changes and additions to the file. This type of tool is especially useful for transactional lawyers when drafting lengthy documents. It can quickly and efficiently point out all of the changes in a document, saving the lawyer a lot of time otherwise spent hunting for the other person's revisions. Here are some redlining tools available for lawyers:

- Workshare Professional (http://www.workshare.com)—one of the leaders in the document comparison field, Workshare offers the ability to compare, review, verify, secure, and audit documents.
- Change-Pro (http://www.change-pro.com/)—from legal technology company Litera, this product has some interesting document collaboration features that we mention in other chapters.
- DiffDoc (http://www.softinterface.com/)
- DocuComp (http://www.docucomp.com/)

You can also compare documents in your own word processing program. Several versions of Microsoft Word have featured two different forms of document comparison tools, including a specific selection for "legal redlining." In Word 2007, that feature is called "legal blacklining," and it's easy to use:

1. Open the document you want to compare.
2. On the Tools menu, click Compare and Merge Documents.
3. Select the Legal Blackline check box.
4. Select the document you want to compare with the open document.
5. Click Merge.

Word then displays a new, third document in which tracked changes in the first document are accepted, and changes in the second document are shown as tracked changes.

Despite their many benefits, redlining tools can sometimes be quite frustrating. They excel when you have a small number of revisions. When you have extensive revisions, these programs are less reliable. When selecting a redlining tool, you will want to test them with the types of revisions and documents you typically use, to see how they handle the load.

Today's document collaboration tools are simply extensions of the ways lawyers have long handled documents. While clearly evolutionary in scope, they are nearly revolutionary in their impact. It is difficult to see how lawyers can avoid using electronic document collaboration tools in their law practices today. If you choose to learn about only one set of collaboration tools in this book, document collaboration tools would be our first recommendation.

Creating a Document Online: Getting Started with the Major Players

8

For lawyers, probably the earliest method of electronic collaboration was the exchange and forwarding of word processing or spreadsheet documents by email. If you and a client were working on a contract or settlement agreement you were negotiating with opposing counsel, the standard way to get the document drafted was to create an electronic file (usually in Word or WordPerfect), then email it as an attachment to the other person for review and editing. The draft could be mailed or faxed to the other person, but today email is the primary tool lawyers use to exchange documents.

After your client received the document, he or she might then email (or fax or print and send) it to another person. If many people needed to review the document, this "forwarding" process could be extensive and protracted. Often, it might be a while before the marked-up draft was returned to the original author.

If the draft required further editing, the original author would make the changes and send it back out to the group, and the whole process would start all over again. And again. And again. Maintaining control of the draft was important. Often it became difficult to determine what draft was actually the most current. Many of you no doubt have participated in meetings and calls where it gradually becomes clear that people are working from different drafts. While this process was and is still commonly used, it is also highly inefficient and unnecessarily time-consuming.

Some lawyers and firms utilized technologies that made electronic documents available on the Internet, often by means of an extranet, so that all participants in the process could access the same document. Some webinar and conferencing tools also made it possible to share documents during the online meeting. However, those examples were very much exceptions to the rule. The need for a simple, easy to use, Internet-based document collaboration tool was apparent.

That changed in 2005, when several new, innovative, and free sites appeared on the Internet. These sites made it possible for users to create documents online and share them with others without having to use email as a distribution channel. Because these sites provide their services on the Internet, there is no need to install them on your own server, or to have everyone download and use the same program. For lawyers looking to create simple documents and share them with others, especially solos and small firms, these sites definitely fit the bill.

Among the first of these sites was Writely. In 2006 Writely was purchased by Google, which later renamed it as Google Docs (http://docs .google.com). Two other good examples of web-based services that provide fully functioning "Office suite" capabilities are Zoho (http://www.zoho.com) and ThinkFree (http://www.thinkfree.com). While these services currently do not offer the power of full-fledged products like Microsoft Word or Excel, they do make creating, editing, and managing a document online a relatively simple matter. In this chapter we'll look briefly at all three offerings, but we'll focus primarily on Google Docs, because we both believe it's the simplest and most user-friendly of the three.

Google Docs

In keeping with Google's standard and well-liked approach, Google Docs has a lean, spare look; but it packs a powerful punch when you dig into its functionality. It contains most of the formatting options available in Word and WordPerfect, including

- 11 different fonts in up to seven point sizes
- Bold, Italic, and Underline functions
- Highlighting and font coloring
- Bulleted and numbered lists
- Tabs and indenting
- Line spacing
- Superscript, subscript, and strikethrough functions

- The ability to insert images, tables, hyperlinks, comments, bookmarks, separators, and special characters

These features are sufficient for most basic legal drafting needs, especially for preparing first drafts of simple documents. However, you'll find yourself at a loss if you want to add page numbers, footnotes or endnotes, a table of contents, an index, or a table of authorities to your document. To do this, you'll need to export the file to a standard word processing program. Fortunately, this is easy; Google allows you to save your document in one of several different formats, including Word, **PDF**, Rich Text Format **(RTF)**, OpenOffice, Hypertext Markup Language (**HTML**), or Text.

For functionality, we like to compare Google Docs to Microsoft's WordPad program included in Windows. Like WordPad, the Google Docs word processor gives you a solid way to get your writing done without too many bells and whistles. It's easy to create a simple first draft in WordPad. However, you will then want to move the document into Word to further format and finalize it. You don't expect WordPad to be able to accomplish all of the things Word or WordPerfect can do. In fact, current versions of the major word processors are quite complicated and have become desktop publishing centers more than writing tools. In contrast, Google Docs should be thought of first and foremost as a writing tool for working on drafts of simple documents. More complex documents should be moved to a full-featured word processor for final processing and polishing, and Google Docs makes this an easy task.

As much as we like Google Docs, there are some drawbacks to using it. For example, it currently lacks a full-text search, as well as a Find and Replace feature (although it currently offers a Replace All function as what it calls an "experimental" feature). There are also limitations to the number and size of documents you can create. Each document has a 500KB size limit (you can embed images up to 2MB per document), and you can create up to 5,000 documents. And note that because Google Docs is an online tool, Google can and regularly does update it with new features. In fact, new features have probably been added since the time this book was published.

In addition to its word processing tool, Google offers the ability to create spreadsheets. While not as full-featured as Microsoft Excel, this tool provides adequate functionality for most practicing lawyers. You can enter data or text, sort information, enter formulas, or insert graphs. Google Spreadsheets offers a large number of formulas for tabulating results, and currently five different types of graphs are available. As with Google Docs, Google Spreadsheets limits the number of documents you can create. You are limited to 1,000 total spreadsheets, and each spreadsheet is limited to 10,000 rows and 40 separate pages. For lawyers who are understandably overwhelmed by the complexity and sophistication of Excel, Google Spreadsheets offers a great alternative for creating simple and useful spreadsheets for common legal needs. These spreadsheets can be shared with others, who can also edit them.

In 2007, Google added a presentation application to Google Docs; it is a more basic version of Microsoft PowerPoint. Users can create slideshow presentations and then edit them in various ways:

- Add text, links, and lists.
- Change the formatting of text (bold, underline, italics—the basics), as well as change fonts or font colors.
- Adjust alignment.
- Insert images.
- Change themes.

Again, think of Google Presentations as a way to build simple, basic presentations that you can share with others. It is not, and is not intended to be, a full replacement for PowerPoint.

One of the best features of the Google Docs applications is that they are available free of charge to anyone with an Internet connection. You must, however, set up a free account with Google—something you may already have done for Gmail or other Google services. If you prefer a more integrated set of utilities, the company offers a product called Google Apps (https://www.google.com/a/). In addition to documents and spreadsheets, the suite contains access to Gmail, Google Talk, Google Calendar, and other collaboration and publishing tools. Google also allows customization of its product to integrate the applications with your existing infrastructure. For $50 per user per year, Google provides access to all of these applications, with 10GB of storage. Recent law school graduates and those of you with children in college may be aware that some universities are moving to Google Apps as a standard software applications package for their students. In the not so distant future, Google Apps could prove an interesting option for law firms with employees or contractors who need only limited applications and email.

The tools offered by Google have their advantages and disadvantages. The biggest advantages to using Google Docs, other than price, are the ease of use and familiar Google look and feel. As we'll demonstrate in the next chapter, Google Docs makes it simple to create and share a document with others. The user interface is friendly and intuitive, and unlike full-featured word processors and Office applications, you won't have to drill down through several menus to find the features you want. However, the simplicity of Google Docs is also a drawback, because it does not offer the advanced functions of Word or WordPerfect, including many relied upon by lawyers. That's why we won't be recommending you ditch your Office suite in favor of an online product anytime soon. Neither Google nor any of the other products comes close to the power of Microsoft's Office tools.

Zoho

In contrast to Google Docs, Zoho offers more of what you would expect in an Office suite—word processor, spreadsheets, presentation creator, email, calendar, and more. Google, of course, also offers email and calendar applications; but they are not yet integrated into the Google Docs site. Unlike Google, Zoho presents its folder list on the same page as its word processor, with sections for My Docs, Templates, Shared Docs, and Public Docs. Zoho offers the same word processing features as Google Docs, plus a few more. Zoho more closely resembles the familiar word processing interfaces of Word and WordPerfect. Zoho's free product provides 1GB of space for your documents, and additional space is available for a fee. Even better, in November 2007 Zoho gave its users the ability to work on documents offline—using, of all things, a synchronization tool from Google. Zoho also has a plug-in that allows you to work on your Zoho documents from within Microsoft Word or Excel. Zoho Sheet is a more fully realized version of Google Spreadsheet, with more features, formulas, and nine different types of charts.

Like Google Docs, Zoho Personal tools are free. If you want a more integrated application suite for use with more than one person, consider Zoho Business (http://business.zoho.com/). Introduced in September 2007, this competitor to Google Apps offers many of the same features, plus a few more. In addition to Zoho's word processing, spreadsheet, and presentation tools, you get a wiki, planner, and notebook applications. On top of all that, you will find chat, mail, and calendar functions. Zoho Business also provides these benefits:

- A single sign-on for all applications
- Multiple levels of security, including **Secure Sockets Layer** (**SSL**)
- Remote backup
- Document and data storage management
- Company-level administration of your applications
- Telephone support

Zoho Business costs $40 per user per year, which is slightly less expensive than Google Apps. Again, in certain offices, Zoho Business might be an attractive option for employees or contractors who do not need many features of standard Office applications. Using Zoho Business in this way can generate significant cost savings without losing any needed functionality.

ThinkFree

The last online Office-type suite we'll explore in this chapter is ThinkFree. This product offers only three tools—Documents, Spreadsheets, and Presentations—but it does them *very* well. When you open a document, you'll swear you're using Microsoft Word, because ThinkFree has so many of its traditional word processing features. Likewise, ThinkFree spreadsheets look and feel just like Excel spreadsheets. Of the three suites, ThinkFree comes closest to the functionality and power of Microsoft Office. There are several flavors of ThinkFree. The free Online edition is similar to Google and Zoho, with up to 1GB of storage. For more flexibility, try the ThinkFree Desktop or the ThinkFree Premium offering. ThinkFree Desktop is a downloadable version of the product that you can install on your computer. After installing it, you can access your documents both online and on your own computer—giving you the best of both worlds. ThinkFree Premium also provides online and offline access, backup of your files and documents, the ability to sync the files you work on offline to their online counterparts, and 24/7 technical support. The ThinkFree Desktop costs $49.95 for each user.

What's different about ThinkFree (and in our opinion, what makes ThinkFree our least favorite Office-type suite) is the technology it uses to display and manage documents. The technology used by Google Docs and Zoho—Asynchronous JavaScript and XML (**AJAX**)—allows you to view your documents instantly. You simply click on a document, and it appears immediately. AJAX works by refreshing only the actual part of a web page that needs to be changed. And AJAX pages create an experience quite similar to using desktop programs. In contrast, ThinkFree uses Java programming in its applications. Your computer must first load that software, and then ThinkFree must retrieve the document from its server, which can take up to 30 seconds.

Other Online Office Tools

While the products mentioned in this chapter are the best known and highest rated, they are not the only Office-type applications available on the Internet. In fact, a new online word processor or presentation tool seems to debut every few weeks. Here are some other sites that provide an online approach to creating and working with documents:

- Ajax13 (http://us.ajax13.com)—offers a full suite of AJAX-based applications—word processor, spreadsheets, presentations, and drawing tool.

- Sheetster (http://www.sheetster.com)—deals solely with spreadsheets. It supports over 180 Excel formulas and exports your document to a true Excel file.

- Solodox (http://www.solodox.com/)—includes project management and other collaboration features.

- SynchroEdit (http://www.synchroedit.com/)—provides "synchronous editing for the web." It allows multiple users to edit a document at the same time, continuously synchronizing all changes so that users always have the same version.

- CuteFlow (http://www.cuteflow.org)—**Open Source software** that facilitates online document circulation. If you must work on a document the old-fashioned way, by circulating it from reviewer to reviewer, this is an interesting online option. To enable the service, you must download it and install it on your own computer server.

Keep an eye out too for Microsoft's coming "hybrid" approach, currently called OfficeLive, that adds online sharing capacity to its standard suite of Office products. By all accounts Microsoft seems to be taking the opposite approach to online document creation, working from the standard Office programs and not simply your browser. You'll be able to use your Office applications with integrated collaboration features rather than just your browser to interact with documents on the Internet.

The tools discussed in this chapter offer free or very inexpensive ways for individual lawyers and law firms to jump into online document creation and collaboration. In our experience, these tools are attracting many users for collaboration on simple documents without the need for complex authoring, numbering, or outlining structure. For articles, memos, letters, and other standard documents needing the input of several people, these online document creation sites offer a quick and easy way to collaborate without the hassle and delays of the traditional email–and–attachment approach. In the next chapter, we'll show you how to get started with Google Docs.

Working Simultaneously *on a Document* 9

Now that you have a good understanding of the major play-ers in the online document creation business, it's time to get started on actually creating your own documents. In this chap-ter, we'll introduce you to the world of online document col-laboration by showing you how to create a simple document. For our example, we will use the popular Google Docs, the tool we used to write this book. We selected Google Docs because it's easy to use. However, we expect you'll find that Zoho and ThinkFree are also user-friendly and simple to learn. Once you have Google Docs mastered, the other tools in this category will be a breeze to figure out. You'll also have a baseline for evaluating and comparing the other products.

Let's jump right in and get started. Before you can create a document in Google Docs, you'll need to register. Fortunately, getting a Google account is easy and free. On the Google Docs home page (http://docs.google.com), just click Get Google Docs Now! and you'll be taken to a sign-up page, where you'll need to provide this information:

- An email address—it can be any email address, but for ease of use you may want to consider getting a Gmail account (http://mail.google.com)
- A password
- Your name
- Your location

That's it! Just enter the security word to prove to Google that you're a real live human being. Google will then create your new account and send you a confirming email. The next time you visit the Google Docs main page, simply provide your email address and password, and you'll be admitted to your personal main documents page.

Navigating the Google Docs Main Documents Page

The Google Docs main documents page resembles what you might see when you open any folder on your computer, or when you're working in an email program like Microsoft Outlook. In fact, the main view will seem familiar to most computer users, which will make it easy to learn and use.

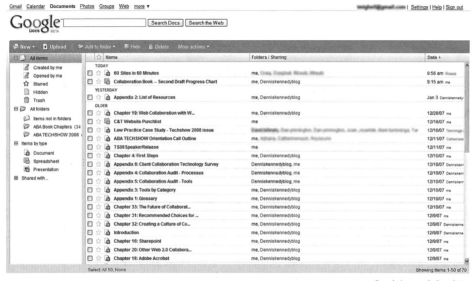

Google images © Google Inc.

FIGURE 9.1   Google Docs Main Documents Page

On the left side of the screen, you can choose a preferred view for the documents you create. The following types of views are available:

- All Items—This view displays every Google Doc you have created. You have the opportunity to filter this to more-specific lists, including:

    - Documents created solely by you.
    - Starred documents—Google lets you mark important documents with a "star."
    - Hidden documents—You can remove documents from your lists by clicking the Hide button on the main documents page toolbar. This page lists all of those documents that you have hidden. When you "hide" a document, you're not deleting it; you're just removing it from the current list, so it's not taking up extra space on the screen. This feature is useful, for example,

when you want to see only the documents associated with a particular project.

■ Trash—When you delete documents they go into the Trash, at least temporarily, until you delete them permanently.

■ All Folders—Google Docs allows you to create folders, so you can separate documents by client, case, or other designation. You can create folders for anything you want.

■ Items by Type—If you want to just view your word processing documents or spreadsheets, you can filter your document list here.

■ Items Shared With. . . .—As we'll discuss, Google Docs gives you the ability to share documents with anyone. With this filter, you can quickly get to documents you share with specific individuals.

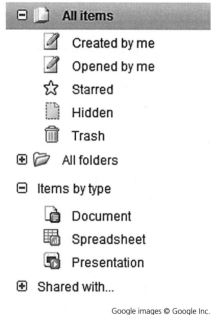

Google images © Google Inc.

FIGURE 9.2 View Showing All Items

On the right side of your screen is a listing of the documents you have created. By default, all of your documents will be displayed with the most recently edited file at the top. You can change the order of this listing to display them by Document Name, Folder, or the name of the person with whom you're sharing the document.

The main documents page toolbar takes the space above this list. This toolbar is where you'll get started with your documents and spreadsheets. Here are the actions you will find:

■ New—Click this button to create a new document, spreadsheet, presentation, or folder.

FIGURE 9.3 Main Documents Page Toolbar

- Upload—You don't have to use Google Docs simply to create new documents. You can upload a document you have already created in Microsoft Word so others can review and make changes to it. Click Upload, and a dialog box will direct you to locate the original file on your computer.
- Add to Folder—Adding documents to folders is easy. Once you have created a particular folder, just click the check box next to the documents to be placed in that folder. Click Add to Folder, then select the appropriate folder, and those documents are now a part of that folder.
- Hide—As discussed earlier, clicking this button will remove a document from the main list. You might use this feature to keep your document list uncluttered so you can focus on just the documents for your current project. A hidden document can be restored at any time by going to the Hidden Documents view, clicking the check box next to it, and checking Unhide.
- Delete—Click the box next to the document you want to delete, and click this button. Note that, as with documents on your own computer, you still have the ability to retrieve a document from the Trash until you permanently delete it by clicking Empty Trash on the Trash page. This feature can be a lifesaver if you accidentally delete a document.
- More Actions—When you're working in a Google Docs document, you have several options for dealing with that document. These options include sharing, previewing, publishing to a website, and exporting to a particular file format, among others. The More Actions button provides many of these functions without the necessity of actually opening the document. We'll discuss these functions in more detail later in this chapter.

Creating a Document

Creating a new document with Google Docs is as easy as it is in your word processing program. On the main documents page, just click New and choose the type of document you want to create. The document appears in a new browser window (or tab, if you're using Internet Explorer 7 or Firefox with tabbed browsing activated). You will see a familiar blank page, on which you can begin typing. By default, Google Docs will title the document with the first few words you type, and the title will appear just above the File menu in the upper left corner. If you want to change the title, just click on it, and a dialog box will appear. Type the new name for your document, click OK, and you're done.

Navigating Within a Document

The features on a Google Docs document provide basic functionality in a word processing file. If you think of Google Docs as a limited word processing program with only the most basic and commonly used functions, the navigation and features will make sense to you. Remember that Google Docs is similar to WordPad, the simple word processing tool built into Windows.

Edit Tab

On the Edit tab, you will see buttons like these:

- Undo Last Edit
- Redo Last Edit
- Cut
- Copy
- Paste
- Bold
- Italic
- Underline
- Font
- Font Size
- Text Color
- Highlighting
- Link (for inserting links to websites)
- Numbered List
- Bulleted List
- Indent Less
- Indent More
- Quote
- Align (Left, Center, Right)
- Remove Formatting (helpful if you are pasting information from another document into your Google Doc)

- Style, including
    - Paragraph Style
    - Page Spacing
    - Text Formatting (Strikeout, Superscript, Subscript)
- Change (Restore or remove extra blank lines, or move items in a list up or down)

Google images © Google Inc.

FIGURE 9.4   Edit Tab

Insert Tab

The Insert tab is next on the screen. When you click this tab, you are given the option to place several different types of objects directly into your document. These include

- A picture or other image
- A link to a URL
- A comment
- A table
- A bookmark, which is a shortcut to another place in the document
- A separator (either a page break or horizontal line)
- Special characters (for example, £, §, or ñ)

Revisions Tab

The next tab is titled Revisions. Here users can view previous versions of the document, see the history of revisions and who made them at a particular time, and compare different versions of a document with each other. Again, the functionality here is very basic.

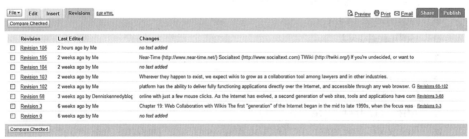

Google images © Google Inc.

FIGURE 9.5   Revisions Tab

Publish Tab

The Publish tab, located at the far right on the screen, allows users to publish their documents directly to their websites or blogs. Just click Publish Document, and a link will be created where anyone can view the document. Here's a great feature of publishing that takes full advantage of the Internet: when the document is updated, the published version is simultaneously revised as if it were synchronized with your working draft in Google Docs. If you change your mind, it's easy to stop publishing your document; just click Stop Publishing, and the page becomes private again.

In general, you will want to publish only when you are done with a document. One big lesson we want you to learn in all collaboration contexts is to keep in mind the distinction between documents that are in process and documents that are finalized and ready for publication. Remembering that will keep you out of trouble and ensure that people see only what you want them to see.

If you have a blog and want to post a Google Doc to it, just enter the appropriate URL and login instructions where indicated. You might have to consult with your blog host, or check the Help materials if you use TypePad or another hosted blog service for details. Once you post it to your blog, your readers will be able to view the document you created as a new post. While this feature may not be used much by lawyers, in the right setting it can be a valuable tool.

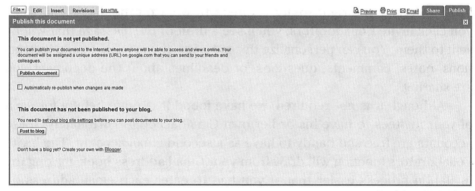

Google images © Google Inc.

FIGURE 9.6   Publish Tab

Sharing Documents with Others for Collaborating

Last, but certainly most important, is the Google Docs Share tab. This function allows you to share your documents with others in several different ways. When you click on the tab, the left side of the screen provides a box where you can Invite People, either as Collaborators or Viewers. If you invite someone only as a Viewer, the document is provided to them in read-only format. A Viewer will not be able to make any edits to the document. Collaborators, on the other hand, can make changes to the document, even while others are viewing or working on the document in different locations.

Google images © Google Inc.

FIGURE 9.7 Invitation Form

To invite someone to share your document, you must enter his or her email address. You can add several people simply by separating additional email addresses with commas. You can invite as many people as you want to collaborate on the document. You can also control whether those you invite will have the right to invite others to work on the document. Once you click Invite Collaborators, you'll see a draft of the message that will be sent to them. You can personalize this message, if you wish, to add instructions, notes, comments, questions, or deadlines about the document you are sharing.

Although it is not required, we have found it is quite helpful for each of your invitees to have his or her own Gmail account. Fortunately, these accounts are free and handy to have as a second email account. The Invite Collaborators function will draw from your Gmail address book, making the invitation process easier than if you had to enter each email address by hand. When you send out your invitations, your collaborators will receive an email with an embedded link to the document, rather than the document attached to an email (although Google does give you the option to paste the article directly into the email). The invitee clicks on the link and is taken directly to the document. Thereafter, when your collaborators log in to their own Google Docs account, your document will appear in their list of documents, making it effortless for them to find and work on your document.

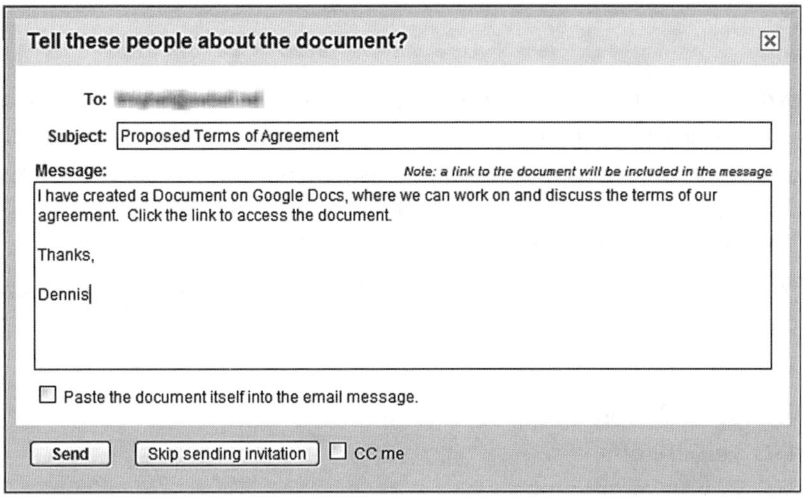

Tell these people about the document?   ☒

To: ▓▓▓▓▓▓▓▓▓▓▓

Subject: Proposed Terms of Agreement

Message: *Note: a link to the document will be included in the message*

I have created a Document on Google Docs, where we can work on and discuss the terms of our agreement. Click the link to access the document.

Thanks,

Dennis|

☐ Paste the document itself into the email message.

[Send]   [Skip sending invitation] ☐ CC me

FIGURE 9.8   Invitee Email

With that step done, you and your collaborators will be able to work simultaneously on the same document. Each user may access the document at his or her own computer, wherever he or she is located. All of the collaborators can view and edit the document at the same time. When you make a change, other users won't see it instantaneously; but they will see it fairly quickly, after the document is auto-saved by Google Docs (Google spreadsheets are saved automatically, so edits on these files can be seen as they occur). Imagine how effective a meeting would be for the users of this document to join a conference call and view and edit the same document at the same time. This is a good example of combining two basic and easy-to-use collaboration tools to create a powerful process that gets work done.

Even better, if you have a personalized Google start page, now known as your iGoogle (http://www.google.com/ig) page, you can add a **widget** to that page that will display the latest activity in any of your Google Docs. It's a good example of the collaborative concept of "alerts," or ways to be notified of activity and changes in tools you commonly use, without the need to constantly revisit the collaborative site.

Other Features

The Preview feature allows users to preview the document, print it, or email it to others. Google Docs also automatically saves your document on a regular basis, thus addressing one of the most common concerns about working online.

Shortcuts

Just like Word and other word processing programs, Google Docs provides a good number of shortcuts for those who prefer to navigate the screen with their keyboard rather than a mouse. Many of the shortcuts are recognizable: Ctrl+A to Select All; Ctrl+B, Ctrl+U, and Ctrl+I for Bold, Underline, and Italics; and the usual Cut (Ctrl+X), Copy (Ctrl+C), Paste (Ctrl+V), and Undo (Ctrl+Z) shortcuts. Here are some of the other more popular Google Docs shortcuts:

- Ctrl+J: Full justify
- Ctrl+Shift+L: Bulleted list
- Ctrl+L: Left alignment
- Ctrl+E: Center alignment
- Ctrl+M: Insert comment
- Ctrl+Space: Remove formatting
- Ctrl+1, 2, or 3: Header style 1, 2, or 3
- F2: Edit active cell (spreadsheets)
- Ctrl+Spacebar: Select entire column (spreadsheets)
- Shift+Spacebar: Select entire row (spreadsheets)

For a complete list of Google Docs shortcuts, visit https://docs.google.com/support/bin/answer.py?answer=66280.

As we've mentioned, we have used Google Docs for several years to work on articles we coauthor as well as on roundtable articles with multiple authors. It was also our tool of choice for the drafts of this book. Its combination of simplicity and power, and the comfort people have in the Google brand, make it a solid choice for simple document collaboration between lawyers and clients, co-counsel, and others.

Hidden Dangers, Security, and Metadata | 10

In previous chapters, we've covered some great online alternatives for collaborating on documents. Google Docs, Zoho, and the others provide the ability to work on a document together in real time, without having to send it out on the "document review" circuit. After reading our recommendations, some of you may be tempted to ditch your current word processing applications entirely in favor of the "online office." Indeed, Google Docs and Zoho offer appealing alternatives that allow anyone in your office access to documents wherever they happen to have an Internet connection. Maybe you're not ready to move your documents completely online, but you might be interested in some form of online document collaboration, or simply storing some of your documents online. What should make you stop and think twice before plunging into the online document arena is that some of those documents contain confidential client information.

Before making the move to online documents, you should consider the answers to a few questions about security and other issues. Can an online office tool be a substitute for a product that resides on your computer? What are the security issues involved with keeping confidential client documents online? How do these services back up my documents—if they do so at all? And do online documents contain metadata? These are serious issues you must consider carefully and determine how you will deal with them. We'll discuss these issues in greater detail in this chapter.

Online Documents and Security

When you consider the documents you create for your clients and cases, the primary issue should always be that of security. Whether you are a solo, a member of a 500-lawyer firm, or part of a general counsel's office, document security should always be your first priority. With online documents, security can be an "iffy" proposition. The services will tell you that your documents are securely maintained in state-of-the-art data centers, but can or should you trust their guarantees? After all, the documents reside on someone else's computer, which usually gives most lawyers an automatic sense of concern, if not heartburn. Let's consider whether documents on online services like Google and Zoho are really as secure as if they were on your own computer, or whether in fact they might be more secure than on your own computer network.

One of the main security issues with Google is how it integrates its services and handles "cookie" data. A **cookie** is a small text file that is placed on your computer by a website so that you can be identified the next time you visit the site. Google often uses the same cookie to access all of its various sites, as part of that user's Google account. To access Google Docs, you must have a login, usually your email address, and a password. However, because people are commonly registered with several Google services (Gmail, Google Calendar, Google Reader, etc.), they may be logged in quasi-permanently to Google. If you walk away from your office for only a second and someone accesses your computer, if you are logged in to Google they can access your Google Docs account and the documents in it. In fairness to Google, the same result occurs with documents that are not password-protected on your computer or office network.

Further, hackers using something called an HTML code injection tool can theoretically gain access to online services by injecting code that bypasses its system security features. While this has not happened in the general Internet community yet, the very architecture of sites like Google Docs makes it possible for hackers to break in and steal your documents. As the user base for these services gets larger, and more documents are stored there, the sites will become more and more attractive to hackers.

For attack from outside sources, Google offers encrypted access to all Google Docs—you can confirm your document is encrypted by seeing the *https://* at the beginning of the URL. As of this writing, Zoho does not offer encrypted documents, although the company is working on it.

A few isolated security incidents regarding Google Docs have occurred in the past few years. One involves the apparent "misplacing" of documents. At least one user reported finding files in his document list that did not belong to him. Upon further inspection, it appeared that Google mistakenly "assigned" the document to him rather than its original author. In another incident in early 2007, documents from about 30–40 users were simply deleted from Google's servers; the documents ceased to exist. Although these appear to be random errors that have not been duplicated since then, they are examples of what can happen to confidential documents if precautions and backup measures are not taken.

Another issue to consider is your legal right to relief if one of these services does happen to lose your documents or compromise their confidentiality. When registering for Google Docs, you must agree to the site's Terms of Service (http://www.google.com/accounts/TOS?hl=en), which include (among other things):

> 15.1 Subject to overall provision in paragraph 14.1 above, you expressly understand and agree that Google, its subsidiaries and affiliates, and its licensors shall not be liable to you for:
> (a) Any direct, indirect, incidental, special consequential or exemplary damages which may be incurred by you, however caused and under any theory of liability . . . this shall include, but not be limited to, any loss of profit (whether incurred directly or indirectly), any loss of goodwill or business reputation, any loss of data suffered, cost of procurement of substitute goods or services, or other intangible loss; . . .

So if Google does lose your documents, you may have difficulty holding Google liable for the loss of profits and other damages you or your client sustain, whether directly or indirectly. While this type of disclaimer is standard on sites delivering services over the Internet, it probably will not give you the comfort level you might need for your confidential documents. There is, of course, some question about whether courts will enforce broad disclaimers and limitations such as this.

Another issue is not one of security but of availability. What if you need to access a document on the road, and Internet access is not available? Even worse, what if Google's computers go down, even temporarily? How will you access your documents? The short answer is, you won't. This, of course, is common to all websites that store your information, your organization's computer network, and your own individual computer; but in this case we're talking about client documents and potential malpractice if that confidentiality is breached. The ability to download your documents in Zoho and later synchronize them with the online repository may solve the availability problem for some users.

Interestingly, the fact is that the levels of security, backup, redundancy, and uptime at a tier 1 data center supporting a service like Google Docs are well beyond what you will find at the vast majority of law firms. Still, to satisfy yourself on the security issues involved, you must do your homework and apply due diligence when using these services.

Automatic Backup of Documents

A critical part of any organization's technology plan is the regular backup of documents created within whatever **document management system** the firm or company uses. It is very easy for documents or computer data to be lost, accidentally deleted, or otherwise removed from a computer system. It is thus essential that every document have a backup in case its original is lost. Ideally, your backup system backs up your documents every night, so there can be no interruption of service to your clients. How do online services like Google and Zoho fare when it comes to backing up your client documents?

Google Docs does not have an official backup policy, but Zoho does. The folks at Zoho create a duplicate of each document that is created, so another live copy exists if the original is deleted. Further, Zoho backs up its data daily, from which documents can be restored. Even better, Zoho has partnered with both OmniDrive (http://www.omnidrive.com) and Box.net (http://www.box.net), allowing users to edit their documents directly from these online storage services; this can provide an extra level of backup for Zoho's online files. For those interested in finding a way to back up their Google Docs, here's an interesting alternative. If you use the Firefox browser, there's a Greasemonkey script called GoogleDocDownload (http://1st-soft.net/gdd/googledocdownload.user.js) that will help you regularly download and back up your Google Docs documents. Greasemonkey scripts are pieces of computer code that let you modify the way web pages look and run in the Firefox browser. This solution requires a lot of work on your part—you'll need to regularly back up the documents yourself—but it can be done.

Metadata in Online Office Documents

Documents created in Word, Excel, or other applications often contain **metadata**, or information embedded within the file. Often this metadata can contain confidential client information, especially if Track Changes is activated or comments are inserted into the document. How is metadata handled with tools like Google Docs or Zoho?

Fortunately, metadata is not much of an issue with these online document creation sites. We cannot find evidence that Google Docs or Zoho keep metadata that travels with the documents, especially once the documents are exported to other formats like Word or PDF.

In Google Docs, however, you and your collaborators are able to review the changes made by others by selecting the Revisions tab. Previous versions found under the Revisions tab can show information you might not want to share with others. You can compare one revision against another, with the differences highlighted in different colors according to each specific editor. Zoho programs work much the same way. As long as your document resides online, these revisions are visible. Once you export the document to Word or some other format, the revision history is erased. For Word, it's as if you were creating a document for the first time. All Track Changes metadata is erased from the document. However, unless you delete the document from its online repository, the revision history will remain. Again, remember that you must take care to understand the exact state of a document when determining who is allowed to work on or view it. For example, you might permit colleagues and a client to work on a draft until it is ready to share with the other side. Next, you would copy that document into a new Google Docs file and then share the new document with the other side. This approach lets you take advantage of the collaboration features of Google Docs while not revealing the revision history from the prior document.

Both Google Docs and Zoho allow users to add comments to any online document. Zoho's Comment feature is fairly basic, providing a simple box to add comments. Google provides more options for commenting. It inserts a timestamp with the comment, along with the name of the person making the comment. That comment can be also be customized with different colors. Google also allows you to insert the comment text directly into the document. When you do this, the comment text becomes a permanent part of the document, so be careful when using this feature. Both Google and Zoho provide the ability to delete comments; and if they are not deleted, they will remain in the online version of the document. However, once the document is exported to another format, the comments do not travel with the document (unless, with Google, you have inserted the comment directly into the document). As with changes and revisions, comments are effectively erased from the document once they leave the online environment. Again, you might want to move your draft, without the comments, to a new Google Doc before sharing the draft with opposing counsel or others not on your side.

Tips for Dealing with These Issues

Online document creation sites can be excellent collaboration tools, allowing users from anywhere in the world to work on documents simultaneously while maintaining version control of the changes made. Even so, you cannot assume that these services will substitute for a secure computer or server-based document management system that provides a tested, reliable backup method. If you plan on using tools like Google Docs or Zoho as part of your collaboration strategy, here are a few tips for keeping your documents safe and secure:

- If you can, limit the number of confidential documents you create or use online. Obviously, the less confidential information online, the lower your chances of having it compromised.

- If you must keep a document with confidential information online, try to limit how long it remains there.

- Develop a backup strategy to ensure that your online documents are never lost. Use Zoho in conjunction with one of the online storage sites, or back up your Google Docs yourself by using the GoogleDocDownload script.

- Once you are done working with a document online, delete it from its online location, if you are sure you will not need to access it there again. Leaving a document online when it no longer needs to be there increases the security risk; what's more, individuals who access the online version will be able to view the revisions and other metadata underlying the original document.

- Understand who your collaborators will be, and determine whether they will be able to access your comments or revision history. Create a new document or export your file into Word or PDF format to deal with these issues.

- Read carefully the terms of use or online agreement for any service you will use.

- Notify your clients in writing that you plan to use online document collaboration tools as part of your representation, and obtain client consent.

- Create a policy for informing clients and others about the risks and special concerns in using these tools.

- Watch for developments and news about security and other issues involving online document collaboration services.

- Make reasonable assessments, and do not underestimate the way that the same issues can arise when using your own computers and networks. Documents on these online services might be far safer than they are on unsecured computers and networks.

With these tips in mind, you should be able to take advantage of the benefits of online document creation sites with a minimum of concern.

PART IV

Collaboration on Cases, Transactions, and Projects

Benefits of Collaboration in Lawsuits and Transactions

11

Although the day-to-day practice of lawyers tends to focus on working with documents of one form or another, most documents are part of a larger project. Legal projects commonly fall into broad categories of lawsuits (dispute resolution) or transactions (deals and planning). In fact, many firms are divided into separate litigation and transactional groups.

Lawyers in large firms work in teams on litigation and transactional matters, with partners, associates, paralegals, secretaries, and other staff comprising the team. Even in the smallest firm, today's cases typically involve some kind of team, even if only a lawyer and paralegal. However, as we have noted, if you focus only on the internal team, or who is on "your side," you will miss the number and variety of people collaborating on a particular matter.

In a lawsuit, you may find yourself working with clients, witnesses, experts, opposing counsel, vendors, service providers, judges, court personnel, and others. As a simple exercise, take a few moments to write down the list of all the people you worked or dealt with in your last lawsuit, whether it settled or went to trial. You'll be surprised at the length of your list. As we move into the era of electronic discovery, that list will grow, as vendors, experts, consultants, IT staff, and records managers become more involved in litigation, and trial lawyers must learn to work with these individuals to ensure that discovery is properly handled throughout the life cycle of a lawsuit. In fact, litigation departments are increasingly hiring dedicated project managers, and more and more electronic discovery vendors are offering project management services to deal with these collaboration and communication issues.

In transactional matters, the teams usually are smaller; but large transactions and mergers might require a small army of people. A transactional lawyer putting together a deal will work with various individuals on both sides of the transaction, including professional services providers, subject matter experts of various kinds, consultants, and others. If the deals have a national or international dimension, as is increasingly common, the number of different people involved is bound to expand. If you are a transactional lawyer, try the same exercise and make a list of all the people who worked with you on your last large transaction.

Collaboration in the legal world occurs not only in the realm of large deals and lawsuits. Estate planners often deal with accountants, financial planners, life insurance agents, appraisers, and trust officers while putting together an estate plan. Divorce and family law matters can also involve a large cast of characters. In fact, lawyers of every stripe must collaborate with others in virtually any matter they undertake to accomplish.

Of all activities engaged in by lawyers, perhaps none is more common than the meeting or conference call. Lawyers spend significant chunks of time scheduling these events, trying to find dates and times that work for all attendees. Scheduling a single meeting might take longer than the meeting itself, just to get people onto the same call or into the same room. Fortunately, group calendar tools that can find a common open time slot in everyone's schedule now make a world of difference in scheduling the meeting. These tools are increasingly being used internally, and Internet-based scheduling tools also have started to attract interest in the business world.

As welcome as reducing the time spent setting up calls and meetings may be, however, there are many other benefits to using collaboration tools in litigation and transactional matters. As in the area of document collaboration, you will want to look first to ways electronic tools can build on and improve existing nonelectronic processes. In other words, look for places that collaboration tools are evolutionary rather than revolutionary. The collaboration revolution in your practice will likely come as a series of small steps.

Break Down the Barriers of Time and Space

Lawyers now work with people locally, nationally, and globally. Many law firms have multiple offices, often worldwide. Meetings and conference calls in the United States may involve coordination with attendees in four time zones. In transactional matters, one or more participants in the negotiation might be from another part of the world. Further, legal work, from the most mundane administrative tasks to legal research and document review, is now outsourced to India and other places around the globe. Coordinating business activities that are taking place literally around the world can be a daunting task.

Enter Technology

One reason email has become so popular and widely used is its **asynchronous** mode of communication. An email sent late in a New York morning can be available first thing in the morning to the recipient in California. Indeed, it's difficult to imagine how global negotiations succeed without email. Collaboration tools like email can make the differences in geography and time zones less burdensome and more manageable. Some lawyers complain about the extra burden instantaneous communication places on them—the evolution of mail to fax to email to instant message certainly requires lawyers to be more diligent in responding to clients and others. When time is of the essence or a deadline is close at hand, however, instant communication and the delivery of documents in electronic format can make all the difference in the world, no matter where in the world you happen to be.

Improve Client Service and Access

A frequent complaint of clients is getting billed for "teleconference with client re: pleadings in Smith case," when all they wanted was to look at a copy of one of the documents filed in the matter. Worse yet, they might have to play telephone tag with the lawyer just to get a copy of the document. Extranets and other collaboration tools enable clients to access their documents and other data at any time. When this material is made available on a secure website, clients can handle the simple requests, like getting a copy of a filing or contract, on their own. Then they need to call their lawyers only about the billable stuff—real legal questions and problems. Improving a client's ability to access documents, manage contracts, track pleadings, review the status of a case or negotiation, or even facilitate an electronic signature process will benefit lawyers and clients alike, and it will help enhance a law firm's value to its clients. Given the collaboration tools available, we are surprised when we see large percentages of general counsel answering "none" to survey questions about the new ideas and benefits offered by their outside counsel. Collaboration tools offer an attractive and often easily implemented benefit a lawyer can provide to his or her clients.

Get More Eyes and Heads into the Process

When it's easy to collaborate, it's easier to increase participation from the people who should be involved in the process. With more people involved, you get different perspectives, more informed judgments, and better decisions. A simple conference call can bring in important business decision makers who would never have participated had the meeting been in person. Online document repositories allow experts to review relevant discovery material without shipping boxes of paper around the country. These tools also allow you to bring people into the process at the appropriate points and be more efficient in your review process, avoiding duplication and wasted effort.

Make Electronic Discovery a Team Effort

Today, electronic discovery in complex litigation matters can easily involve millions of documents, email, and other files. You don't have to be a math major to realize that one person cannot review that amount of material, at least not in one lifetime of billable hours. Collaborative review tools, document repositories, workflow management programs, and the like make electronic discovery feasible and realistic, especially as the "team" grows larger and spreads to many geographic locations.

Make Due Diligence a Team Effort

Electronic discovery gets all the press, but transactional lawyers tasked with performing due diligence increasingly are finding that they too are reviewing large numbers of electronic documents. They may also be advising clients about records management and other data issues. The need for collaboration tools similar to those used in electronic discovery definitely exists in this area as well.

Keep Everything Together

A deal negotiation may consist of an electronic flurry of document drafts, exhibits, schedules, email, and even stored voice mail. We have moved well beyond the single manila file or "Redweld" that contains everything related to a particular matter. Collaboration tools can help assemble and make accessible in one place all of the materials relevant to a deal or a litigation matter. This idea of electronic file keeping may well provide sufficient incentive to make the move to some type of collaboration tool attractive.

Stop Reinventing the Wheel

As all the team members move into working on a matter, it always takes time for them (especially if they are lawyers) to get up to speed. Many firms give young associates the "file" and instruct them to "familiarize themselves with the case." As lawyers rotate on or off a case or deal, clients subsequently see bills with many lawyers spending many hours catching up on the case, often by spending days reading through boxes of documents. Collaboration tools that focus on workflow, show what has already been accomplished, and clearly identify key documents can drastically reduce the time spent in review, and they produce better results.

Improve Training

Collaboration tools can keep histories, record notes and comments, and even extract lessons learned from earlier matters. They can also help you define and implement processes, spell out necessary steps, and improve quality control. As a result, these tools often have the side benefit of improving training of young lawyers, lateral attorneys, and others who are added to the team after the matter is commenced. Watch for the impact that audio and video will begin to have in training firm or company employees.

Improve Accountability

Collaboration tools can help you track where changes were made on a matter or project. You can discover who worked on a particular task, how well they did, and how efficient and productive they were in completing the task. With this knowledge you can then provide training where needed, or assign the right people to the right tasks. Workflow tools are good at revealing logjams and choke points. The better you can track the work of the team and see its members' progress, the better you can manage the project. You'll also reduce the number of surprises. Clients are pushing lawyers to lower bills and improve efficiencies, but value billing is possible only when you understand the processes and work involved. We believe the continued emphasis on improving legal work processes will drive the implementation of collaboration tools in the practice of law.

Close Projects Efficiently

When a project is completed, lawyers tend to drop everything and walk away, moving on to the next matter. We have heard many lawyers over the years say how they wish they could put together a nice portfolio with a summary of the matter and its results, along with the relevant documents, to give to their clients at the conclusion of a matter. At the same time, we have heard many clients say they wish their lawyers would do exactly that for them when a case is closed. Collaboration tools make it easier to close out a project and allow lawyers, clients, and others to follow the trail of the matter, easily access relevant documents, and generally provide a sense of closure that an itemized bill does not.

Collaboration tools would not be interesting to us if they did not produce better results than we currently experience in lawsuits or transactions. Consider the impact of the benefits of collaboration tools set out above. The combination of these benefits leads to an improved chance of winning the case, negotiating a better deal, getting better results, and creating happier clients. Who can argue with results like these? It is the increased chances of these results that puts collaboration tools on the radar of litigators, transactional lawyers, and other legal professionals. In the following chapters of Part IV, we survey the landscape of the main categories of collaboration tools used in lawsuits and transactions.

Instant Collaboration— from Conference Calls to Instant Messaging

12

Choosing the right collaboration tool often depends on the type of collaboration required, the context for the collaboration, and its timing. The timing of collaboration can be separated rather neatly into two categories: **synchronous** (occurring at the same time or in real time) and **asynchronous** (not occurring at the same time). These are big words to describe concepts that actually have been part of the practice of law since its beginning. Face-to-face conversations and working meetings are forms of synchronous collaboration. They are immediate and require the actual presence of the participants. There is a contemporaneous exchange and back-and-forth to the conversation. With asynchronous collaboration, work is done by message and contemporaneous presence is not a requirement. For example, a lawyer sends a letter, delivers a document by courier, or even leaves a file folder with a sticky note on a colleague's chair where it can be seen first thing in the morning.

Today's practice of law is increasingly asynchronous in nature. As we discuss throughout this book, email is the primary collaboration **platform** lawyers use today. Email is also an excellent example of asynchronous collaboration. As practices become more global in nature and law firms have increasing numbers of offices, it becomes more difficult to coordinate meetings and conference calls. So asynchronous collaboration techniques will naturally receive more attention than synchronous tools will, for good reason. However, synchronous collaboration tools are still quite important and have a place in a lawyer's practice.

Real-time collaboration is best utilized when time is of the essence, when a quick conversation can answer a question or sort out a problem, or when the information that needs to be conveyed does not lend itself to being written down. Real-time collaboration also helps us overcome the lack of nuance, the tendency to misinterpret, and the potential for misunderstanding we often find in email. In many cases, conversation tends to be more polite when it is immediate and in real time.

In this chapter, we focus on the real-time collaboration tools of conference calls and instant messaging, and the important role they play in facilitating instant collaboration across wide geographic distances.

Conference Calls

If email is the primary asynchronous collaboration platform, then the *sine qua non* of today's real-time collaboration is the **conference call**. The conference call is both a blessing and a curse. It is a simple, effective collaboration tool that takes advantage of one device critical to the practice of law—the telephone. It is logical to assume that because telephone calls work well for conversations between two people, they should serve as a great collaboration tool for calls involving many people.

There's little doubt that conference calls help us get work done more efficiently, but they can be maddeningly frustrating. Lawyers and businesspeople complain about conference calls as often as comedians joke about airline food. The question "Are you still on the line?" is heard in every call when someone new is added to the conference. Another familiar line is "I'll call you back if we are disconnected." However, the inability to handle basic conference calling today will make you as quaint and irrelevant as the lawyer who has his secretary print out his emails and reply to them herself.

Lawyers find conference call options in nearly every phone they use today, including home and cell phones. In most offices, regular phone service, **PBX** systems (Private Branch Exchange) and **VoIP** systems (Voice over Internet Protocol—Internet-based telecommunications) offer conferencing options. Skype and other Internet telephony services, both free and pay, are good alternatives. These Internet-based services, while generally very stable, do have their drawbacks. A brief Skype outage in 2007 revealed that the stability of the Skype platform was so strong, its users took Skype availability for granted. It also showed how many small businesses rely on Skype for business communications, especially for international calls.

The basic conference call features involve pressing buttons, putting people on hold, and then calling and adding more people to the conference. This process often ends up wasting time, dropping connections, and causing general frustration. Either keeping a cheat sheet on hand with the phone commands and instructions or having someone who can handle setting up the conference call for you are your best bets if you choose to initiate the call yourself.

The preferred way to handle conference calls today is with a professional service. These services, both free and fee-based, are available from telephone companies, dedicated conference call companies, and others. With these services, you receive a dial-in number and a participant or event code to call in at a prearranged time. Most of these services provide a toll-free phone number your participants can call. Additional features offered include operators for support, the ability to record the call, and scheduling features and reminders. The costs for these services will vary.

With conference call services, you can easily email participants to invite them to a call. Depending on their email system, participants may be able to add your invitation directly to their calendars, with the relevant numbers and dial-in information all in one place. At the appointed time, the attendees simply call the toll-free number, enter their participant or event code when prompted, and are then placed into the conference. The meeting organizer does not need to place a call to each participant individually.

A great feature of conference call services is that you can create a truly professional conference call, even if you have the smallest, least technological operation in the world. A service we like, Conference Calls Unlimited (http://www.conferencecallsunlimited.com), offers a wide variety of plans to suit your needs and budgets, flat-rate fees, "hold music," announcements of names on entry and departure, and the ability to take attendance and to allow large numbers of call participants. Many of these conference call services also offer webinar services, "whiteboarding," and other real-time collaboration tools, as we'll discuss in greater detail in the next chapter. Here are some of the other conference call services currently available:

- AccuConference (http://www.accuconference.com)
- AT Conference (http://www.atconference.com)
- Budget Conferencing (http://www.budgetconferencing.com)
- ConferenceCall.com (http://www.conferencecall.com)
- ECI Conferencing (http://www.calleci.com)
- FreeConference.com (http://www.freeconference.com)
- Global Conference (http://www.globalconference.com)
- Raindance (http://www.raindance.com)
- Star Conferencing (http://www.starconferencing.com)
- Teleconference.com (http://www.teleconference.com)

Conference calls have clear benefits for lawyers, especially lawyers who already spend most of their time on the phone. They take the most commonly and widely used real-time collaboration tool—the telephone—and make it more powerful and useful by multiplying the number of people who can participate in the discussion at the same time, no matter where they happen to be. When everyone needs to hear the conversation and give their input, a conference call definitely does the trick.

On the other hand, conference calls have their limitations. As an audio medium, the sound quality is often poor or even unacceptable. You also lose the benefits and nuances of face-to-face communication. And time zone differences can create problems of logistics. Even more aggravating can be the difficulty of commanding attention on a conference call. The typical conference call is a vivid illustration of the term "continuous partial attention," as people frantically multitask during the call—answering email, surfing the Internet, sending instant messages to other conference call participants, or doing other tasks (including participating in other conference calls at the same time!). From putting up with the annoying music when someone puts their phone on hold to take another call to hearing people place orders at the drive-up window of a fast-food restaurant, we all have stories of the negative aspects of conference calls.

▼▼▼▼▼
Conference Call Etiquette

Not surprisingly, a whole set of etiquette has sprung up to deal with conference calls. Here are some of our favorite tips to make sure you are a considerate and effective conference call attendee.

- Try to find a quiet place for the call—background noise will distract the other attendees.
- Try *not* to use a cell phone—the background noise from a cell phone can also be distracting. Also, poor-quality speaker phones can be worse than cell phones. Do a listening test on whatever phone or microphone you plan to use, even if you only call your own voice mail for a quick listen.
- Use the mute button on your phone—there are few things as annoying as having to listen to a call participant talk to his or her assistant or giggle about what's being said on the call.
- Remember to cancel the mute function when you do speak.
- Some headsets feature noise-canceling microphones that will keep background noise to a minimum and ease neck and shoulder strain on long calls.
- Identify yourself when you speak—don't assume everyone recognizes your voice.

- Don't shuffle papers or type on your computer keyboard—it's noisy! This is another reason to use your mute button.

- Don't put your phone on hold to do something else, especially if your company has "hold music"—the other participants effectively will be prevented from talking until you come back on the line.

It's important to remember that conference calls can be either fully participative or one-way in communication style. The classic one-way conference call is the teleseminar or **webinar**. Participants can call in to hear a presentation and have the ability to ask questions or make comments at your discretion. This alternative is useful with certain types of projects, to deliver educational content or updates on a project. Your current conference calling service may already offer these webinar features.

Although audio calls are still predominant, the distance to video conferencing gets smaller every day. In many ways, lawyers with grandchildren in other cities pioneered the use of videoconferencing in the law. With an inexpensive webcam (typically under $50), a fast Internet connection, and teleconferencing software, these lawyers could see their grandchildren and communicate with them. Other lawyers found out that while on vacation, they could connect to the website of the kennel boarding their pets and watch real-time videos of their dogs.

Today videoconferencing is increasingly used in the practice of law, although it still represents a small fraction of the volume of conference calls conducted daily. Many larger firms, especially those with offices in multiple locations, have built elaborate videoconferencing centers with state-of-the-art cameras, screen sharing, and the like.

However, you don't have to work for a megafirm to discover the power of the video conference. With an inexpensive webcam, broadband Internet access, and free software like Skype, you can be videoconferencing in a matter of minutes. While we expect videoconferencing to remain a small but steadily growing segment of overall conferencing, under the right circumstances it is a viable collaboration tool for every lawyer.

Instant Messaging

The last few years have seen explosive growth in the use of another real-time collaboration tool—**instant messaging** (or IM). Instant messaging is typically associated with teenagers and young adults, who live by it to such a great extent that they are abandoning both email and voice mail. As the generation raised on instant messaging enters the business world and the legal profession, and as business professionals begin to realize the value of these instantaneous communications, instant messaging is poised to take off as an important real-time collaboration tool.

Lawyers tend to shy away from instant messaging. Do lawyers really want one more way to be instantly available? The crush of email and voice mail is already so great; why open up another avenue for people to contact us at any time of day or night? Add to that the extremely casual nature of instant messages, the fact that instant messages are discoverable just like email, and the potential security risks of using instant messaging tools, and it's no surprise that instant messaging has been slow to catch on in the legal profession.

This stereotype of instant messaging ignores the real value that it can bring, especially if you use IM for its best intended purposes. It's another case of using the right tool for the collaboration that is needed.

What is especially intriguing about instant messaging is the way it straddles the line of asynchronous and synchronous communication. People can carry on an instant messaging conversation in real time, or they can send each other messages that can wait until the other is available to respond to them. The conversation also tends to be even more informal than email. In some ways, instant messaging is more an enabler of real-time collaboration than a channel for working with others at the same time.

A common misconception is that with instant messaging, you will have people firing IMs at you all day long. Fortunately, few of us are that popular. Instead, instant messaging software allows you to take control of who can have access to you, and when. At the same time, you can also see which of your contacts are available when you need to talk to them. Instant messaging software uses an invitation approach to help you set up your contact list of people with whom you want to communicate.

We'll use our favorite IM client, Skype, as an example in this chapter. Let's say Tom wants to IM Dennis using Skype's instant messaging features. Tom searches for and locates Dennis's Skype IM address in the Skype directory (or, even better, gets it directly from Dennis). To initiate the first contact with Dennis, he clicks "Add Skype Contact," which notifies Dennis that Tom wants to add him as a Skype contact. Dennis can either accept, or ignore and block, all future requests from Tom. Fortunately, he accepts Tom's requests, and Dennis and Tom are now "friends" who can begin to IM each other.

Now that they are IM friends, Tom and Dennis will be able to see when each of them is online and available for instant messaging. Skype offers a number of settings to indicate your availability, including Online, Away, Do Not Disturb, Not Available, and even Invisible. When Tom sees a green

"Online" icon by Dennis's name on his list of Skype contacts, he can initiate an instant messaging session with him.

Tom starts the conversation with Dennis by simply double-clicking on Dennis's name in IM (or chat) mode. A small text box appears, in which Tom can type a message. When he hits Enter the message is sent to Dennis, who is notified that Tom is contacting him. When Dennis clicks on the notification, the instant messaging window opens. Dennis can read Tom's message and type his reply in the text box. His response appears in Tom's Skype session window, and they can then continue to type messages in real time. It's not much more complicated than that.

Skype also keeps a dedicated history of your instant messaging transcript, so you can go back to an earlier conversation to see what was said or simply pick up where you left off. This archiving function has both good and bad points; although it is an appealing tool for brainstorming sessions and keeping track of what has been said in a conversation, it is, like email, a discoverable electronic communication.

Although we may think of instant messages as the short, acronym-filled bits of text our children send to each other, a message could be as long and detailed as an email (although we don't always advise this, because it reduces the true usefulness of the instant messaging program—if you want to send something of email length, send an email). You can also copy and paste text from another document and send a hyperlink or even a document or other file within the instant messaging session. There is a surprising amount of flexibility in instant messaging tools.

Further, the IM conversation is not limited to two people. It is easy to add additional participants to the same instant messaging session, making IM an interesting medium for ad hoc discussions. Dennis and Tom might be IM-ing each other and see that someone who could add something to the discussion is online and available. One click, and that person is invited and added to the conversation.

For those who work in a larger firm or organization, consider how instant messaging might be useful for intracompany communication. Rather than walking down the hall or downstairs to another floor, you can send an instant message to your colleagues in a fraction of the time. Instant messaging is especially handy when you don't need an answer immediately (for which you would use the phone), but need it sooner rather than later (for which an email would suffice). Some companies provide secure instant messaging services that can be deployed across your entire firm's network.

An open instant messaging session can also be a channel for an ongoing discussion in a way that phone calls cannot, and in a more connected way than the same discussion in an email thread. A 10- or even 45-minute delay in responding to an instant message is perfectly acceptable. A 45-minute silence on a phone call would be uncomfortable at best. For back-and-forth discussion, instant messaging is a better choice than email, because it is quicker and can be focused on certain aspects of a conversation as it develops. If you have a conversation by IM while you are having an extended email exchange with someone else, you will quickly see the benefits of the quickness of instant messaging. But that quickness can also be a negative; the speed and informality of IM sometimes lead to miscommunication.

Instant messaging can also enable the use of other collaboration tools. You might IM someone to see if he or she is available for a call, or to direct them to review or use content in another collaboration tool. Instant messages have also gone mobile, with many services offering the ability to IM on your cell phone, sometimes via Short Message Service (SMS, also known as a text message). Instant messaging also works well with those who have "continuous partial attention," allowing people to carry on multiple instant messaging sessions, IM while on a phone call, and do other types of multitasking.

Although we use and prefer Skype for our instant messaging conversations, there are dozens of IM services out there—from free, well-known tools to enterprise instant messaging products that can be deployed across a firm or company network. Here are a few of them:

- AOL Instant Messenger (http://aimpro.premiumservices.aol.com/)
- Apple iChat (http://www.apple.com/macosx/features/ichat/)—for Mac only
- Gizmo Project (http://www.gizmoproject.com)
- Google Talk (http://www.google.com/talk)
- ICQ (http://www.icq.com)
- ineen (http://www.ineen.com/)
- Jabbin (http://www.jabbin.com/)
- KoolIM (http://koolim.com/)—a web-based instant messaging aggregator that lets you access one or more of the popular IM services through your web browser—helpful if your company's firewall will not permit using a stand-alone IM client
- Meebo (http://www.meebo.com)—a web-based aggregator similar to KoolIM
- Miranda IM (http://www.miranda-im.org/)—an Open Source IM client
- Trillian (http://www.trillian.com)—an instant messaging aggregator—you can access one or more of the popular IM services from this platform
- Windows Live Messenger (http://get.live.com/messenger/overview)
- Yahoo! Messenger (http://messenger.yahoo.com/webmessenger promo.php)

Some instant messaging products are designed specifically for enterprise or firm network use. They include

- Akeni (http://www.akeni.com)
- Jabber (http://www.jabber.com)
- Lotus SameTime (http://www.ibm.com/developerworks/lotus/products/instantmessaging/)—from IBM and common in corporate settings.
- Microsoft Communicator (http://office.microsoft.com/en-us/communicator)
- Openfire, by Jive Software (http://www.jivesoftware.com/products/openfire/)
- Sonork (http://www.sonork.com/)

Instant messaging definitely belongs in the lawyer's toolbox of real-time collaboration tools. Properly understood and used, it is a perfect channel for quick real-time collaboration. While we expect to see the simple phone call and its bigger sibling, the conference call, remain the primary vehicle for real-time collaboration among lawyers for the foreseeable future, we hope you'll agree the real-time collaboration space is richer, more varied, and more versatile than you'd expect. In the right situation, any of the tools mentioned in this chapter might be the ticket to completing a project faster and better, which is of course the point of using collaboration tools in your practice.

How to Hold a Meeting on the Internet 13

No matter what type of law you happen to practice, at some point you will have to attend a meeting. You might think first of client meetings; but you also meet with staff, colleagues, co-counsel, expert witnesses, consultants, the court, and others. A meeting can be an expensive proposition, especially when you meet with people in other cities or even on other continents. The client typically ends up shouldering the costs of these meetings, which include travel expenses as well as the billable hours spent by lawyers and others in traveling to the meeting. Other, more intangible costs also are involved—usually involving time. For example, the time spent traveling is often wasted because it can usually be spent more productively back at the office. Even more frustrating is that the actual time spent in the meeting frequently pales in comparison to the amount of time involved in travel and logistics.

Until recently, lawyers and their clients accepted traveling long distances for meetings as a necessary evil and an unavoidable cost of doing business. With the rise of the Internet as a collaboration tool, however, more and more lawyers and businesspeople are finding it easier, cheaper, and more efficient to hold meetings online rather than in person. Surprisingly, this turns out to be the case even where long-distance travel is not involved. Where once the parties would have to spend hours (and sometimes days) traveling to and attending a meeting—and sometimes coordinating the travel of other attendees—now they can simply turn on their computers at the appointed time, sit down, and join the meeting from the comfort of their own offices, homes, cars, or hotel Internet connections. Online meetings aren't just for big firms or large companies. Solo and small firm lawyers are also increasingly attracted to this new phenomenon not just for its convenience, but because it can provide them with a virtual "conference room" they may not have in their own office space. In this chapter, we'll outline some of the ways you can hold a meeting on the Internet, from basic screen sharing to full-fledged online conferencing.

The Basic Meeting—Simple Screen Sharing

Some meetings are simple. Two people get together to review a document, exhibits for trial, or transaction files. Several collaboration technologies are available that will allow you to hold simple meetings online, with a minimum of effort. Many of these tools use a process known as **screen sharing**, which is generally defined as the ability to transmit the contents of your computer screen to the computers of one or more individuals. Essentially, screen sharing enables you to show presentations, documents, images, or any other software running on your computer, while remotely connected users can see what you are doing, in real time. The result is that you can accomplish "virtually" most of what you can do if you were meeting in person with your attendees. Some typical features of screen-sharing applications are similar to what can be done in a face-to-face meeting. Consider the following:

- Desktop sharing—Gives you the ability to share a document in its natural program or even the entire desktop with others, or just specific applications, if you do not want your attendees to see other parts of your computer.
- Changing presenters—Some services permit the host to give control to any attendee, who can then instantly share his or her screen with others—it's like turning over a presentation to someone in a physical meeting.
- Text and voice chat—Many of the screen-sharing services allow attendees to chat with the host or with others during the meeting, using either public or private chat or even voice chat for formal discussion, side chats, and back-channel conversations.
- Annotation tools—The host and attendees can mark on the screen in the same way meeting participants can use a dry erase marker to write on a whiteboard to an in-person meeting.
- Recording—A helpful feature is the ability to record sessions, so that participants or those who couldn't make the meeting can view it at any time.

- Download or installation—Many services do not require the download of specific software to take advantage of screen-sharing functionality, but some do have stand-alone software that adds extra features to the meeting experience.

- Screen sharing is platform neutral—Because most screen sharing takes place within a web browser, it does not matter which operating systems are in use by the attendees. Windows, Mac, and Linux users can all attend the same meeting, much as any invitee can enter the conference room where a physical meeting is being held.

Here's one caveat for all screen-sharing programs: to get the most out of an online meeting, a high-speed Internet connection is essential. If you are on a slow Internet, Wi-Fi, or cellular modem connection, your online experience will be balky at best and impossible at worst. As a practical matter, you simply cannot use a dial-up connection and expect to participate meaningfully in online meetings.

Before we get to some of the more full-featured services, let's look at the most basic of screen-sharing applications. Many of these tools use the **Virtual Network Computing** (VNC) desktop-sharing system as their engine for sharing screens. This system transmits keyboard and mouse events from one computer to another, allowing the person sharing the screen to control the other's computer. It's fast because you are transferring only a small amount of information—keystrokes and the like—from computer to computer rather than running the full underlying applications over the connection. Many IT help desks use programs like these to assist the company's employees with computer problems. By using the VNC tool to access someone else's computer, IT professionals are able to solve the employee's technical difficulties and save time in the process, instead of having to leave their desks to fix problems on individual PCs.

CrossLoop

A great example of this type of tool is CrossLoop (http://www.crossloop .com), a free application used between no more than two computers. It's very basic and dead simple to use. Both users must download and install the CrossLoop software. The program has two tabs and two basic functions—Access and Share. If you are sharing your own screen, click on Share, and let the other person know the access code indicated (for security purposes, this code changes every time you start the program). When both of you click Connect, you'll receive a request to allow the other to view your computer screen. After you grant access, a viewer opens up on the user's computer, which shows everything currently displayed on your computer desktop. You can then show documents, demonstrate programs, or give a presentation. If your counterpart wants to participate, he or she can control anything on your computer, using your own cursor. When you're done with the meeting, simply click Disconnect, and the two computers are no longer connected. If instead of hosting you want to view someone else's computer, it's as easy as clicking Access (the other person has first used the Share function on his or her computer), typing in the access code given to you by the other meeting participant, and clicking Connect. The viewer will launch on your computer, and you'll instantly have access to the other person's computer.

Reprinted with permission from crossloop.com.

FIGURE 13.1   CrossLoop

Adobe Acrobat Connect

A more-advanced screen-sharing program is Adobe Acrobat Connect (http://www.adobe.com/products/connect/). Acrobat Connect does not require any software download. All users need is a web browser and a fast connection. Users are given a URL where the meeting will occur, and the presenter can then share his or her computer screen within the web browser. Connect is different from CrossLoop because the meeting organizer can share his or her screen with more than one user, enabling multi-party meetings. Here's a quick overview of its features, and how we use it to conduct screen-sharing meetings.

When the organizer of the meeting logs in, he or she will have the opportunity to invite meeting participants by email, if they do not already have the URL of the meeting room. Participants cannot enter a meeting without the organizer's permission. When they are granted access, a pop-up window provides telephone information for the companion conference call, if desired. Adobe has fee-based phone lines available in the United States, United Kingdom, France, and Germany. Once the participants enter a user code, they will have access to the online meeting room.

The main screen is divided into several components. The largest area is where the organizer's screen is shared. On the left side are several windows, including one for a webcam, a list of attendees, a chat box, and a place to take notes. Any of these windows (called pods) can be expanded so that they are easier to use. The attendee list also allows users to indicate their status, including "I have a question," "Go faster," "Speak softer," or even "Stepped away." To begin the screen sharing, the organizer simply clicks Share My Screen. You can choose to share either your entire desktop, or individual windows or applications. You will need to download a small **plug-in** to enable the screen-sharing process.

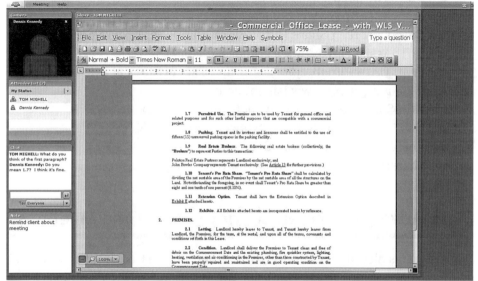

Adobe product screenshot reprinted with permission from Adobe Systems Incorporated.

FIGURE 13.2 Adobe Acrobat Connect

Once you are sharing your screen with the meeting participants, they can see everything you are doing on the computer screen, in real time. Attendees are able to look at documents, spreadsheets, images, or anything else you want to show them. Other users can take control of the organizer's screen to demonstrate something, make a change to a document, or share their own screens instead. Annotation tools are not available in the basic Connect product, but users of Connect Professional are able to mark up the screen they are sharing with others.

Acrobat Connect provides good, basic screen-sharing functionality with a comfortable and easy-to-use interface. If you upgrade to Connect Professional, you'll receive even more great features. Instead of sharing a document on-screen, you can upload a version that's converted to Adobe Flash and shared with all attendees. The Professional version also allows file sharing during the meeting. Web-based audio of the call is available and can be recorded for archiving or future use. PowerPoint programs can be uploaded and viewed by all participants, with support for video, animations, and high-resolution graphics.

Other Basic Screen-Sharing Tools

Other free or low-cost screen-sharing applications are available. Several of the following are designed primarily for tech support, but they are perfectly acceptable for screen sharing:

- BeamYourScreen (http://www.beamyourscreen.com)
- BLive (http://www.blive.com/)
- Bomgar (http://www.bomgar.com/)
- Bosco's Screen Share (http://www.componentx.com/ScreenShare/)
- GoToAssist (http://www.gotoassist.com/)
- Invitt (http://invitt.com/)—for up to six invitees at once
- ISL Light (http://www.isllight.com)
- NCH Software (http://www.nchsoftware.com)
- Netviewer (http://www.netviewer.net/)
- RealVNC (http://www.realvnc.com/)
- ShareItNow (http://www.shareitnow.com/)

More-Advanced Screen Sharing—Real-Time Meetings

The programs already mentioned (other than Adobe Connect Professional) give you basic functionality and get the job done when the focus is on simple screen sharing. They are less serviceable when you want integrated, back-and-forth, real-time communication as the key component of your meeting. If you're interested in a more powerful online meeting experience, there are some tools that can take you to a different level. Probably the biggest names in the online meeting space are GoToMeeting, WebEx, and LiveConference. We'll take a quick look at them here, along with some worthwhile competitors.

GoToMeeting

GoToMeeting (http://www.gotomeeting.com) is a well-known online meeting tool that can literally have you in an online meeting in a matter of seconds. Like the screen-sharing programs discussed earlier, GoToMeeting enables you to share your computer desktop with other attendees and show them specific applications or anything else on your computer. And that's only the beginning. With GoToMeeting, you can change presenters at the click of a button, so your attendees can see someone else's desktop. Drawing tools let users highlight and point to items of interest on the screen, and the Chat feature allows you to chat with specific participants or with all attendees. The program can be recorded, including any audio that is broadcast during the meeting, so that it can be saved for others to view. Depending on your subscription level, you can have up to 200 people attend your online meeting.

GoToMeeting is available on a 30-day trial basis free of charge, but after that you'll have to select a subscription option. The basic individual plan costs $49/month; corporate meeting accounts are also available for larger businesses and firms. GoToMeeting works on both PCs and Macs.

WebEx

WebEx (http://www.webex.com), another big player in the online conferencing world, is popular among large corporations and law firms. WebEx will actually host a meeting for you, providing behind-the-scenes support to plan, start, and run the meeting, so you can concentrate on the actual meeting itself. The service also integrates live audio, video, and data for multimedia presentations and teleconferencing. In addition to subscription and corporate pricing, users can purchase the pay-per-use meeting option, at a price of about $1.50 per minute for a three-person meeting. For more flexible pricing options, try the WebEx product MeetMeNow (http://www .meetmenow.com). It offers many of the same services as GoToMeeting, for the same prices.

Other Online Meeting Tools

Here are some other recommended web conferencing services:

- Convoq (http://www.convoq.com/)
- eBLVD (http://eblvd.com/)
- GatherPlace (http://www.gatherplace.net)
- Glance (http://www.glance.net)
- GoMeetNow (http://www.gomeetnow.com/)—available for Windows, Mac, Linux, UNIX, and even iPhone users
- HelpMeeting Presenter (http://www.hostpresentation.com/)
- InstantPresenter (http://www.instantpresenter.com/)
- Microsoft LiveMeeting (http://office.microsoft.com/livemeeting)
- Persony (http://www.persony.com)—offers a one-time license fee of $199, instead of subscription pricing
- PresenterNet (http://www.presenternet.com/)
- Spreed (http://spreed.com/)
- Vyew (http://vyew.com)—free for up to 20 participants. Plus and Premium pricing is available starting at $6.95/month, with increased attendee capacity and no ads. One nice feature of Vyew is

the Vyewbook, where content from meetings is automatically saved for review, edit, or further comment.

- Yugma (http://www.yugma.com)—offers free basic web conferencing for up to 10 users, with subscription pricing between $9.95 and $89.95/month, for between 10 and 500 attendees

Advanced Web Conferencing

The tools we mention in this chapter are fairly easy to implement, either by yourself or with the help of your IT department and others. More advanced conferencing options are available if your budget permits. Companies like Aspen Conferencing (http://www.aspenconferencing.com) integrate audio, web, and video capabilities to create a fully participatory meeting experience. Screens and even individual applications can be shared; and with whiteboarding and the ability to view your other meeting participants by video, it will seem as if you are all together in the same room. Even more high-end options are available to larger law firms, which are likely to implement custom-designed conferencing tools that integrate with multiple offices. Imagine being able to sit at a conference table and, on the floor-to-ceiling monitors across the table, see your other meeting participants as if they were actually in the room with you. You can stop imagining—this is now a reality in many firms and organizations around the world.

There's no question that online meeting tools have become some of the biggest time and money savers among the various collaboration technologies. They enable instant collaboration, connecting individuals from anywhere in the world to share documents or otherwise discuss important matters. And they ought to be successful tools—after all, every professional industry revolves around the idea of the meeting to get work accomplished. Hopefully, one of the tools mentioned here will work for the way you meet with others in your law practice.

Simple Project Management: Basecamp 14

The idea of project management has been around for some time, but until recently it was relegated to fields such as construction or engineering. As corporations began to appreciate the value of project management, more and more adopted this strategy and have improved efficiencies and profits as a result. Nearly every Fortune 500 company has some sort of project management department or structure, and there's even a Project Management Institute (http://www.pmi.org) with hundreds of thousands of members.

What is **project management**, and why should lawyers care? A project is essentially a temporary or short-term endeavor that requires a team of individuals to achieve a particular result. A good manager is necessary to the success of any project. Here are some basic activities of a project manager:

- Establishing project objectives
- Identifying the steps needed to achieve those objectives
- Putting together a team who will work on the project
- Developing a project plan
- Setting deadlines for completion of the plan
- Reporting plan progress to team members
- Reviewing project results

Now read this list again, but this time substitute the words "client matter" for "project" or "plan." Sound familiar? Lawyers engage in some form of project management all the time in dealing with lawsuits, transactions, and other legal matters.

There is a trend in legal services, especially electronic discovery, toward the use of actual project managers in the handling of electronic evidence. In many ways, law firm partners who manage associates, paralegals, and staff are good examples of project managers. So why don't lawyers use classic project management approaches, principles, and tools in their practices?

While lawyers may appreciate the efficiencies of project management, in general they are reluctant to take the time necessary to actually "manage" the project. Lawyers often see "management" work as something separate from or outside the scope of the "practice" of law. Some lawyers may not consider management time the same as billable time, which makes it feel like even more of a burden than it already is. The best lawyers also often have exceptional project management skills, even if they do not consciously recognize or value those specific skills. Project management is one of those valuable legal practice skills not taught in any law school or continuing education class. Further, legal project management tools don't get a lot of recognition.

Many of the project management tools you see today are high-end, expensive enterprise applications built on complex database software or programs like Microsoft Project, a well-known project management program. However, Microsoft Project is not part of the standard Microsoft Office suite used in most firms, so you won't find it in many law firms. Some lawyers and firms adapt case management software, public folders in Outlook, or other standard legal programs for certain aspects of project management. Fortunately, various project management tools have appeared on the Internet in the past few years. They can take the uncertainty out of managing a project and make the process an easy, user-friendly experience.

In this chapter, we will discuss project management by focusing on one of the most popular, inexpensive Internet project management tools and showing you how lawyers might use it for collaboration. It's simple to use and has been well received by the primarily solo and small firm lawyers who have tried it. This project management tool is Basecamp (http://www .basecamphq.com), a web-based service from a company called 37 Signals. It provides an interface common to other project management tools, so you can get a good idea of what other sites offer by giving Basecamp a test drive. Basecamp is also relatively inexpensive to use, and it can provide you with a good return on investment (ROI) or "bang for your buck," which is always nice to find in a technology tool.

The Basecamp service is free to use for one project, and it is available in other packages that cost up to $149/month for an unlimited number of project pages. Basecamp offers the following features:

- Storage for file sharing—from 250MB to 50GB
- Unlimited number of people or clients can access your project pages

- Real-time chat
- **Secure Sockets Layer** (SSL) security—the data sent between Basecamp and the computers of you and your collaborators is encrypted
- Time tracking
- Unlimited number of writeboards (online whiteboards or collaborative document spaces)
- Campfire—real-time group chat tool for businesses

Basecamp offers a free 30-day trial, so you can give it a test drive before deciding to purchase. After you register, the first thing you'll want to do is provide access to the members of your project team. This can be done by clicking All People, and then Add People. All members of your team will receive an email with login instructions.

When you create your first project, you'll start with the **Dashboard**, which gives you access to everything going on in all of your open projects. The Dashboard page displays upcoming and late milestones, and the latest activity broken down by specific project. Click on Create a New Project, which is in the right-hand margin of the page. Just give the project a name—the case title, the transaction description, the subject matter of your project—and you're all set. You can create more projects now, or just start with the first one. All of your projects will be listed on the right side of the screen—to get started with one, simply click the project name, and you'll be taken to that project's individual page.

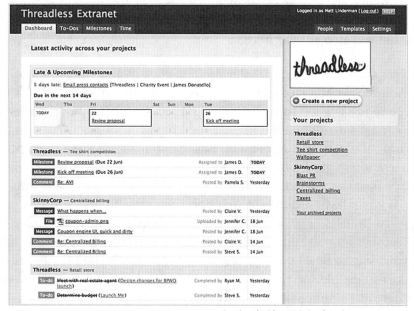

Reprinted with permission from basecamphq.com.

FIGURE 14.1 Basecamp Dashboard

The project pages are easy to navigate. All of the functions are lined up in familiar tabs across the top of the screen. For each project, you have these separate areas:

- Overview—A mini-Dashboard, showing all the recent activity for that individual project.
- Messages—A discussion board where team members can discuss issues and post files. The messages are threaded so conversations are kept together.
- To Do—A place to create to-do items. You can filter the list to see only the tasks assigned to you.
- Milestones—Major objectives of the project are posted here, with specific tasks for each milestone posted in the To Do area.
- Writeboards—A place where team members can create group documents. Although this is a handy feature, we recommend a more full-featured word processor like Google Docs for sustained online document collaboration. Writeboards can be great for brainstorming, making initial outlines, and collecting ideas.
- Chat—Team members who are online at the same time can chat about issues in this area.
- Time—Available to premium account members only, this feature helps keep track of time that is being spent on an individual task, or the complete project.
- Files—Any file can be uploaded to this area, so that all files for one project are in the same place, accessible to all team members. If you attach a file to a message in the Messages area, a link to that file will also appear here.

To get started with a particular project, click on the Milestones tab and select Add a New Milestone. You can add up to ten milestones at a time. A **milestone** is assigned to a particular person, and it is due on a specified date. It can be a deadline for a filing, a meeting with the client, or a date for a first draft of a contract agreement. Basecamp makes it easy to create the milestone and assign the task to a particular member of the team; you can even have Basecamp send a reminder 48 hours before the task is due.

To Do lists have a different function than milestones. You can create multiple To Do lists, with as many separate tasks as you want under each list. Milestones let you know what specific tasks need to be done and when. When you assign a new task, you can designate a particular member of your team as responsible for the task, and Basecamp will automatically email him or her with a notice of the newly assigned task.

Keeping Notified with Basecamp

One of the best features of Basecamp is its ability to notify any team member of new information whenever it is posted to the project page. As we discuss in greater detail in Chapter 27, your collaboration tools become much more valuable to your users if they can have site updates delivered to them without having to visit the site itself.

Basecamp provides several methods for notifying team members of new information. The first is email notification. When you post a message or upload a file to a project page, you have the option to notify some or all of your other team members. Everyone who receives an email of your new post or file will not be able to reply directly to that email. Instead, they must log in to make their comment. This might seem to be a drawback, but it's a great feature that keeps all parts of the conversation together. You don't have the content of individual emails escaping the attention of other team members.

Those of you who use **RSS feeds** to keep updated with the latest news and information will appreciate Basecamp's RSS notification feeds. There's an RSS feed for every project page that is created. You can easily subscribe only to those projects in which you're participating; or, if you want to keep track of everything that's going on in all of your projects, you can subscribe to the Global RSS feed at the bottom of the Dashboard page. Unlike the email notification feature, the RSS feeds notify you of everything that happens on a project page or even site-wide, depending on the type of subscription you choose. Simply select the notification feature that works best for you.

Basecamp also provides a calendar to keep you on schedule and see when milestones are due. One current downside of Basecamp is the lack of a calendar that integrates with your computer's calendar—something you will find in other collaboration tools. However, if you use a program that supports the iCalendar standard—Outlook 2007, Apple iCal, Backpack Calendar (http://www.backpackit.com/calendar), or Mozilla Calendar (http://www.mozilla.org/projects/calendar/)—you can subscribe to the milestones on any particular project page, and they'll be imported directly into your regular calendar. There's also a Global iCalendar at the bottom of the Dashboard page, if you want to get milestones from all project pages at once.

Using Basecamp in a Law Firm

How would lawyers use Basecamp or a similar online project management tool? Litigators could set up a project page for a particular upcoming trial, so that all of the issues, tasks, court deadlines, communications, and case files (pleadings, exhibits, depositions, etc.) regarding that case could reside in one place. Transactional lawyers who are working on a particular acquisition could post the different versions of transaction documents online; actually draft documents or share meeting minutes, ideas, action items and the like in the writeboard area; or chat about issues from their desktop. More and more, lawyers are working "virtually" from their home office, and sites like Basecamp allow groups of lawyers to work together on matters without ever having to leave their home office. In such situations, project management sites are superior to traditional forms of collaboration such as email, because they provide a centralized repository of information that is not scattered among multiple computers.

Whether you are working with trials or transactions, Basecamp can serve as an "extranet" for easily and securely communicating case information to your clients, co-counsel, experts, or other individuals. We discuss extranets in detail in later chapters, but Basecamp's basic features will give you a taste of what to expect when using an extranet. Clients or others can be given access to any portion of the project pages, and access can be restricted only to projects they are permitted to view. The advantages to providing this type of online access to clients are immediately apparent. They will have 24/7 access to case files and the calendar of upcoming deadlines or court dates. They can leave messages for—or ask questions of—you on the message board. They can actually participate in their legal matters, which is always important to clients. In this way, Basecamp can also work as a marketing tool, demonstrating to your clients that you have a transparent practice and that everything they want to know about their case is available to them at any time of the day. An extranet is often too expensive for a solo or small firm to use, but Basecamp fills the gap admirably, providing extranet-type services for a fraction of the cost.

Alternatives to Basecamp

Although Basecamp was one of the first online project management sites and is still one of the best, it's not the only game in town. Here are a few other project management sites worth checking out before making a final decision on the tool that best serves your needs:

- ActiveCollab (http://www.activecollab.com)—an Open Source project management tool, with more flexible pricing options
- Zoho Project (http://projects.zoho.com)—another great free offering from Zoho
- Project360 (http://www.project360.com)—similar to Basecamp in plans and pricing offered, although Basecamp plans provide more

storage space for documents. Many of the Project360 features are more extensive than those of Basecamp.

- Central Desktop (http://www.centraldesktop.com)—provides quite a bit more features than Basecamp, including the abilities to collaborate on documents in real time and to hold web meetings and audio conferences

- GoPlan (http://goplan.info/)

- Project2Manage (http://www.project2manage.com/)—a free project management tool with most of the standard features described in this chapter

- Huddle (http://www.huddle.net/)—a U.K. service that offers features similar to those of Basecamp

- Solodox (http://www.solodox.com/)

- Sosius (http://www.sosius.com)—less a project management site, and more a site for storing information and sharing it with others

Lawyers today can choose from a wide variety of project management tools. Your choices range from simple online calendars that help you schedule meetings to enterprise-level behemoths. Don't forget that Microsoft's Project and SharePoint tools are two very popular and well-regarded options. Increasingly, project and workflow management software can be found in electronic discovery tools and other traditional legal software, such as case management programs. Project management tools can assist you in scheduling, delegating and monitoring tasks, keeping track of deadlines, and measuring productivity and other metrics—in ways that are sure to appeal to lawyers.

Another great benefit of project management software is that it gives everyone on the team a single place to find all of the relevant information about a project. This may be the best advantage of these types of sites, and what leads businesspeople to select them for project management over the usual scattershot approaches that can leave team members trolling through email, calendars, document and case management programs, specialty databases, spreadsheets, and various other places to find relevant information. Of all the collaboration tools we discuss in this book, project management tools may have the most potential to benefit practicing lawyers and the people with whom they work.

Setting Up a Simple Extranet or Deal Room | **15**

If it is not obvious to you by now, the Internet is at the heart of nearly every collaboration tool we discuss in this book. As law firms add offices in multiple locations and lawyers work from both home and on the road, the Internet provides the actual platform on which collaboration is accomplished. Email, websites, audio, video, messaging, and many more collaboration technologies are facilitated over the Internet. People know how to use the Internet, and it is a continuously evolving, highly flexible channel for communication and collaboration. More importantly for our purposes, it is an environment in which lawyers and millions of others are comfortable.

In this chapter, we will discuss one of the most basic of Internet collaboration tools—the extranet. Extranets are used for collaboration by law firms of all sizes, and they are steadily increasing in popularity. Once you understand the nature of extranets, you will appreciate their ubiquity, versatility, and importance as part of the lawyer's collaboration toolbox.

In simplest terms, an **extranet** is a private, secure website. While they are available over the Internet and accessible through a browser, extranets can be used only by a limited, permission-based audience. In other words, extranets are private websites on the public Internet. If you have the URL for an extranet site, you can navigate to it; but you cannot access it and view its contents unless you are an authorized user with appropriate access rights.

Why do we believe extranets are the building blocks of collaboration? At the root of nearly every online collaboration tool, including web applications like Google Docs, is the fundamental notion of an extranet—even if the tool does not go by that name. No matter which online tool you use, you must navigate to it on the public Internet using your browser. For most sites you must register as a user and create a password to gain entrance. It is only after you are accepted as a registered member of the site that you can use the content and features available there. Any time you register for an Internet site with a user name and password, you are essentially working with an extranet. These sites include web-based email, personalized pages, subscription and membership-only sites, social networking sites, and more.

The user name and password requirement illustrates the authentication features inherent in all extranets. **Authentication**, the verification of identity, is a necessary component of any secure collaboration tool; and of course security is critical to any activities in the legal profession. Lawyers need to be certain that only the appropriate people actually have access to the information provided on the site. They also want to make sure that the person who has permission to enter the site is actually the person who is gaining access.

To understand how this works, we must consider the concepts of authentication and authorization. Authentication works hand in hand with authorization, and both components are part of the larger idea of identity management, which we discuss in greater detail in Chapter 28. **Authorization** takes place when a person is given the right to access and use certain content, and nothing more. This right of access is sometimes referred to as user rights or privileges. When you visit an extranet, you see only what you are permitted to see. You cannot do anything beyond your level of authorization. Extranets can also track what you view or do while on the site.

Because it is at its heart a website, an extranet has the same capabilities as other sites you see on the Internet. Extranets use graphics, video, audio, animation, web design, scripting, and anything else a regular website offers. They also connect to databases; provide email, instant messaging, and RSS features; allow you to upload and download files; and much more. And because extranets use web design techniques like cascading style sheets and **Extensible HyperText Markup Language** (XHTML), they can be customized to the user's personal wishes.

In theory, an extranet is infinitely customizable. As a practical matter, however, most basic extranet tools tend to be provided as complete all-in-one applications, with a limited degree of customization. Some law firms are able to create a higher level of personalization by producing their own extranet sites. As with many collaboration tools, you can host an extranet site on your own server or have a third party host it for you, which is most common for basic extranet users.

To recap, an extranet combines the best elements of a modern, versatile public website with the security and control of a private, internal application. This unique combination of qualities leads us to say that extranets are the basic building blocks of online collaboration. Although you will not necessarily see most online tools referred to as extranets, you will definitely recognize the basic extranet concepts in nearly every online collaboration tool—Internet availability, registration and authentication, authorization and control, and versatility in what can be done on the extranet.

Extranet Features

Extranets are extremely versatile. You can set up as few or as many as you like. You can set up a single extranet and let many people use it for their particular purposes, or you can set up multiple extranets, one for each client or matter. The second approach is more popular among lawyers, firms, and their clients, for several reasons.

When choosing an extranet, lawyers typically consider two types of configuration. The first, at least conceptually, remains "outside the firewall." The extranet is sealed off from a firm's internal systems and applications, sometimes residing on an external computer. To make a document available on the extranet, it must be copied out of the firm's document management system and uploaded to the extranet, where others—including clients—can access the document. If editing on the extranet is allowed, any changes would occur on the extranet's document, but typically not to the original document still residing in the document management system. The emphasis of an external extranet is on security, allowing the extranet user to access the relevant information without inadvertently or improperly gaining entry to the firm's internal network.

The second extranet configuration recognizes that the "stand-alone" version creates certain inefficiencies and can be cumbersome, forcing you to make copies and creating duplication of effort and documents. With appropriate security, this second type of extranet provides limited and controlled access to a firm's internal systems, including document management and, in some cases, even time and billing systems. The client may be allowed access to archived documents, work in progress, billing records, and even real-time billing information.

Many extranets also provide some type of communication or "awareness" tool. Users might be able to send messages to others on the project, use discussion boards, send instant messages, or otherwise communicate with each other. When changes are made or someone has completed a task on the extranet, alerts might be issued by email or **RSS feed**.

Other extranet features include group calendars with the ability to schedule meetings and calls, online "case files," project management and workflow tools, news updates, collections of useful links, and research and form banks. Extranets are endlessly versatile and flexible, and they can be customized to your specifications.

Lawyers typically use extranets for defined and limited groups of outsiders, usually clients but also experts, opposing counsel, or anyone with an interest in a particular matter. Firms often "brand" their extranets with their logos and colors, or even with the logos and colors of their clients. Firms may routinely roll out new extranets based on a standard design template, which reduces the incremental costs of providing additional extranets. A significant number of large firms routinely create extranets for each of their new clients as a matter of course when a new file is opened. Solos and small firms are also experimenting with these tools, using the Basecamp services described in the previous chapter as an inexpensive form of extranet. Some firms are using extranets as marketing tools, demonstrating to their clients that they are interested in providing transparent access to the client's important case information, which the client can access at any time.

As we've stated, extranets are infinitely customizable, but in most cases they reveal just the amount of information needed and provide only the tools necessary to complete the particular project. New features can readily be added as they are needed or requested.

Using an Extranet in Your Law Practice

How would a lawyer use an extranet in his or her practice? A lawyer might open a client extranet to make sanitized versions of research memos and updates to articles available for download. A firm might upload copies of the client's complete file, accessible only by that client. As we'll discuss shortly, a litigation extranet might provide clients, experts, and even co-counsel with access to deposition transcripts or even video of depositions. An extranet can give a client instant access to time and billing information, electronic bills, expense receipts, and message boards to leave comments for its attorneys. Rather than preparing huge closing binders for real estate deals, a firm could instead provide access to an electronic copy of the closing documents on an extranet. And an extranet can provide updates of legal developments and case summaries of interest to the client. In short, just about any type of information that would be of interest to the client can be posted to an extranet.

The beauty of an extranet as a collaboration tool is its simplicity. Collaborators require no new hardware or software other than their computer, an Internet connection, and a browser. They can access their extranet wherever the Internet is available, and at any time. An extranet's business hours are 24 by 7 by 365.

Extranets are also becoming popular in the corporate setting; law firms are actually being pressured by their clients to offer extranets. The collaboration-savvy firm will no doubt be receptive to requests from clients and corporate legal departments to provide extranets as a part of its legal services. As the Internet increasingly changes our expectations about customer service, lawyers must keep up with new developments in technology and be prepared to meet client demand. For example, many consumer websites show how many units of an item are in stock before you order it, and then let you track the shipment of your order with the click of a button. Why shouldn't clients likewise be entitled to see their lawyer's current billings and work in process with a click of the mouse or in a dashboard, **applet**, or widget on an extranet entry page?

Another common division of extranets is by practice categories—litigation and transactional extranets. Extranets used for transactions are often referred to as **deal rooms**. Although used for different areas of legal work, each type of extranet has at its heart the same idea: to create a place to share files or store documents, where authorized people can review, revise, and otherwise work on them. The extranet can also serve ultimately as a permanent online archive for this material.

Let's discuss further how an extranet can be used in the context of litigation. At its most basic, a litigation extranet can be used as a repository for pleadings, transcripts, and exhibits. As we've already discussed, audio or video depositions might be collected there, along with research, memoranda, and notes. In the case of electronic discovery, the actual electronic documents can be stored and reviewed directly on the extranet, often with the ability to use powerful search and review tools. Extranets are also used in multi-jurisdictional cases, to allow co-counsel or other lawyers representing the same client in similar cases across the country to access the client's core document collection. Everyone involved in the lawsuit will appreciate the benefits of an extranet; and perhaps the biggest benefit is being able to obtain documents on demand, without having to call or email the lawyer for a copy.

Deal rooms offer similar benefits to transactional lawyers and their clients. In a single online location, all parties to a negotiation or deal can access relevant documents, keep track of revisions, review the progress of negotiations, and simplify the exchange of documents. Combining the extranet with an electronic signature tool will enable the parties to close transactions securely without shipping paper documents around the country or the world. At the close of a deal, clients and others involved in the transaction can retain access to the deal materials whenever they are needed.

In addition to providing convenient, even comprehensive, collaborative spaces, extranets offer significant side benefits in cost savings and marketing. By providing documents online, extranets can save the costs of paper, printing, copying, faxing, overnight shipping, postage, and other expenses associated with transmitting paper documents. Extranets likewise can reduce the need for travel and travel costs. Using extranets to electronically bill your clients may even help you be more efficient in billing and collecting your fees. Best of all, extranets are a means by which lawyers can provide their clients with innovative ways to save them money. How many times have you heard clients talk about ideas lawyers bring to them for saving money? Not often, we'd guess.

One of the most frequent client complaints about lawyers, about which many lawyer disciplinary complaints are filed, is that lawyers do not keep clients informed about what is happening with their matters. Extranets help solve that problem by creating a channel for regular, always accessible communication, updates, and alerts on lawsuits and transactions. An extranet that keeps your clients up to date, provides them with news and developments, and even allows them to collaborate on projects and documents will show them that you are paying attention.

We've already mentioned that extranets can help you market to your clients, but the idea is worthy of further discussion. When you offer an extranet at the outset of representation, you are demonstrating your commitment to keeping the client informed and aware of what is going on at all times. An extranet can tie a client to your firm, not just to the attorney with the personal relationship. If clients become used to the benefits and conveniences of their own customized extranet, they will find it more difficult to go with a lawyer who is leaving your firm or change to another firm without the same level of service.

Extranets require commitment. They must work flawlessly, or the client will lose trust, not just with the extranet but with the lawyer providing it. You must pay attention to message boards and update content regularly on the site. As you provide features and your clients use them, your clients may suggest new features and expect you to add them. This may place additional demands on your systems or staff, but it is worth the effort. While you need to approach the idea of extranets with your eyes open, you'll find the benefits usually will outweigh the risks and difficulties.

In Chapter 18, we'll discuss some of the extranet tools and services being used by law firms and organizations.

Commonly Used Collaboration Platforms

Email as a Platform 16

Many years ago, email was dubbed the "killer app," as the computer application destined to have the most impact on our daily lives. The fact that more than 20 billion emails are sent on a *daily* basis proves the truth of that assertion. In this chapter, we'll discuss the idea of email as a collaboration platform, the pros and cons of using email as a collaboration tool, and some practical tips for getting the most out of your email use.

Of all the collaboration platforms we discuss in this book, none is more important or more ubiquitous than email, for several reasons:

- Simplicity—Email is easy to use (although it may be more difficult to *manage,* as we'll discuss below). Of all computer applications, email is perhaps the one that people "get" the most. And after you learn it for the first time, all other upgrades or variations are basically the same, so the learning curve for keeping up with email is almost nonexistent.

- Interoperability—No matter what operating system you use, you can send email. Further, you can use email from a stand-alone application or via web-based sites like Gmail, Yahoo, or others. It's also accessible from anywhere you are—from your computer, your mobile device, or, increasingly, your cell phone—at any time.

- Speed—Email is all but instantaneous today. We can send an email while talking on the phone and discuss its contents in a matter of seconds. Regular mail and overnight delivery simply are not fast enough to keep up with lawyers today.

- Time Shifting—Email does not require your collaborators to be present when you communicate with them. Email allows you to get your work done and forward it to your collaborators, who can then work on their part of the project on their own time.

- Single Point of Access—Many people prefer to maintain only one **silo** of information, and for most people email is that silo. Once information has to be sought out by regularly visiting several places or begins to come in through RSS feeds or other channels, confusion begins to set in.

- Personalized Organization—You can organize your email the way you like, not according to someone else's idea of how information should be categorized. You can also choose who to include in conversations, by sending your message only to those people.

- Universality—Email is universal, and it's in your face—do you know anyone who doesn't use email? The downside is, it's *always* in your face, demanding your attention. Users have the ability to determine how often they want to be disrupted by their email, and unfortunately many choose to be disrupted far too often.

- Carry a Payload—The ability to attach documents and other files makes email an effective vehicle for collaboration. Email combines a communication element with a content transportation element.

- Comfort—Email just works. Simply open a blank email, type a few words, click Send, and you're done. You won't find many programs on your computer that are so easy to use.

But email is not without its challenges. Spam makes up 60–80 percent of the email we receive, depending on which survey you believe. Email arrives daily, loaded with viruses, **spyware**, and **adware**. Scam artists send us messages that actually look like they came from our bank or credit card company. The problems with email have gotten so bad, some have suggested that "email is dead."

As useful as email may be as a standard communications tool, it is generally considered to be a poor collaboration platform, based on its lack of "pure" collaboration features. Nonetheless, email remains the most common medium of collaboration; the death of email, especially among lawyers, is far from imminent. In most settings, you will not only be collaborating by email, it will be the preferred and requested method of collaborating and sharing information with others, despite its shortcomings. For collaboration purposes, you must understand and address the weaknesses of the email platform while taking advantage of its strengths.

Email as a Collaboration Medium

Let's look at some reasons email is a less than ideal collaboration medium. Say you have a project to work on with five people, and you choose to do so by email. Here are some problems that could arise.

Technical Difficulties

You send a document for review by email. It might be blocked by one of your recipients' spam filter, rejected because the attachment is too large for another recipient's inbox, or trapped by aggressive security settings on someone else's firewall. Not all of your recipients might get the document, or they might receive it too late only after having to search for it.

Email Is Not a Document Manager

After all of your recipients receive the email, they edit their individual versions of the attached document on their own timetables and without knowing the changes others are making. As they finish, they send out five different versions to all members of the team, with comments in five different messages. You can also expect several of the reviewers to edit versions sent by others, resulting in a constantly expanding number of document revisions. At that point, where's the most recent version? Email is a poor document management system.

Improper Use of Technology

Reviewers may forward drafts to the wrong people, reply only to the sender rather than to all, or make any number of other basic email faux pas that can result in confusion, miscommunication, and wasted time. If members of your team fail to turn on Track Changes before editing their document, you or other team members will have to spend precious time figuring out their changes.

Failure to Copy All Team Members

If team members fail to copy everyone on their comments and edits, you quickly reach a point where people are looking at different drafts or missing out on key parts of the discussion. If the collaborators continually fail to use the Reply to All option, you could end up with several different discussions, each going to different groups, with everyone thinking that all members are involved and on the same page. Of course, the reverse problem—copying people who should not be copied—can cause its own set of issues.

Continually Restarting the Project

Email does not provide a good way to add people to projects in midstream. For example, if three new people join the project, to get them caught up you will have to send them the current draft, prior drafts, forward earlier key emails, and generally try to recreate the email thread. The recipient then has to sort the messages in the proper order and try to get caught up.

Confusion in Conversation Flow

The asynchronous, ongoing nature of email can make it difficult to reach consensus or finality. For example, suppose you ask for final comments by the end of the day. Three members of your team respond quickly to the topic, all of them agreeing with your approach. The next day, other responses trickle in with new thoughts that change the approach you want to take. If a key team member does not reply to an email, it can hold up the process as people wait for the reply. If someone later goes back to find the reason for a decision, they might not find all of the related email replies.

Decentralization of Information

Everyone has to manage her or his individual email archives, and this process often results in important information being deleted, lost, or misplaced. Conversations on the same topic can be scattered in time throughout folders in your inbox. Unless you use a conversation threading feature in your email program, it is difficult to trace and follow the flow of conversation. Further, having all of this information in individual, personal silos means the team cannot share or search it. In comparison, a discussion forum excels in letting users insert their feedback into the correct place in the hierarchy of the conversation, where it can be easily followed and searched at a later time. We cover discussion forums in greater detail later in this chapter.

Email Safety

Email raises a number of safety and security concerns, from misaddressing the message to the possibility of having it intercepted before it reaches the recipient. Unless you use encryption to protect your messages, whenever you send an email you risk the possibility that it will be received, intercepted, or read by individuals other than your intended recipient. The ease with which people can forward email with sensitive information is another source of concern. The best way to secure your email is to encrypt it—a practice that is still rare in the legal profession. This is due in large part to ABA Formal Ethics Opinion 99-413, which has been broadly interpreted as stating that lawyers do not need to encrypt email to preserve its confidential status. While we expect the use of encryption to grow in the coming years, its use will probably be limited to extremely sensitive matters rather than for all email.

Email Makes Us Lazy

Of all the technology tools, email is the easiest and most comfortable for lawyers to use. However, comfort sometimes leads lawyers (and all professionals, really) to be lazy about their communications. Unlike written letters, email makes it easier to be informal, quick, and even flip. Many email communications we receive from practicing lawyers do not even contain proper grammar, spelling, or punctuation. Likewise, when you receive an email there's no one looking over your shoulder to make sure you respond to it in a timely manner. Unfortunately, email leaves a written, timestamped, and traceable record of your lazy habits, and flip email replies can come back to haunt you.

Many of these problems are not necessarily inherent in the use of email itself. Rather, they are primarily problems with the people using email, and with expectations not being properly communicated at the outset of the project. As you read this chapter, you may be thinking of better, more efficient ways to collaborate on a project than by using email. What's clear, however, is that for many lawyers the other tools we mention in this book will not replace email for collaboration in the foreseeable future. Email is still a necessary and perhaps primary communications platform for many collaborative efforts.

Making Better Use of Email

We are not here to bury email or to proclaim that it is dead. We merely point out that the constraints and weaknesses of email as a collaboration platform will continue to be a concern, and they are not likely to go away anytime soon. For this reason, we think it's wise to reconsider how you currently use email, how you might use it in the future, and how you can make the transition to using tools better suited than email to your individual projects.

When you think about ways to make better use of email as a collaboration tool, one option is to combine your email communications with a discussion forum or mailing list. These tools allow you to add team members as subscribers, and you can create a single email address for that team. Users send all email to that address, which automatically distributes the message to the entire team, thus eliminating the CC issues discussed earlier. Online email list tools (often called listservs) also typically provide archiving tools. When anyone sends a message to the list, a copy is posted automatically to the online archive. Archived conversations are organized in threads; so users visiting the archive can review what has been said, in the order it was communicated. Two free web-based tools that will create archived mailing lists for you are Yahoo! Groups (http://groups.yahoo.com) and Google Groups (http://groups.google.com). These online discussion groups can be made public or private, but for purposes of your projects you will probably opt for the private group. For those of you who are able to host a mailing list on your own computer servers, consider using Open Source programs like MailMan (http://www.list.org/) or Majordomo (http://www.greatcircle .com/majordomo/), which can allow you to create your own highly customized mailing lists.

Another option is a service like 9cays (http://9cays.com), which makes it simple to create an online discussion forum out of any email conversation. To start a 9cays conversation, simply include a dedicated 9cays email address in the initial email to your group—that's it! The 9cays server will create a web page to hold all of the email messages. Group members are given login information so they can access the online message archive. Messages are private and cannot be accessed unless permission is given. Additionally, if an email has an attachment, it will be saved on the 9cays server and can be viewed online. The 9cays service is currently free to use, but future versions will include fee-based premium features.

Also available are some advanced email tools that might be appropriate in your setting. A good example is Prolify (http://www.prolify.com), which provides a software platform that allows users to continue to use email as the main medium of collaboration, with the added benefit that all activities can be monitored through administrative dashboards or even in planning tools like Excel or Visio. Prolify is intended primarily for larger organizations with the need for enterprise-wide collaboration.

Using the discussion forum option definitely addresses some of the problems with using email as a collaboration platform. However, to be truly effective the discussion forums must be appropriately utilized by every member of the team; once an email is sent to an individual's personal inbox, the chain is broken, and the utility of the discussion forum is weakened or destroyed. It's surprising how quickly a group email effort can break down and fall into disuse once people start sending individual emails outside the system.

Tips for Email Productivity

Email has some shortcomings as a collaboration platform, but we're not going to see any significant movement away from email as the primary collaboration channel for lawyers anytime soon. While we recognize that other collaboration tools we discuss in this book may better serve your needs for individual projects, we also recognize that email is a popular medium that works well enough in most cases. With that in mind, we've put together some of our favorite productivity tips to help you manage your email better and use it more effectively.

Face Up to the Email Volume Problem

Our first tip is often the hardest for people to implement. You must admit that, on your own and without additional automation and strategies, you are powerless to stop the never-ending onslaught of email and spam. Let's face it, we will never be able to read every single email we receive for the rest of our lives. And why would we want to? The earlier you admit that sometimes your workload exceeds your resources, the closer you are to dealing effectively with your email and focusing on the messages that matter most to you and your projects.

Perform Regular Email Triage

Next, consider using triage for your email. The word "triage" comes from the battlefield term, which describes the system emergency personnel use to respond when the medical resources available are limited. Medical triage is divided into three primary groups:

- Those who can survive with immediate help
- Those who are not seriously injured and can wait for attention
- Those who are beyond help

Email triage should work in much the same way as you process the contents of your inbox each day. Ask yourself, which messages must I deal with immediately and get out of the way? Which messages require further action, but can wait for an answer or response? And finally, which messages can I delete immediately, because they require no response or are of no future use to me? By thinking like a medic, you can work through your inbox in a fraction of the time it usually takes.

Get Things Done

If you do not think a triage approach will work for you, try productivity guru David Allen's methods in his book *Getting Things Done*. Where email is concerned, the goal of getting things done (or GTD, as it is often called) is to work toward having an empty inbox by focusing on the action each email requires and moving the messages out of your undifferentiated inbox to folders where you can take action on them. Every time you check your email—ideally, at certain designated times during the day rather than as each email arrives—try to do one of four things:

- Read and delete immediately any noncritical email.
- Respond to or otherwise deal with the email, if it can be done in 2 minutes or less.
- If it will take longer, turn the email into a task or appointment (if you use Outlook).
- File away into a folder those emails you need to keep for future reference.

If you can follow these simple rules, you too can keep your Inbox clean. If you must keep email in your actual inbox rather than in folders, make sure you have only a screen's worth of messages visible; if your inbox contains email "below the fold," you may forget it's there and fail to act on it.

Stop Intrusive Notifications

The notification tools in email programs are designed to let you know when new email is available. They are also an endless source of distraction and interruption, especially for those of us who receive hundreds of messages each day. The response to these notifications is somewhat Pavlovian; every time we hear that little sound, see an envelope appear in our system tray, or receive a pop-up notification that a new message has arrived, we are convinced we have received the most important email in the history of the world. As a result, we stop immediately to check our email as it arrives—to the detriment of our other work. BlackBerry users often have their devices set to vibrate whenever any email arrives, leaving them in a constant state of distraction as they struggle internally with whether and how often to check their messages. Imagine using the old America Online audio notification "You've got mail!" and hearing it hundreds of times a day. Turn off these notification reminders, and the focus on your work will improve.

We also recommend that you set a realistic schedule for checking your email during the day, so that you have some control over email and how it interrupts you. Don't check your email every 5 minutes unless you are expecting important messages to arrive soon. Set your schedule to check email at times when you can best deal with it. Some people check email only several times a day—in the morning, immediately before or after lunch, in late afternoon, and at the end of the day. Others check email once every hour to keep the messages to a manageable amount. If you currently feel pressure to constantly check for and respond to email, we recommend reducing the number of times you check your messages during the day. It will give you a greater sense of control over your inbox as well as your time.

We recognize that it's hard not to want to check your email immediately or answer the phone every time it rings. It's even harder to resist responding to instant message requests. But resist the urge, and turn off the notification features of your email program. Most of your messages do not require an instantaneous response, or the sender would have called you on the phone. Your clients will appreciate a well-thought-out response that arrives a little later more than they will a fast, off-the-cuff response that you might have to correct later.

Create a Folder System

Success with email requires a consistent, useful form of organization. If you try to keep a clean inbox, it's apparent that the email you keep must go somewhere. That's why it's important to create a set of folders that will keep your messages organized. There are many ways to set up folder systems, and using an approach similar to your other filing systems will probably work best for you. However, try to avoid naming your folders based on the sender of the email. A better method is to name them after specific topics, projects, matters, time periods, or clients. You want to use a system that will help you find an email when you need it. But be careful not to place folders within folders—it's too easy to forget them. Create subfolders only if you refer to them often.

Use Rules and Other Automated Tools

Your folders are the place where a properly configured rules system comes into play. The Rules Wizard of Outlook, and similar tools in other programs, provides a powerful means for filtering and sorting your email. For example, you can set up a simple rule that will automatically move messages from a certain sender, or with a certain word in the subject, to the appropriate folder without having them even appear in your inbox. You can use rules to filter out junk mail or to send email to any folder you want, based on a wide variety of criteria. Some email programs allow you to flag important emails for follow-up, color-code messages as they arrive, set up "saved search" folders to help you organize related emails in one place, and change the view so you see your messages in the actual conversation thread.

Stay Near Zero

Once you've followed the preceding tips and pruned your inbox to a manageable number, if not zero, where do you go from there? Try to take a lean approach to email. Keep your work email inbox devoted to work matters. We often recommend creating a separate personal email account to use for email newsletters, family, and friends. Also consider trimming your newsletter and mailing lists. Do you really need all the newsletters you receive?

If you subscribe to an email discussion list, especially a high-volume list, consider changing your subscription to the "digest" option and receive only one email each day containing all the messages, instead of many messages all day long. For those subscriptions that you must keep, consider using a rule or filter to shuttle them directly into an appropriate folder, where you can deal with them later. You might also find out whether an RSS feed is available for your newsletter, to eliminate the email entirely from your inbox.

Learn How to Use Cc and Bcc

A popular rule savvy email users often employ is one that automatically sends all email on which they are copied to a separate folder. The theory is that your most important email is sent to you as the main recipient, not as a Cc (carbon copy). The Cc function is used far too often, and often inappropriately as well. The term "fat finger" arose because of the common, often embarrassing instances of someone clicking Reply to All without checking who was on the Cc list. We've all heard stories of snide comments and criticisms sent to the wrong people, often to thousands of people on a public mailing list. Although it has its drawbacks, the Cc function is a primary way people collaborate using email. It effectively conveys the same messages and attachments to everyone who needs them. At the same time, it should be used sparingly and carefully. Check each message, especially on forwarded email, to ensure you are copying the right people.

An often under used function is the Bcc: (blind carbon copy) field in an email. Have you ever received a message addressed to hundreds of people, with all of the addresses listed in the To: field of the message? Not only has the email sender revealed your address to hundreds of other people, he or she has also revealed potentially sensitive information about who is part of a particular collaboration team. Rather than expose all of those addresses to your recipients, add them to the Bcc: field instead. You'll save your recipients a lot of hassle. As the name implies, Bcc is also a good option when you don't want your recipients to know the identities of everyone who is receiving your message.

Use Care When Selecting Reply to All

The carbon copy issues go hand in hand with the Reply to All feature. Reply to All is both a blessing and a curse. Not having to type all those email addresses saves you a lot of time, and it ensures people are not left off the distribution list. On the other hand, Reply to All also makes it easy to send confidential information to unintended recipients with the click of one button. We cannot stress enough the importance of confirming your recipients before you send an email.

Email Helpers

If you need a little help with the Reply to All issue, we suggest you try the helpful Sperry Reply-to-All Monitor (http://www.sperrysoftware.com/ Outlook/Reply-To-All-Monitor.asp, $14.95), which will show a pop-up message asking if you really want to reply to all before you send the message. In addition, Sperry (http://www.sperrysoftware.com/Outlook) offers several helpful email add-in programs, including one of our favorites, the Attachment Monitor. How many times have you sent an email and then realized you forgot to attach the document you were sending? The Attachment Monitor will remind you to attach a document or file if it detects words like "Attached is" or "Enclosed is" in your message.

Email sometimes feels like an overwhelming burden; but as we've discussed in this chapter, you can start taking control of it with just a few simple steps. If you look for ways to improve your email experience rather than seeking an email "solution," you can make small, helpful improvements that will lead to overall increased satisfaction. There are many other useful tips and tools for improving your relationship and skills with email. We've collected some of these resources in Appendix 2. We also recommend that you consider taking a training class about the email program your organization uses. It should pay for itself in making your life a little easier.

We firmly believe that email is and will remain critical to the collaboration process, even though there are definitely better tools for most types of collaboration. Email enables collaborators to communicate with each other, and it provides a mechanism for alerting members of a collaboration team when new actions or events occur. As an independent collaboration platform, however, email is less than desirable. By incorporating smart email practices into your general collaboration strategy, you'll take advantage of all the benefits email has to offer while minimizing its drawbacks as a communications medium.

SharePoint 17

SharePoint is a portal-based collaboration platform from Microsoft. It might be the most widely available collaboration tool for legal professionals, primarily because it is attached to the Microsoft Office suite of tools. SharePoint has drawn a lot of attention from large law firms, particularly over the past few years and especially among those firms running a Windows Server environment with Office and Exchange. We've noticed large audiences at presentations on SharePoint at legal technology conferences we've attended.

SharePoint uses the familiar Microsoft interface and is contained almost entirely within the web browser, making it easy for anyone with an Internet connection to access. It can be used internally or externally. SharePoint also integrates well with Microsoft Office products, including OneNote, and it can be configured to pull data from other law office programs, databases, websites, and other sources. Even right out of the box, it provides a wealth of collaboration tools as well as easy ways to personalize and customize the tools.

A basic SharePoint portal page is composed of modules called **web parts**, which are components that implement a specified function, such as a task list, discussion board, calendar, or shared document area. SharePoint sites are quite customizable, which means users can add the web parts they need for each specific project. A SharePoint site can be used within a firm or company via the organization's intranet, made available to clients on an extranet, or published to the Internet for more public use.

The SharePoint family is composed of three different applications. Windows SharePoint Services (WSS) is the basic application, and it's a free add-on to the Windows Server. WSS offers the basic portal infrastructure, allowing collaborative editing of documents and document organization as well as creation of to do lists, alerts, and discussion boards. The Microsoft Office SharePoint Server (MOSS) improves upon WSS, adding better document management, search functionality, navigation features, RSS, and support as well as the ability to create wikis and blogs. For power SharePoint users, the Microsoft Office SharePoint Designer (MOSD) is an HTML editor that helps users design their own SharePoint sites.

SharePoint is portal based. It lets you create a single portal or dashboard from which you can access all of the information you need for your project. In other words, SharePoint gives you a "home" page for your project. It also provides enterprise search, document and content management, and workflow tools, all featuring strong integration with Microsoft Office.

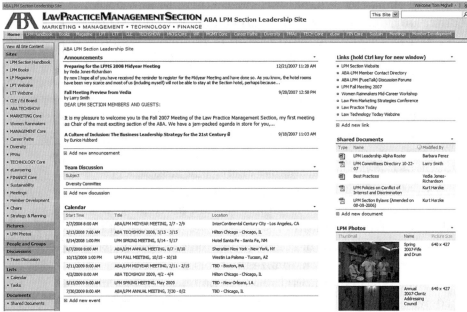

Microsoft Product screenshots reprinted with permission from Microsoft Corporation.

FIGURE 17.1   SharePoint Portal Home Page

What makes SharePoint such a powerful collaboration tool? It is fully customizable, allowing you to create exactly what you need for your project and nothing more. A SharePoint page is built by taking the web parts and combining them into a single web page. Here are some of the modules you can add:

- Discussion forums
- Task lists

- Calendars
- Document libraries
- Links to external pages
- Wikis

Because SharePoint is a Microsoft product, it integrates well with Microsoft Office applications. With MOSS, users can view and edit Office documents directly within a web browser, making it simple to work on documents from anyplace with an Internet connection. The SharePoint services can also be accessed through Microsoft Outlook, and users of Office 2007 can synchronize their Outlook calendars and task lists with their SharePoint counterparts. Another advantage of using SharePoint in a firm environment is the product's ability to fully index all of the documents stored in its library, so that users throughout the organization can search across all libraries and user groups. This document management capability will definitely be of interest to legal professionals. Individual pages or the entire site can be searched via the search box at the top right of the page.

SharePoint is ideal for those interested in a more full-featured project management tool than Basecamp or some of the other web-based applications. Separate pages can be created for different aspects of the project, so that each page has its own dedicated discussion forum, task list, calendar, and document library. Each user can customize the project pages to her or his specifications, moving them to different areas on the page or minimizing web parts that do not apply to them. There is a specific web part that will filter tasks, showing only those for the particular user. And there are several ways to work with the data outside of SharePoint:

- Edit in Datasheet—allows users to bulk edit the information using a datasheet format.
- Connect to Outlook—synchronizes the items for that particular web part and makes them available offline in Outlook.
- Export to Spreadsheet—downloads the documents into Excel for analysis and editing.
- Open with Access—uses the popular Microsoft database program to work with your data.
- View RSS feed—creates a feed that will alert you whenever something is added to or changed within that particular item—for example, when tasks are added or completed.
- Alert Me—sends email alerts whenever something changes on the site.

The SharePoint document libraries are particularly powerful. The Check Out feature permits you to take a document from within SharePoint to edit it on your computer or somewhere else. While a document is checked out, other users do not have access to edit it. Users can also access the version history of each document, to review and perhaps restore previous versions of a document. If sensitive documents are uploaded, the permissions for those documents can be managed so that the document can be restricted for certain users.

How might a law firm use SharePoint? A firm could easily use Share-Point as the foundation for its intranet to provide a wide variety of information to employees. The firm might also personalize each lawyer's experience by creating a web part that gives easy access to wanted information. For example, a lawyer could see a display of work in progress, accounts receivable, and other financial matters for top clients pulled directly in real time from the firm's time and billing software. News items, practice-specific resources—internal and external—and forms can be displayed in a handy "resources" box. The SharePoint search function allows easy search across all firm databases, including the firm's documents, accounting, and HR materials. Firms are reporting fast search functionality across millions of documents.

Software platforms typically have third-party integrators that develop software to make the platform work with legal-specific software. As an example, Microsoft and third-party developers are looking at SharePoint as a platform for electronic discovery tools. Here are some of the companies that already provide integration with SharePoint:

- Handshake Software (http://www.handshakesoftware.com/)
- SocialText (http://www.socialtext.com)
- XMLaw (http://www.xmlaw.com/)
- SV Technology (http://www.svtechnology.com/)
- eSentio Technologies (http://www.esentio.com/)
- Hubbard One (http://www.hubbardone.com/)
- MindJet (http://www.mindjet.com)

One benefit of using a SharePoint portal is the ability to make use of the institutional knowledge inherent in any law firm. Users can set up internal blogs to share knowledge, and any member of the firm can access and search this information. Since the information is captured by the system, it is no longer necessary for firm employees to know the "right person" in order to gain access to important information. A simple search of the firm's intranet is all you need. It's a simple but effective form of knowledge management.

SharePoint is an immensely powerful tool for collaborating within a law firm or organization, and its ease of being customized has attracted large law firms in particular. In addition, third-party providers have begun to develop legal-specific applications for SharePoint. Because of its scalability and ability to work with third-party applications, we expect that over the next few years many large law firms and some smaller firms will implement SharePoint as their intranet of choice and begin to take advantage of the collaboration tools and integration with Office in creative and productive ways. Small firms and solos should also consider hosted SharePoint sites to take advantage of this platform at a modest monthly cost.

If you're interested in learning more about SharePoint, visit SharePoint-pedia (http://sharepoint.microsoft.com/pedia/Pages/Home.aspx).

Collaborating Inside and Outside the Office: Extranets and Intranets

18

As we discussed in Chapter 15, the extranet is a fundamental building block of online collaboration. Its internal counterpart, the intranet, is also a valuable collaboration tool for lawyers. Although the extranet is designed to allow collaboration outside a firm or organization and the intranet facilitates collaboration within a company's computer network, both tools share one crucial attribute: to access either, all the user needs is a web browser. They also share other common collaborative features: document sharing, communications and project management tools, resource libraries, and other items that assist people in working together. Together, they are two of the most important collaboration platforms available to lawyers.

In this chapter, we discuss extranets and intranets, and some of the products available in these areas.

Extranets

The Basecamp Example

We covered Basecamp in great detail in Chapter 14, but primarily as a project management tool. However, innovative lawyers and others increasingly are using Basecamp for its outstanding extranet features. Some solo and small firm lawyers use Basecamp to set up extranets for each of their clients, and these lawyers swear by the results. Basecamp provides an easy-to-use, secure, relatively inexpensive solution to the problem of giving your client access to their case files and information.

Hosted SharePoint Portals

Another example of a simple extranet is the hosted SharePoint site. For less than $100 a month, you can share documents with clients, post calendars, and discuss case matters, all in an environment similar to the Basecamp application. Many Internet Service providers (ISPs) offer hosted SharePoint services, so you may be able to set up an extranet using the same company that hosts your firm or company website.

Document-Sharing Extranets

You and your firm may not be ready to dive into the extranet world. That's okay—there are ways to dip your toes into the extranet pool without making a full commitment. The easiest way to start is to provide simple document-sharing and transfer services to your clients. Sometimes all clients want is access to pleadings, memos, filings, or other documents—or a way to download large document attachments without using email. From a confidentiality standpoint, a lawyer might not be comfortable emailing estate tax returns, medical information, financial records, supporting documents for patent filings, or other sensitive material by email or even regular mail.

In these situations, a simple extranet established for the sole purpose of sharing documents might be all you need. There are several routes you can take to share and transfer documents using an extranet.

Many document management systems now provide outside (or "web") access to anyone with an Internet connection. You can leverage that capability to give external collaborators limited, secure access rights to your network, so they can view and obtain copies of documents from anywhere at any time.

As an example, Worldox, a document management program commonly found in small and mid-sized firms, features a Worldox/Web tool that provides external access. To use this functionality, simply make a client or other collaborator a "user" and give them limited rights to access your Worldox system over the Internet. Users can take advantage of the search features of the system, check files in and out, upload and download documents, and create audit trails. For particular sets of outside users, you can even create a user group that controls their document-viewing rights and establishes the desired level of security. User access can also be tracked and monitored to ensure there is no abuse of the system. For organizations using a **document management system**, the system's "web access" system might be a good first step into the use of extranets.

"Temporary" Extranets—File Sharing

Documents can be shared in a variety of other ways via the Internet. We routinely use YouSendIt.com to share audio files in connection with our podcast. Once you create a free account, you can upload a large file (one too big to be sent by email—on YouSendIt, the free limit is 100MB). The file is stored on the YouSendIt site and assigned a URL. YouSendIt emails that URL as a link to the people with whom you want to share the file. The recipient is then able to download the file, simply by clicking on the link in the email, for up to seven days (when the file is deleted from the site). It's a simple and free "temporary" extranet application that solves a specific problem, and it is likely to become more common as lawyers receive and send more audio, video, and other large files. We discuss YouSendIt and other file transfer services in Chapter 21.

Legal Extranets

Extranets targeted to and customized for the legal profession have had a long history, at least in relation to the life of the Internet. Several companies specializing in this area date to the mid to late 1990s. One of the companies we examine in this chapter, AMS Legal (http://ams-legal.com/), traces its roots to one of the first legal extranet companies, LegalAnyWhere.

When you compare a service like the AMS Legal Collaborator with generic extranet products, you will notice some fundamental similarities. You will also see an order-of-magnitude increase in the sophistication of the tools and sensitivity to the concerns of the legal profession. Collaborator actually integrates with leading legal document management systems as well as Microsoft Outlook, providing direct access to documents, calendars, and messaging systems. Versions of Collaborator are available for large firms, small firms, and corporate legal departments. There is a heavy emphasis on industrial-strength security, as you might expect from a company operating in the legal industry.

Collaborator also provides a lot of power, flexibility, and ease of use. Where most basic extranets permit only limited customization, AMS Legal allows you to fully personalize a site, design it to match your firm website, and even create custom "skins" to match a desired look and feel. You can also customize the links to a user's entry page as well as to the individual matter pages. The user's entry page is populated automatically with new items or changes to the site.

With Collaborator, you can share edited documents, which can be synchronized with the document management system, redlined, and even made read-only. User permissions on individual documents or on folders can be set to restrict access where necessary. Versions of documents can be created, timestamped, and logged. Calendars can be tied to documents or matters, and the system will create ticklers to remind users of upcoming events or deadlines. Integration with Outlook makes it easy to transfer calendar items to and from the extranet; calendars are created for each matter, showing only the dates relevant to that matter.

To communicate with others on the extranet, Collaborator offers secure threaded discussion boards that maintain a transcript of the entire thread. This system enables you to collect and manage discussions in one place without the need to track email or worry about inappropriately forwarded messages. You also can attach or create links to documents referenced in the discussion threads.

Collaborator also allows you to create and assign tasks to participants, who are notified by the system of the assignment. Automated reminders of the tasks are designed to help team members meet deadlines and prioritize tasks.

Collaborator's structure is such that users can create new extranet sites quickly and with a minimum of effort. This and other useful administrative features enable you to roll out sophisticated extranets any time you need them for clients or matters.

While a legal extranet like AMS Legal Collaborator costs more than some of the more basic tools we've discussed, it is still reasonably affordable when compared to custom-developed extranet products. In addition, you get the benefit of AMS Legal's long history in the legal profession, and extranets specifically designed with lawyers in mind. Its integration with Outlook and popular legal document management systems will also be important to firms and legal departments looking for a unifying extranet product.

Another legal extranet service is TrialNet (http://www.trialnet.com), which covers the whole litigation process, from case initiation and matter management to electronic billing for legal services, all in one seamless product. You can purchase either the entire package or specific modules à la carte. TrialNet's service creates a single "case file" that everyone associated with the case—both inside and outside the firm or law department—can access, review, and use anywhere and at any time, wherever an Internet connection is available.

Corporate counsel or law firms can create and assign matters or cases and organize them easily into files and subfiles. TrialNet's matter management tools include document management, secure email, calendaring, automatic notification, and reporting. TrialNet also integrates with your own data and financial systems, to connect with existing files on a particular matter. Inside or outside counsel both can contribute to the case file, manage information, and track activity.

TrialNet also provides expanded extranet services, with additional collaboration tools that can be accessed by *any* member of the TrialNet system. Expert databases let you collect and share witness information, transcripts, and strategies on dealing with an expert. Law and medical libraries offer starting points for case-related research, including articles, briefs, and medical defense proposals. A terrific feature is the virtual conference room, with threaded discussions and ways to talk to other lawyers on the network through counsel-to-counsel postings. You'll also find client-sponsored databases with standard discovery responses and corporate policy documents.

Electronic Discovery Extranets

As discovery of electronically stored information continues to grow in importance, extranets increasingly will be used as document repositories for shared document review and other aspects of electronic discovery production and evidence management. Electronic discovery vendors with hosted services are already referring to their offerings as "e-discovery platforms."

Specialty Extranets

Extranets can also be narrowly tailored to deliver focused services or specific information, or to provide training. A pioneer in the use of specialty extranets is Bryan Cave, with its well-regarded eCave family of extranets. These tools provide training, simple decision trees, answers to common questions, and other materials that enable clients to get answers to simple questions and to bring appropriate questions to their outside lawyers when answers aren't otherwise available.

Here are some other companies that provide legal extranets:

- Merrill Lextranet (http://www.legalintranet.com/)
- NetDocuments from LexisNexis (http://law.lexisnexis.com/net -documents)
- Xerdict Technologies (http://www.xerdict.com/)

Intranets

While the extranet might seem like the more important collaboration tool because it lets lawyers work with others around the world, it would be a mistake to take for granted the significance of the intranet, a tool that has been widely used by large law firms for many years. In fact, the intranet may be one of the most important internal collaboration tools a law firm or company can use, because it provides an "always-on" platform where employees can go to find information, get documents, and communicate with other employees—all without having to walk down the hall, send an email, or pick up the phone. How often do you receive an email in your office that starts out, "Has anyone here researched the issue of . . ." or "Does anyone here have experience with Judge Smith . . ."? Intranets are designed to maintain information like this in one central location, which hopefully will put an end to these email queries.

In simplest terms, intranets are the opposite of extranets. An **intranet** is a private, secure, internal website for sharing information and services within an organization. Some organizations think of their intranets as private versions of the Internet. An organization's employees can access an intranet through their web browsers, but they are not actually on the Internet when they do so. Many firm intranets are designed in-house (by large firms or companies) or by web design companies (for smaller firms and solos). The security concerns that are so critical when dealing with extranets are not as pressing with an intranet. Because everything takes place within the firm's firewall, it is generally protected from outside attack or compromise.

Law firms use intranets for a wide variety of purposes:

- General firm or company information—News about clients, firm manuals, company policies, health benefits information, training materials, directories, and even classified ads can be posted on an intranet.
- Practice Pages—Separate pages can be set up for each practice area, with news, RSS feeds, and communication tools for lawyers practicing in that area.
- Research—Law libraries can upload vast repositories of research, including web links, research guides, court rules, and more.
- General Internet resources—These often include weather, airline, and travel sites.
- Ongoing litigation—An intranet can serve the same purpose as an extranet for members of a firm or law department. For each case, a separate page can be created that provides access to calendars and deadlines, links to the document management system with relevant case files, and a discussion forum for team members to talk, among other features.
- Time and billing—Through the intranet, all employees have some level of access to the firm's time and billing software, so they can instantly view a client's current financial situation.

Intranets have many benefits. They help employees to be more productive in their work by giving them easy, quick access to firm institutional knowledge on their own schedules. Employees can receive the information when it suits them rather than being deluged by a constant stream of email. Because messages between employees are all kept in one place on the intranet, it is easy to keep track of discussions—unlike the case of email. Intranets save money because they reduce the amount of paper that must be produced when printing out procedure manuals, forms, and other firm documents. With the information on an intranet equally available to all employees, teamwork is a natural consequence.

When we say that extranets and intranets are the basic building blocks of collaboration tools, we do not exaggerate in the least. They provide around-the-clock access to important case and firm information, in an environment that is familiar and easy to use. They can be used by just about anyone who works with a lawyer: other attorneys, clients, experts, and other people associated with legal matters can all benefit from being able to access an extranet or company intranet. Most important, these private, secure websites take advantage of and build on everyone's familiarity and comfort with working on the Internet. One or both of these tools should definitely be a part of your overall collaboration strategy.

Adobe Acrobat 19

For years, Adobe Acrobat has been the leader in the creation, editing, and management of Portable Document Format (PDF) files. Lawyers have recently come to appreciate the value of PDF, as it has become the de facto standard for court filings and secure document exchange. PDF is increasingly becoming a standard in electronic discovery as well, making inroads against the TIFF format for scanned documents. Both the Adobe Reader and the Adobe Acrobat PDF programs can be found in many law firms and corporate legal departments as part of the standard desktop application package.

While many lawyers today are familiar with PDF and utilize the format in their practice, they may not realize that recent versions of Acrobat introduced several tools that enable collaborating on documents. Like Microsoft Word does with word documents, Acrobat allows users to review, mark up, and comment on PDF files, both within your organization or by email review. Additionally, as mentioned in Chapter 13, Adobe introduced its Adobe Connect conferencing product in 2006, which provides an online screen-sharing space for larger numbers of document reviewers. Let's take a look at some key Acrobat tools and how Acrobat has evolved into a collaboration platform. While we will be focusing on Adobe Acrobat 8 in this chapter and recommend that lawyers use the most current version, Acrobat versions 6 and 7 have many of the same features mentioned in this chapter.

Review and Comment

Why use Acrobat for document review and other collaboration? Why not instead create a document in a program like

147

Google Docs, where everyone can contribute to the editing of the document? The answer is simple: control. If you want to make sure that a document isn't altered, but still allow others to review and comment on it, you're far better off working with PDF files than Word documents. With a PDF you can be assured that the document will remain unchanged while others are making suggested edits to it.

To take advantage of Acrobat's reviewing toolbar, select View, then Toolbars, then Comment & Markup.

Adobe product screenshot reprinted with permission from Adobe Systems Incorporated.

FIGURE 19.1 Acrobat Reviewing Toolbar

This toolbar offers the following options:

- Sticky Note—The easiest way to leave comments. Just click anywhere in the document with this tool; when you begin typing, text for the note is inserted. When you're done typing, click to minimize it. You'll still see a small note icon in place on the page. To see the comment, hover your mouse over it or click on it to reopen the note.

- Text Edits—For documents that have been scanned directly to PDF, you can strike out text you want to change, or insert text you want to add. This feature will not work on an image-only PDF.

- Stamps—You can create your own stamps to insert anywhere on a document, or use some of the preconfigured stamps offered by Acrobat. Some of these include stamps marked "Reviewed," "Received," "Approved," and "Confidential." Many of the stamps will insert your name or the date and time when you add the stamp to your document. It's also easy to create your own custom stamps. One great use of this option is creating a stamp from your own signature. Simply scan a copy of your signature as a JPEG image and convert it into a stamp, which you can then use to "sign" PDF documents you create.

- Highlighter—Highlights text in the color of your choice.

- Callout Tool—Creates callout boxes in your document.

- Text Box tool—Creates a text box so you can add extra text to your document. This tool is useful when working with an image-only PDF.

- Cloud tool—Draws a cloud around an object or text as another way to highlight material.

- Arrow, Line, Rectangle, and Oval tools—Draws these objects within your document. These tools can be configured to any color, size, or thickness.

- Pencil tool—Use the pencil for free-form drawing anywhere on your document.
- Show—This tool allows you to filter the markups on your document—by markup type, by reviewer, by review status, and by the status of the particular markup.

As you work with the Comment & Markup toolbar, all of the edits, revisions, and comments you make to the document are visible on the screen. Another way to view these changes is to use the Comment list at the bottom of the screen. The Comment list is particularly helpful if several people have worked on the document, and you need to view all of the changes and comments from all reviewers. To activate the Comment list, either click the Comments button at the lower left of the screen or select View, then Navigation Panels, then Comments. A window will appear underneath your document, with a full listing of all of the marks you or others made to the document.

The Comment list is a powerful feature that offers some great options for dealing with comments and changes in your document. First, click the button Expand All, so you can view all the details of a particular change, including its date and time. The Next and Previous buttons allow you to move from change to change, and the Reply button provides a text box where you can comment on someone else's comment or change. There's a trash can where you can send any deleted comment. The Set Status and Checkmark buttons provide a means of dealing with each comment and marking the ones you have already read. You can use Sort to arrange the comments by Author, Type, Date, Color, or Status, and there's also the ability to search through the comments. Finally, if you want to keep a copy of the Comments for a document, Acrobat offers several options for accomplishing this: you can print them out, save them to a PDF file, or export the comments to a Word, AutoCAD, or data file.

Sending a Document Out for Review

Using the Comment & Markup toolbar isn't very useful if you're using it all by yourself. To get the most out of Acrobat's reviewing tool, you'll need to send the document out to others. With Acrobat there are three ways to share a document for review.

Email Review

The first document-sharing method is the easiest. You simply email a copy of the PDF document to others. When the reviewers email their changes and comments back to you, Acrobat will automatically merge all of the edits into your original document for you. To begin, click the Comments menu and select Attach for Email Review. You'll be asked to fill out some identifying information (name, email address, company, etc.), and then to click Next. On the following screen you'll be given an explanation of the email-based review, that your recipients will receive a set of instructions on how to begin reviewing the document, and that anyone with Adobe Reader 7 or later can review and comment on a PDF. Select the document you want to share, and click Next.

The next screen allows you to invite reviewers to your document by entering their email addresses. When you click the Customize Review Options button, you can specify the email address to which reviewers should return their comments. Make sure the box next to the instruction "Also allow users of Free Adobe Reader 7.0 or later to participate in this review" *is checked.* Click OK. When you're done adding email addresses, click Next.

The last screen is a preview of the invitation that will be sent to your reviewers. You can change the subject line of the email the reviewers will receive, and you can edit the instructions to your liking. Click Send Invitation, and you're done. Your reviewers will receive an email with the PDF attached. When they open the PDF file, the Comment & Markup toolbar will be visible, and they can then make their changes to the document.

▼▼▼▼▼
Tip

If you're working from an original Word document that you'll have to continue editing once the review is completed, consider having your reviewers use the Text Edit tools to insert and delete text in the PDF file. When your reviewers return the changes, you can integrate them directly into the original Word document.

Once the reviewers are done with their changes, they'll click the Send Comments button on the Comment & Markup toolbar; the document will be attached to an email and mailed back to you.

Shared Review

If you're reviewing documents within your firm, law department, or other organization, Acrobat's Shared Review feature is likely a better option than the email review. With a shared review, the comments are stored in a central location—a folder on your network or a SharePoint workspace, for example. The location of the comments is programmed into the PDF file so that whenever the document is opened, it can automatically find where the comments are being kept on the network. This system allows you to distribute the document not only via your document management system but also by email or by placing the document on a server. It does require, however, that all reviewers have some sort of network connection to the location of the PDF as well as the commenting server.

A benefit of the shared review is that you don't always have to be connected to your network. Say you take a document with you to work on while you're traveling across the country by plane. The next time you reconnect your computer to the network, any comments you have made, as well as comments made by other reviewers while you were gone, will automatically be synchronized with your document. In a way, your document is alive because it can be continuously updated with the comments and changes others are making to the document. Acrobat has also included the handy Review Tracker (select Comments and then Review Tracker) that shows the status of the review either from all reviewers or from any individual reviewer.

Browser Review

A browser review is exactly what it sounds like—a document review in which anyone with an Internet browser can participate. To create a browser review, you must have an online repository where the document can be located. To start, select Comments and then Upload for Browser Review. You'll be prompted to locate your file, and then upload it to your preferred destination. You'll also have to designate a Comments Repository online—if the repository is not configured, Acrobat can attempt to do it automatically when you click the Configure button. If Acrobat can't configure the Comments Repository, you'll have to do it manually. This can be accomplished by going to Edit, then Preferences, then Reviewing. Once you accomplish these steps, you can invite reviewers, as with the other types of document review.

Document Security and Control

In developing the Acrobat product, Adobe correctly anticipated the needs of lawyers and others in the business world to be able to create secure PDF files that protected the confidential or proprietary information contained within the document. Acrobat 8 offers several different means of securing your documents, depending on your particular needs and circumstances.

The first way to secure a PDF file is to restrict access or permission to it. With Acrobat you have several options for accomplishing this. The most common is simply to password-protect the document; in doing so you can also set security options so that users are restricted from opening, editing, or printing the PDF. With this security in place, a recipient with the password can open and view the document but cannot copy, print, or do anything else with the file. This level of security is ideal for sending out sensitive or confidential documents, or when you are concerned the information may be improperly used for other purposes. For more advanced security, you can encrypt a document with a "certificate," so that only a specific group of users has access to it; or you can "certify" the document, which allows the document author to restrict further changes to it. If Acrobat is available to your employees on the network, or if you want to share PDF files with clients or others outside your firewall, the Adobe LiveCycle Manager will create server-based security policies that permit access to PDFs for a limited period of time.

If you want to secure several documents all at once, Acrobat 8's Security Envelope is the way to go. The Security Envelope takes multiple files and places them in an encrypted "envelope," which can be opened only by those with sufficient access rights. To create a Security Envelope, simply select the files you want to include, choose a template (eEnvelope with Date Stamp, eEnvelope with Signature, or Interdepartment eEnvelope), determine the security policy you want to apply to the envelope, and you're done. Acrobat will assemble your files into a neat package and send it along to your recipient.

Acrobat also deals with the tricky issue of **metadata** by examining documents for hidden content. Acrobat will check each PDF file for metadata, either on demand or when you attach it to an email, and will remove the hidden content from the document. It can also remove digital signatures, information added by third-party plug-ins, and other special types of information.

Acrobat has long been a useful tool for lawyers and other business professionals. The rise of e-filing and standardization of the PDF file has only increased the utility of this application. Now that the latest versions of Acrobat have added collaboration features, it is nearly an all-in-one tool for creating, sharing, and working on documents with others. There are other programs that will convert documents to PDF, but none are as powerful in the area of collaboration. For more information on how to use Adobe Acrobat, see *The Lawyer's Guide to Adobe Acrobat,* Third Edition by David L. Masters (American Bar Association, 2008).

Wikis: Web Collaboration **20**

The first generation of the Internet began in the mid to late 1990s, when the focus was on getting information online. The main benefit of the Internet during that time was the simple fact that for the first time, resources that were previously only in print format were now available online with just a few mouse clicks. As the Internet has evolved, a second generation of websites, tools, and applications has come forward that is taking all of that information and making it interactive. This second generation is often referred to by the name **Web 2.0**, and it refers to web-based communities, sites, and hosted services that aim to facilitate collaboration and sharing between users.

For our purposes here, probably the most important feature of the Web 2.0 phenomenon is the idea of the network as platform. This platform has the ability to deliver fully functioning applications directly over the Internet and accessible through any web browser. Google Docs, Zoho, and the other online document creation tools discussed earlier are good examples of the network-as-platform idea. Other **platforms** mentioned in this book—web conferencing, project management, extranets—are other types of applications that can be operated directly from your **web browser**. Another important feature of Web 2.0 technology is the idea of rich Internet applications. These are technologies—with names like AJAX, Adobe Flash, Adobe Air, Ruby on Rails, and Microsoft's Silverlight—that improve the user experience in browser-based applications. In other words, these technologies make web-based applications easier, more user-friendly, and even more fun for anyone to use. They also give applications on websites the feel and functionality of desktop applications.

Another part of Web 2.0 is the notion of user-generated content. Visitors to Web 2.0 applications are now creating and editing content on these sites in a way that has been called the read/write web. Over the next two chapters, we'll be taking a look at collaboration tools made possible by new Web 2.0 technologies, starting with a prime example of a user-generated content application, the wiki.

What Is a Wiki, and Why Should I Care?

Wikis may be the best-known, yet least-understood, example of Web 2.0 technologies. Many lawyers have heard of wikis, but don't know what they are, much less how to use them in their practice. The term "wiki" comes from the Hawaiian *wiki-wiki,* meaning "fast." That's an appropriate term to describe the way this web-based tool can be used. In its simplest terms, a **wiki** is a web- or intranet-based tool that can be edited by anyone and can be used to link from one page to another. Its inventor conceived of a wiki as the simplest form of usable database. It also illustrates the read/write aspect of Web 2.0. You can read the entries and you can edit them. Perhaps the best-known wiki is Wikipedia (http://en.wikipedia.org), the encyclopedia that anyone can edit and a cultural phenomenon as well. Wikipedia contains well over 2 million articles, each of which is accessible and editable by anyone with information to contribute. Some of the founders of Wikipedia started their own competitor, Citizendium (http://en.citizendium .org), which aims to become "the world's most trusted knowledge base."

Some consider the wiki to be among the most powerful collaborative tools currently available. Wikis have been rapidly adopted by major corporations, nonprofits, and informal groups. Companies like Microsoft, Disney, Nokia, Xerox, eBay, Sony, and others are deploying wikis for their employees. In these companies, wikis are not just for working on projects or communicating with other employees. They are also being used to track news, post corporate policies, and create strategy documents. Microsoft has also incorporated wiki tools into SharePoint.

The defining characteristic of a wiki is how easy it makes the tasks of creating and updating pages. With Wikipedia, for example, anyone can access a page and edit it without any initial review or assurance that what's being posted is accurate or trustworthy. This has led many critics of the wiki format to complain that because the system can be tampered with so easily, it cannot be considered a reliable source of information. Supporters of wiki technology respond by saying that the collaborative nature of the wiki makes it difficult for inaccurate information to remain live for very long. Wiki authors and editors tend to be a devoted following, and errors and false statements are quickly corrected most of the time. There is no question that many people find Wikipedia a useful reference resource.

Most wikis have a similar structure, usually displayed in tabs across the top of the page:

- The main page, where the information can be viewed, and links to other pages are placed.
- A Source tab, where the text can be edited, revised, deleted, or otherwise formatted. To edit a wiki page, users should have a basic understanding of Wikitext, which is a simple but not very intuitive markup language that applies formatting (font, bold, underline, italics, indent, etc.) to plain text.
- A History tab, where users can view the changes made by other wiki editors.
- Some wikis (like Wikipedia) have a Discussion tab, where users can debate and otherwise talk about the article and changes made to it.

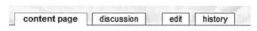

FIGURE 20.1 Wiki Tabs

Why should lawyers care about and use wikis? To answer that question, let's break it down by how lawyers already use wikis: as either consumers or producers, or as both. Let's look first at the idea of consuming wikis. Most lawyers will get more benefit out of wikis that have been created by others. Here are some of the law-related wikis available, as well as other general-topic blogs that lawyers will definitely find useful:

- 7th Circuit Wiki (http://www.ca7.uscourts.gov/wiki/)—The first wiki produced by a federal court of appeals provides access to the Practitioner's Handbook and Current Events in the jurisdiction.
- Civil Law Dictionary (http://civillawdictionary.pbwiki.com/)—A wiki from Louisiana, on civil law.
- Congresspedia (http://www.sourcewatch.org/index.php?title=Congresspedia)—A Wikipedia-like site covering the U.S. Congress.
- CopyrightExperiences(http://commons.umlaw.net/index.php?title=Main_Page)—A site for legal academics to share their copyright experiences with law journals and other legal publishers.
- Internet Law Treatise (http://ilt.eff.org/)—The Electronic Frontier Foundation publishes this summary of the law related to the Internet.
- IP Daily Update (http://ipdailyupdate.pbwiki.com/)—Daily commentary and news on intellectual property law.

- Jurispedia (http://en.jurispedia.org)—Worldwide coverage of legal information.

- LawLibWik (http://www.editthis.info/lawlibrary/)—A collection of wikis created by law libraries, law schools, and on various legal topics.

- PatentLawPractice (http://patentlawpractice.wikispaces.com/)—A frequently updated list of intellectual property resources.

- Readable Laws (http://www.readablelaws.org/)—A wiki dedicated to translating legislation into plain English.

- TaxAlmanac (http://www.taxalmanac.org/)—An online tax research resource and community for tax professionals.

- Wex (http://www.law.cornell.edu/wex/)—From Cornell Law School, this is a Wikipedia for the law; Wex is a freely editable encyclopedia and dictionary of legal terms and concepts.

- WikiCrimeLine (http://www.wikicrimeline.co.uk)—The goal of this U.K. site is to bring together all relevant criminal law materials together in an easy-to-search website.

- Wikilaw (http://www.wikilaw.org)—Concentrates on U.S. law, with topics ranging from Alternative Dispute Resolution to Wills, Trusts & Estates.

- Wiki Law School (http://www.wikilawschool.com)—Designed primarily for law students, this wiki provides outlines on the legal topics covered in law school.

- WikiLeaks (http://www.wikileaks.org)—An "uncensorable system" for safe mass document leaking and public analysis.

- WikiPatents (http://wikipatents.com/)—Uses the wiki format to encourage users to comment, rate, and otherwise discuss patents and prior art.

More legal wikis are becoming available as lawyers and legal information providers see the value of the Wikipedia model. Before you use a wiki as a consumer, it's good to know a few things: the people who are editing the wiki, whether there is an active community supporting the wiki, and whether the information is current or comprehensive. It's essential for a wiki to reach some kind of "critical mass" and have some "life" to it. Otherwise, it can be become an information ghost town.

Does it make sense for a lawyer to create a wiki? Obviously, maintaining a publicly available wiki takes a lot of work, much of it probably nonbillable time in most firms. A key to producing a successful wiki is to attract and encourage a community that supports it, internally and/or externally. The user community for that wiki must be vigilant not only in keeping it updated with current information but also in keeping errors from finding their way into the wiki entries. These issues alone would be enough for most lawyers to shy away from starting their own wiki—time is a precious commodity that lawyers do not have enough of. While a public-facing wiki might not be appropriate, however, an internal or private wiki may be a unique and innovative way of communicating with lawyers in your firm, clients, or anybody you want to share information with.

How can lawyers produce wikis in their practices? A number of possibilities exist. Lawyers can set up wikis to provide their clients with an online "idea space" to place their thoughts, ideas, and other information relating to a particular matter. Lawyers working in different cities on a matter can use a wiki as an extranet to share ideas on transactions or pending litigation. Some lawyers have used the wiki format to prepare a course syllabus for law school classes, or to write a book with multiple authors. If the authors place the individual chapters into a wiki, everyone can access and edit or add to the book at their own speed and convenience. We considered that approach, but rejected it and chose the simpler Google Docs method, largely because there are only two of us. We also knew we would have to submit our drafts in Word format and did not want to experiment with pulling chapters out of a wiki into a Word document. From the standpoint of administration, many firms and companies are using wikis to post human resources or office policies, or other internal documents that are periodically revised by firm management.

A good example of a firm currently producing a wiki is the U.K. firm of Allen & Overy. Their Group Space wiki area provides attorneys and knowledge management staff with regularly updated information about training programs and recommended reading. It's also a place for users to share their business plans, carry out consultations, and compile reports from all of their offices. These are all great ways for offices in many disparate places to communicate. Workers in other companies are finding their email use greatly reduced after the introduction of a wiki. Rather than wade through a flood of email, some with documents, spreadsheets, or presentations attached, users simply visit the wiki for that particular case or project and see at a glance everything that's going on.

Setting Up Your Own Wiki

Before deciding to implement your own wiki in your practice, you need to make one critical determination: whether the wiki will reside on your own computer server or on a web-based platform. A self-hosted internal wiki is attractive for collaboration among lawyers and other legal professionals in the same firm or corporation. It provides the greatest level of control and security because the information resides behind the company's firewall. The disadvantage of the internal wiki is that it is not accessible to clients or others who may have something to contribute to its content. For those who wish to collaborate with others around the country or the world, a web-based wiki may be the answer, especially a wiki hosted in the form of a secure extranet application.

When you are deciding the type of wiki that's best for you, here are some questions you need to answer:

- Do you need a page history? A page history is critical for public wikis, to ensure that previous versions can be restored if someone vandalizes the wiki or posts inaccurate information. It may be less necessary for those wanting to use a private or personal wiki.
- Is it a WYSIWYG (what you see is what you get) process? Many wiki products use Wikitext to format text, but the process is not intuitive and may be off-putting to non-techie users. Some wikis offer a WYSIWYG editor, so you can more easily see the formatting in your document and easily make the edits you want.
- Is the wiki provided as software or hosted? Running your wiki on your own server gives you more control, but will take some installation know-how. A hosted option is definitely easier to use, but you are forced to accept the settings/options that service offers.

Here are some examples of the different types of wiki products available.

Web-Based Wikis

There are literally dozens of wiki tools available over the Internet, from the most basic to some that are pretty advanced. Some of the sites we have tried and like are (sites that charge for their wiki products are denoted with $$):

- ClearWiki (http://www.clearwiki.com/)—$$
- EditMe (http://www.editme.com/)—$$
- Netcipia (http://www.netcipia.com)
- Nexdo (http://www.nexdo.com/)—free for personal use, $$ for professional version
- PBwiki (http://pbwiki.com/)
- StikiPad (http://www.stikipad.com/)—free and $$
- ServerSideWiki (http://www.serversidewiki.com/)
- tiddlyspot (http://tiddlyspot.com/)
- TiddlyWiki (http://www.tiddlywiki.com/)

- Wikia (http://www.wikia.com/)—join a wiki community, or create your own
- Wikispaces (http://www.wikispaces.com/)—$$

Enterprise/Internal Wikis

If you're looking for a more robust, full-featured, *secure* wiki product, an enterprise application is the way to go. These companies offer additional services beyond those provided by web-based wiki tools—high-end, server-based wikis permit notification by email or RSS when new content is posted, and they can serve as intranets, document repositories, and project management tools.

Keep in mind that all of these services require you to purchase either a license or renewable subscription to use their product. Here are some companies that can install wikis on your network or other server:

- BrainKeeper (http://www.brainkeeper.com/)
- Confluence (http://www.atlassian.com/software/confluence/)
- eTouch Systems (http://www.etouch.net/) (Also available as a web-based version)
- instiki (http://instiki.org)
- MindTouch (http://mindtouch.com)
- Near-Time (http://www.near-time.net)
- Socialtext (http://www.socialtext.com)
- TWiki (http://twiki.org/)

If you're undecided, or want to compare wiki products before making a final decision, definitely check out WikiMatrix (http://www.wikimatrix.org/). By simply answering a few questions at the WikiMatrix site, you can find out which wikis will best fit your needs. You can then compare them side by side, or discuss them with other users to learn about their experiences with the various products. For those who have already used a wiki and are more interested in spurring wiki adoption in their firm, corporation or organization, WikiPatterns (http://www.wikipatterns.com) provides a toolbox of patterns for wiki users, as well as a guide to the process of wiki adoption.

The use of wikis in the legal profession still seems to involve more discussion than implementation. For at least the next few years, we expect lawyers to be more consumers than producers of wikis and for most wiki efforts to take place safely within internal firewalls for internal collaboration efforts. A wiki can be a powerful tool in the right setting, but it is not a universal or one-size-fits-all tool. Consider our own example and how we chose not to use a wiki to write this book. However, we would definitely consider using a wiki to maintain a listing or directory of collaboration tools or for similar purposes, and we may well use a wiki as part of an online version of this book. One place to watch for wiki development in the legal profession will be the wiki features built into Microsoft SharePoint. Wherever they happen to exist, we expect wikis to grow as a collaboration tool among lawyers and in other industries.

Other Web 2.0 Collaboration Tools 21

In Chapter 20 we began a discussion of **Web 2.0**, the term used to designate Internet technologies that enable information to be used, displayed, and managed in new and innovative ways by turning the Internet itself into an application platform. While the **wiki** is probably the most commonly used example of a Web 2.0 collaboration technology, there are hundreds if not thousands of other sites with the Web 2.0 moniker, and they all have one word in common: "sharing." In this chapter, we'll take a look at other Web 2.0 tools that help users share information with each other.

File Transfer and Sharing

Internet users have been sharing files for years. Through the use of **P2P** (peer-to-peer) networks, music and movie fans have made their files available to others through sites and networks such as Napster, Kazaa, Limewire, and BitTorrent, raising concerns and litigation about the legality of exchanging songs, movies, and other materials protected by copyright. In fact, peer-to-peer networks are not generally considered to be illegal in themselves, but lawyers have become wary of them because of infringing or other illegal activities being conducted by a limited number of people on a small number of networks and systems. In fact, Skype and Microsoft Groove are just two well-known examples of peer-to-peer applications commonly used in business settings.

Peer-to-peer networks work by allowing others to access files on individual computers and share them directly from computer to computer, rather than hosting the files on a traditional web server. When someone wants to download a song or other file owned by someone else, they send a request through the network to the computer where that file is located, and the download begins. This collaborative method of sharing files has been with us for quite some time and predates what we know now as the World Wide Web.

What then is the new Web 2.0 spin on file sharing? The major feature of these new file-sharing tools is that the files themselves can be stored online, temporarily or for indefinite periods of time, at the same place or at a persistent URL. As the cost of server space continues to decline, more and more companies are providing large quantities of online hard drive space at dirt cheap prices and, in some cases, for free. One site we use frequently is YouSendIt (http://www.yousendit.com), a service that allows you to send large files to other people without having to use email. Many mail servers have limits on the size of files they can send or receive, which can result in big problems when you need to forward a large document or media file to a client. For example, closing files in real estate or banking transactions can exceed 100MB, even when the documents are converted to PDF. Most email servers would reject a file of that size, which is what makes YouSendIt (and other services like it) such a blessing.

To use YouSendIt, simply upload your file to the website. YouSendIt then sends an email to the recipient with notification that a file is available for download. With the free version, the file is kept on the YouSendIt computers for seven days, so it must be downloaded within that time. That's all there is to it. Now you can easily and cheaply share large files with others without having to burn them to a CD and stick them in the mail. YouSendIt is free for files up to 100MB. There are paid plans (from $9.99 to $29.99/month) allowing you to send files up to 2GB in size. All transfers are encrypted to provide security as your file travels between your computer and that of your recipient.

There are literally dozens of file transfer sites now online, all offering services similar to that of YouSendIt. Here are a few of our favorites:

- Adobe Share (http://share.adobe.com)
- MailBigFile (http://www.mailbigfile.com/)—100MB limit
- Driveway (http://www.driveway.com/)—500MB limit
- TransferBigFiles (http://transferbigfiles.com/)—2GB limit
- EatLime (www.eatlime.com)—1GB limit
- SendSpace (http://www.sendspace.com/)—300MB limit

Some companies weren't satisfied with merely giving you temporary online file storage space. Many new companies are now providing sites where you can actually store your files permanently and share access to your storage with others. For fairly reasonable prices, users can upload files to an online storage area where they can be instantly shared with others, and the files are accessible to them from any computer connected to the Internet. Here are some of the major sites providing sharing and storage services:

- Box.net (http://www.box.net)
- MediaMax (http://www.mediamax.com/)
- MegaUpload (http://www.megaupload.com/)
- xDrive (http://www.xdrive.com)
- Microsoft Live Spaces (http://home.services.spaces.live.com/)
- Mac (http://www.apple.com/dotmac/storage.html)
- Google GDrive—expected in 2008

To learn about or explore more online backup, sending services, and storage/sending services, visit "Online Storage: 80+ File Hosting and Storage Sites" (http://mashable.com/2007/07/28/online-storage/). Online file storage services offer great alternatives to email for large files, especially since many email accounts will not accept attachments greater than 10MB. As lawyers increasingly deal with larger and larger files, these tools will likely find greater use and adoption.

Online Calendaring

As we've discussed often in this book, the calendar is among the primary tool of the collaborating lawyer. Whether the calendars are used to schedule meetings or hold important dates and deadlines, it's important for all members of the team to maintain a consistent calendar. With Microsoft Outlook it is possible to share calendars, but what if the collaborators work in different places? Dozens of web-based calendars are available, and some of them provide great functionality for those who want to work together. The biggest player in this area is Google, with its Google Calendar (http://www.google.com/calendar). As with most Google Tools, this calendar is extremely easy to use, and it can be used in conjunction with your regular email program. Yahoo (http://www.yahoo.com/calendar) also offers an excellent calendar program that uses a plug-in to synchronize with your calendar in Outlook.

Online calendars are designed primarily for individual use, but most of them offer the option to share them with others. Some online calendars were designed for group activities and can be accessed by any number of users. These group calendar sites allow you to create multiple calendars, get reminders by email or on your phone, provide RSS notification of new events or calendar items, and easily export to many standard calendaring programs. Here are few online calendars that we like:

- 30 Boxes (http://30boxes.com/)—one of the most popular Web 2.0 calendars
- Airset (http://www.airset.com)
- CalendarHub (http://www.calendarhub.com/)
- Kiko (http://www.kiko.com/)
- Now Software (http://www.nowsoftware.com/)
- Planzo (http://www.planzo.com/)

Mind Mapping

Mind maps are diagrams that are used as part of the brainstorming process, to generate a visual representation of ideas as an aid in problem solving, decision making, and even project management. Although mind maps have been used for hundreds of years, technology has recently brought them back into prominence. There are dozens of mind-mapping software applications; MindManager (http://www.mindjet.com) is one program we have both used and can recommend. In fact, we used MindManager to map and outline the ideas and chapters for this book. However, if you want to brainstorm with someone halfway around the world, these stand-alone applications may not be the best answer. Various mind-mapping sites have sprung up on the Internet, allowing users to brainstorm on a mind map at

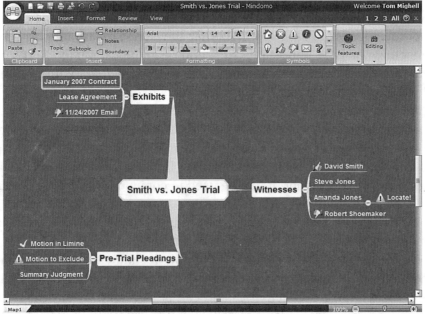

Reprinted with permission from mindomo.com.

FIGURE 21.1 Example of a Mind Map Using Mindomo

the same time. In addition to basic mapping, you can add images, links to other sites, and even files to parts of the map, as well as notes or comments. Many of these sites also offer RSS notification, so users can be alerted when new information is added to the mind map.

Here are some of the noteworthy mind-mapping or brainstorming sites on the Internet (sites that charge for their products are denoted with $$):

- bubbl.us (http://bubbl.us/)—free mind-mapping tool
- GroupSystems (http://www.groupsystems.com/)—$$—enterprise-level decision-making tools
- Mind42 (http://www.mind42.com)—online mind mapping that is easily customizable. Invite collaborators by email to join in the brainstorming, and make your mind maps public.
- MindMeister (http://www.mindmeister.com/) (Free-$$)—basic mind-mapping tool, with premium features for subscribers
- Mindomo (http://www.mindomo.com/) (Free-$$)
- Wridea (http://www.wridea.com/)—more of a basic brainstorming tool, with project management capabilities

Many of these sites offer free mind-mapping tools, with advanced features available for a fee. Give the free trials a shot before diving into the premium services.

Blogging

Blogs are traditionally known as journal-type sites that one or more individuals use to publish regularly updated information on a particular topic. Law-related blogs, sometimes called "blawgs," have proliferated at an amazing rate over the past few years, as lawyers realize that blogs can be excellent tools for communicating with the public or other lawyers or even for marketing their practices.

When it comes to collaboration, however, blogs do not automatically come to mind. But they certainly can be used in collaboration efforts. Blogs are quintessential collaborative applications because they promote a two-way form of communication. They provide a means for readers to comment on posts, adding their own thoughts to what the author has posted. Multiple individuals can author a single blog, so that several different points of view can be presented. Consider the use of a blog within a law firm or organization, and how lawyers can use blogs to collaborate with each other. For example, a practice group could set up an internal blog on a particular area of law, and the lawyers in that group could contribute new items that they came across either in their practice or through reading legal publications. A trial or transaction team could set up a blog for that matter, keeping each other updated on developments in the case. The possibilities for internal collaboration are quite varied. A blog in some cases might work as a good alternative to a simple wiki because it is so easy to use.

The subject of blogging could take up an entire book on its own, so we won't try to cover it all in a few paragraphs. Instead, we'll suggest two resources where you can learn more about blogs—and lawyer blogs in particular. The first resource is a book by Greg Siskind, Deborah McMurray, and Rick Klau titled *The Lawyer's Guide to Marketing on the Internet* (the third edition was published in 2007 by the American Bar Association Law Practice Management Section). The book contains great ideas for marketing a legal practice on the Internet, as well as substantive materials on starting your own blog. For a constantly updated resource on lawyer blogs, try Real Lawyers Have Blogs (http://kevin.lexblog.com/), the blog of Kevin O'Keefe, President of LexBlog. Kevin consistently provides great information on how lawyers can use blogs to their advantage, both for marketing as well as collaboration purposes.

We will mention one blogging tool here, primarily because we are intrigued by its capacity to enhance collaboration among large groups of people. Twitter (http://www.twitter.com) can best be called a "micro-blog" site, because the messages here are limited to 140 characters, like standard text messages. People are using Twitter to update their friends and others on what is going on in their lives. This usually results in mundane messages like "I'm heading out to dinner," or "I'm watching the Cowboys beating the pants off the Rams!" But what makes Twitter such a great collaborative tool is that when you send out a message, anyone who has subscribed to your feed can receive your updated status report by text or instant message, email, and even RSS feed. It occurs to us that Twitter may serve as a good tool to update team members on the status of a project. The messages are short and sweet and can be delivered nearly anywhere you can receive information. Look for more and more tools like Twitter to start offering easy ways to collaboratively communicate with others.

Social Networking

If you have children (or are a savvy web user yourself), you may have heard about sites like MySpace or Facebook. What's the big deal with these sites? They are examples of **social networking** tools, services that have established huge communities of individuals who share the same interests and activities. Most of these sites have very different populations, but they all have a similar structure. Users set up their own "profile" page, where they provide the information they want to share with their "network." When members discover their friends on the service, they add each other to their profile page as a "friend"; as these groups of friends grow, the members can create networks that are quite large and extended.

There's an element of trust involved in social networking. The idea is that if I trust the opinions and recommendations of my friends, it follows that I should be able to trust the opinions and recommendations of my friend's friends, and *their* friends, too. The members of these networks communicate with each other, share information, provide references, make recommendations, and discuss various topics. As you can see, the very nature of the social network is collaborative. What if lawyers could harness this power and use it in their practice, or as part of their professional development?

Some lawyers have already begun this experiment at Facebook (http://www.facebook.com). Once a social networking site for college-aged adults, Facebook has recently become popular with users of all ages who want to connect with others on the Internet. In 2007, businesspeople, including lawyers, began testing the potential of Facebook as a business platform. You can connect with your business contacts in a variety of ways and set up public and private groups with discussion boards and other tools. For example, the Between Lawyers group boasts more than 100 members, and a group called The Civil Law has more than 700 members. Firms both small and large are finding their lawyers drawn to Facebook. As of the writing of this book, 8 of the Top 10 firms in the AmLaw 100 had Facebook networks with hundreds of members.

In addition to Facebook, another social network attracting lawyers is LinkedIn (http://www.linkedin.com), a professional networking service. Users can communicate with others in their own networks about jobs, submit questions to the collective knowledge of the group, or make recommendations about members of their network. Central to LinkedIn is the notion of six degrees of separation—that each of us knows people who know other people, and we are usually within just a few clicks of knowing someone who can introduce us to someone we want to know better. LinkedIn has always been focused on business users. Over 15 million individuals have profiles on LinkedIn, so the potential to find new clients, experts, business opportunities, and job listings is tremendous. You can also find biographical and other information about collaborators and others you are working with or might want to work with. The basic network service is free, but users can get more options and an increased ability to contact others by purchasing an upgraded plan, which runs between $19.95 and $200.00 a month.

As of the publication of this book, one state bar has offered its own social networking service to lawyers. The Texas Bar Circle (https://texasbar.affinitycircles.com/) is a network for licensed Texas lawyers only, with resources for them to join groups, look for jobs, and communicate with each other. With over 2,500 current members, the Texas Bar Circle provides excellent networking opportunities for Texas lawyers. We expect other state bars, and perhaps the American Bar Association, to wade into this space in the near future.

Want to create your own social network? A company called CollectiveX (http://www.groupsites.com) offers a GroupSites program that permits users to create a free social network. The basic network includes member profiles, calendars, discussion forums, **email blasts**, the ability to share files and other media, and more. A premium account removes advertising from the group pages as well as adding security and other features. There's also an Enterprise edition that will organize and manage multiple groupsites across an entire organization.

Other Web 2.0 tools involve mapping information and aggregating or combining data in a wide variety of ways. You might use Web 2.0 tools to locate experts; publish or share information; create charts, slides, and other presentation materials; and distribute audio (podcasts), video (videocasts), or screen captures (screencasts). Expect the number of Web 2.0 tools to continue to grow, expand, and surprise you in their diversity, creativity, and usefulness.

Specialized, High-End, and Alternative Collaboration Platforms

22

In addition to the general collaboration platforms we have covered in this section, lawyers may choose among various specialty collaboration platforms that focus on specific tasks or areas of practice. In particular, electronic discovery is an area to watch for steady development of collaboration platforms. In this chapter, we take a quick tour of ten representative examples of alternative collaboration platforms lawyers can use to work with others.

Practice Management Programs

Many lawyers and law firms use practice management programs like TimeMatters (http://www.timematters.com), PracticeMaster (http://www.practicemaster.com), AmicusAttorney (http://www.amicusattorney.com), and others. These programs help you administer a law practice, and they provide a wide range of tools that let you manage files, delegate tasks, coordinate projects, direct workflow, and take care of other collaboration tasks. If you already have these tools, it might be worth reading the manual or talking with your vendor representative to discover whether you already own a great collaboration tool.

Microsoft Project and Microsoft Office

The title says it all, doesn't it? Project (http://office.microsoft.com/en-us/project/default.aspx) is a workflow management tool widely used in the business world, yet seldom seen in the legal industry. From Gantt charts to other visual tools, Project offers a sophisticated set of collaboration and project management tools that are easily adapted to the legal setting. Microsoft Office 2007 (http://office.microsoft.com) also offers collaboration tools nearly everywhere you click, including integration with SharePoint and the new Microsoft Groove peer-to-peer (**P2P**) communication tools. Law firms also are experimenting more with Microsoft OneNote (http://office.microsoft.com/en-us/onenote/default.aspx), a note-taking tool that features some multiuser collaboration functionality. It may cost you a few hundred dollars extra to take advantage of these additional tools, but the expense is definitely worth it when you consider the cost of other stand-alone tools or platforms.

CaseMap

The LexisNexis CaseMap (http://www.casesoft.com) litigation strategy and management tool has carved out a unique niche for litigators over the years. CaseMap boasts a high-level process to organize and help others understand the facts, people, issues, research, and other key components of a lawsuit. When properly configured, a CaseMap file contains everything you need to analyze your case, including exhibits and deposition testimony. When deployed on a network CaseMap allows everyone on the litigation team to add and review information as well as create customized reports for review by clients, experts, and even mediators or the court itself.

Litera

Litera's (http://www.litera.com) document workflow platform provides for near real-time collaboration on documents. It enables everyone working on a document to make or suggest revisions simultaneously, while keeping track of revisions and comments all in one central location. Litera eliminates the need to email documents to the team, by keeping the "live" document in one place. Changes can be made to that document when everyone agrees, making it easy to move forward in negotiation by freezing the agreed-upon document provisions and keeping alive only the areas in need of resolution. You might think of Litera as "redlining on steroids," but it's definitely a fascinating glimpse at today's advanced collaboration tools, and where the future might be taking us.

Mind Mapping

As we discussed in Chapter 21, mind mapping is a collaboration technique whereby a diagram is used to represent ideas, tasks, resources, and other items used in the brainstorming process. Mind-mapping tools come in either stand-alone or web-based formats. One of our favorites, MindJet's MindManager (http://www.mindjet.com), is an excellent mind-mapping program that now integrates into Microsoft SharePoint for even more collaborative potential.

WorkShare

WorkShare (http://www.workshare.com) admittedly is a primary player in the world of redlining tools. However, digging deeper into the WorkShare feature set will unearth a variety of collaboration tools. You can compare a number of document types, including PDF, and multiple users can work with the documents being reviewed. WorkShare also addresses security issues that can arise during document collaboration.

Catalyst Secure

Document repository companies represent another form of collaboration platform. These companies provide storage for your case file documents as well as sophisticated tools for managing electronic evidence. Catalyst Secure (http://www.catalystsecure.com) is a good example of a repository that does more than just store your documents. As a specialized form of extranet, a document repository provides access to discovery documents for review by everyone working on a case. However, these repositories now also offer workflow and project management features as well as communications and other collaboration tools in one common, secure location.

Electronic Discovery Tools

Lawyers and their clients have quickly found that electronic discovery is a team effort. As a result, e-discovery vendors are moving quickly to provide collaborative tools in their electronic evidence review products. In fact, we believe that the astounding growth in e-discovery makes it one of the best areas to watch for new developments in collaboration tools. Workflow management, services that allow reviewers to work from different locations, and enhanced security are only a few of the collaboration features that are found in these up-and-coming EDD products.

Knowledge Management

The granddaddy of high-end collaboration tools has to be **knowledge management** software. The idea of knowledge management (a system that identifies, stores, and distributes a firm's institutional knowledge) has long offered much promise to lawyers, but its history at law firms and companies has largely been disappointing. This is partly because lawyers have unrealistic expectations about what knowledge management tools can deliver. However, there's no question that knowledge management software offers powerful tools for sharing knowledge within your organization. If you simply focus on the collaborative aspects of these tools, especially if you already own them, you will likely find a powerful platform at your disposal.

Enterprise Content Management

If knowledge management is the granddaddy, then **enterprise content management** (ECM) is the "big iron" of collaboration software. A sophisticated database application platform can manage all of an organization's content and can slice and dice that content in ways to suit your every need. The players on this field include companies like Oracle, and the costs of such a system can be quite high. However, corporate legal departments, especially those in companies where ECM is already in place, might find that it is a dominant collaboration platform for them. The power and ability to customize these tools puts them at the high end of the collaboration tools food chain.

The list doesn't stop there. We expect as time goes on and the Web 2.0 world continues to expand, new and better collaboration tools will appear that improve on previous technologies. And that can only benefit law firms and companies looking for better ways to work together. The lesson to learn here is that collaboration technologies can exist in many unexpected places. The more you become aware of what's out there, the better your chances of finding the tools that will work for you.

PART VI

Developing a Collaboration Strategy

Must-Have Features for Your Collaboration Tools **23**

In this chapter, you will learn how to make good choices when identifying and implementing collaboration tools in your practice or company. We'll highlight those features of collaboration technologies we consider to be must-haves, and provide a simple "feature calculator" table to help you compare the different tools you are considering.

Although everyone's collaboration needs are different, there are some general features we believe are essential, no matter which tools you choose. We have touched on many of these features in previous chapters, but in this chapter we'll be more explicit. Consider this chapter as the starting point to begin developing your collaboration strategy, and a good way to organize your thinking. In some cases, the tools already used by your collaborators will drive your decisions. However, the collaboration tool (or tools) that brings you the best results will be the one that embodies most of the features we discuss in this chapter.

No—or Very Small—Barriers to Entry

Barriers to entry include costs, new software or hardware implementation, training requirements, cultural changes, time delays, and a variety of other factors. Collaboration is about working together, and any tool that makes it easier to work together is always better than one that makes it more difficult. It is surprising how that point is often lost when people evaluate and discuss collaboration tools.

With some **Web 2.0** collaboration tools, you can be up and running, at no cost, in a few minutes. You can set up an account with Google Docs, upload a document, share it with others, and have real-time, online document collaboration in less time than it will take you to read this chapter. All you need is an Internet browser and an Internet connection. The barriers to entry with many Internet tools are indeed low.

Consider the barriers to entry of each of the collaboration candidates on your list. How quickly and easily can you start using the tool? Given the criteria of your decision-making process, how soon can this tool be in place and utilized by your employees? Although you might be able to set up and use Google Docs in just a few minutes, if your technology committee requires six months to study security and other issues, then your actual barriers to entry might be quite high. Preparing a simple timeline for the expected implementation process will allow you to better assess the expected barriers to entry for different collaboration tools.

Reducing—or Not Increasing—the Silo Factor

The rise of new Internet tools and applications—social networks, calendars, webmail, and so on—has created a **silo** effect in our use of these tools. The information we want to use on these sites is kept in different, largely unconnected places that we must visit individually to access. The phenomenon is often described using the metaphor of silos—the cylindrical structures that hold grain and other bulk material separate from each other. As with grain silos, we must visit our "Internet silos" one after the other to load and unload information. The silo effect is present in the office as well. Lawyers experience this effect as they try to locate necessary information in their email applications, document management systems, databases, time and billing programs, intranets, web resources, and the like.

As the number of silos increase, we see two common effects. First, locating information becomes much more difficult because you must move from silo to silo to gather what you need for the job at hand. Second, there comes a point when people have too many silos, and they will refuse to create another no matter how compelling its benefits.

In many ways, the best collaboration tools help you connect to and draw information from many silos. They either reduce the number of silos you must visit or, perhaps just as important, create the illusion that you are using fewer silos. The idea of the **portal** or **dashboard** helps with this issue—it allows you to access all the information stored in different silos, all from a single starting point. Does the tool you are evaluating reduce, maintain, or increase the number of silos of information? Be wary of tools that multiply the sources of information users must visit.

Common Platforms

A key theme in this book is that decisions about collaboration tools and processes should not be made in a vacuum. The very notion of collaboration means that you will be working with someone else. To do so, you must keep in mind that not everyone uses the same **platforms** as you. More importantly, you must factor in the possibility that others are using different platforms when you consider the collaboration tools you will use.

Heated discussions often occur over which platform is "better"—Word or WordPerfect, Macintosh or Windows. As the history of computer use in the legal profession has shown us, the answer to that question is usually determined by which platform is more ubiquitous, and especially which one is being used more by our clients. You can still adopt a platform that you think is better, even though it may be less popular in the business world. But you must take into account the conversion, compatibility, and convenience factors for those with whom you will be working. If you don't, you may find yourself without many collaborators.

Internet-based collaboration tools are especially attractive because everyone has equal access to that platform. In addition, look for tools that utilize common platforms like email, Microsoft Office formats, **PDF**, **SQL** databases, and other commonly used platforms and formats.

Leverage Existing Software

One of the biggest trends in software development since 2000 has been the continued incorporation of collaboration features into new software versions. Collaboration tools that suit your current needs might well already exist in the latest version of a program you now use, or they might be just a version upgrade away. Recognizing this fact, as well as exploring the help screens and manuals of your programs, might give you a simple and inexpensive start on improving your collaboration toolbox.

Using existing programs offers plenty of benefits other than reduced cost. Training and installation will be minimal, if necessary at all. Additional hardware or software likely will not be required. Users will also see that they are gaining additional functionality from a program they already like, which will increase their acceptance of the tool. This is one more way to reduce the barriers to entry, as discussed earlier.

On the other hand, the presence of these features alone does not mean your search for collaboration tools is over. The collaboration features may be poorly implemented, an afterthought, or just not what you need. You may already be frustrated with the existing software, and upgrades might require a substantial hardware or software investment. Consider the complete picture.

Getting Data In and Out

Collaboration tools often let you move information from one program or platform into another program, site, or platform to which others have access. A simple example is when you copy an existing Word file into Google Docs, where it becomes a document that can be shared and worked on by others you invite. When the collaborators are done working with the Google Docs document, it can then be exported and "published" as a Word file. Your document and information effectively make a round trip and can be used or kept in the format best suited to your present needs.

Compatibility and conversion of documents has long been a tricky and often frustrating concept, as anyone who has tried to move documents between Word and WordPerfect can attest. Evaluate your potential collaboration tools with an eye toward how easy it is for you to get your information in its current format into the collaboration program or platform. The one-click "Send to" menu choice is a good sign that the collaboration tool plays well with other programs.

Getting data out of collaboration tools is also a growing concern, especially in the case of Internet-based or Web 2.0 applications. What happens if a hosted service provider goes out of business? How can you retrieve your documents and data in a usable format? And if you want to move from one web-based tool to another, how easy will it be to move your data?

Integration with Your Existing Tools

Good collaboration tools provide a seamless and largely transparent experience when working with other programs. Collaboration features in a program might be accessed by clicking on a button, following a hyperlink, or, with programs like CaseMap, simply clicking on the "Send to" option in a drop-down menu.

Ideally, you want to select collaboration tools explicitly designed to work with other programs that you use. Vendors often make this information readily available, and even tout integration as a selling point—and it *is* a selling point. Out-of-the-box integration with your existing programs promises a happier path than a tool that requires customization, tweaking, and work-arounds.

Accessibility and Portability

Accessibility and portability are two related yet slightly different features that should be part of any collaboration tool you select. People increasingly work in different places, at different times, and on different devices, including smartphones and laptops. A good collaboration tool will make documents and data available to your users when and how they need it, and it will enable users to move documents and data from one device, location, or platform to another.

Internet-based tools provide excellent solutions to accessibility and portability problems. All you need is a browser and Internet access; no other software is required. On the Internet, information is available 24 hours a day to anyone who has access. The proliferation of web-enabled cell phones and smartphones increasingly makes working on the Internet an appealing reality.

When assessing your tools for accessibility and portability, look for features such as version control, synchronization, and replication. These functions can ensure you have the current, working version of a document as well as the ability to work offline. Consider how, when, and where your users and their collaborators will access documents, and how they will need to move the files around. Will new servers, remote access, or additional software be required to make the tools work in your environment? Do Internet tools make sense in your practice for you and your clients? Since the benefits of collaboration tools can be multiplied by increasing their accessibility and portability, you will want to think carefully about how these tools will work in your specific context.

Security and Related Concerns

Lawyers routinely handle sensitive, confidential, and privileged materials. Security, controlled access, encryption, and data integrity are critical issues when selecting collaboration tools. Security plays an especially large part in the decision of whether to use services hosted by third parties or to host collaboration applications on your own. The simple fact is that third-party services typically offer security, backup, and disaster recovery features far better than those currently implemented by the average law firm or lawyer.

Due diligence is required when evaluating the security features of any collaboration tool. Monitor developments in these areas, and understand at least the basics about security issues. High-level encryption as well as the use of digital certificates and secure websites are features you should expect with a third-party service. When you see that a company "uses 128-bit encryption and Secure Sockets Layer (SSL)," you know you are dealing with people for whom security is a serious issue.

Some important security issues to watch for in the near future include identity management and authentication. Can you be certain that your collaborator is who she says she is? Does your collaborator have the rights and access only to the material to which he is limited? These will be significant security questions you must answer when evaluating collaboration tools.

Easy to Learn and Easy to Use

We advocate an approach to collaboration tools that reduces the amount of "friction" the tools create for users to actually work with each other. Good tools make it easy to collaborate. Tools that are easy to learn and use also reduce the barriers to entry, so they are likely to be used and stay used over the long haul.

Ease of use and of learning are obviously highly subjective factors. Usability testing over the years indicates tools that build from our existing user experiences tend to work well for new users. For example, lawyers are comfortable and seem to do well with interfaces and features that look, act, and feel like Microsoft Outlook. As a result, dozens of legal-specific software applications now base their user interface on that of Outlook. And if books, web training, videos, or classes are readily available on a particular software program, it's a good bet that program or platform will be easier to learn than a program for which not much information is available.

The best collaboration technologies are the ones that get used. Try to find tools that are easy to learn and easy to use.

Sensitivity to Legal Issues and Law Practice

Legal-specific collaboration tools often have features and other touches that work well for lawyers. It could be something as simple as referring to "clients" rather than "customers," or calculating filing deadlines for a case, but collaboration tools that take into account the ways that lawyers work offer many advantages to legal professionals. Vendors are aware of this fact; one example is Microsoft Word's "legal blacklining" feature, developed to assist lawyers in document comparison activities.

For each category of collaboration tools that you evaluate, determine if there are any tools designed specifically for the legal market. Many exist. As we have discussed, some extranet providers design products solely for lawsuits and deal rooms. Make the presence of legal features a significant factor in your evaluation of collaboration tools.

What Your Collaborators Are Using

While such evidence is not necessarily dispositive, you must give some weight to the tools used by your collaborators. We offer no great insights here. This is an obvious point, and one that embodies the very nature of collaboration.

Your decision should reflect what's best for you, but the tools your collaborators use will often factor into that decision. In fact, taking a look at what your collaborators are doing has its own advantages. You can learn the pros and cons of a tool from someone who has used it, or even have the opportunity to use the tool before committing to a purchase. In the case of a close call, knowing that your collaborators use a certain product might turn out to be the deciding factor.

Built for the Long Haul

Something that scares people about Web 2.0 and Internet-based tools is how most of the companies are really new, and more and more are appearing on the web with amazing speed. On the other hand, consolidations and mergers among legal software companies do not provide us with any more comfort when considering the longevity of software applications.

There's no crystal ball when it comes to the long-term prospects of vendors and their services. However, we do think a company's experience and commitment to the legal market are important factors in selecting collaboration tools. The examples we discuss in this book reflect our best guess at tools and platforms that will be around for the long haul. It's a good idea to make research about company prospects and industry trends a major part of your evaluation process.

Pulling It All Together

Your individual needs, your collaboration partners, and your expected and actual use of these tools will drive your selection decisions. We do not believe in one-size-fits-all answers, although we do make some general recommendations in Chapter 32. Instead, we offer the calculator on page 183 to help you compare different collaboration tools using the features we think are most important.

To use the tool, simply list each vendor or product you are considering. You can add more sets of columns if you have more than two candidates. Assign a score from 1 (lowest) to 5 (highest) to rate how well the product does for each feature on the list. Place that number in the "Score" column for each. Then determine the actual importance of each feature to you on a scale of 0.1 (lowest) to 1.0 (highest), and place that number in the "Weight" column. Multiply the score times the weight for each feature, and you will get the weighted score. Place that number in the "Weighted Score" column for each feature. Add up the total weighted scores for the vendor or product, and enter the number in the "Total" box under "Weighted Score." You might also do this for the "Score" column to compare raw scores. Repeat the process for each vendor or product you are comparing. When you finish, you will have an easy-to-use comparison of the vendors or products, with total scores and a way to compare individual features.

If you duplicate this tool as a spreadsheet, you columns will automatically total if you make any adjustments. If you use the spreadsheet in Google Docs, for example, everyone involved in the process can collaborate on the ratings calculation and share the tool when you sit down and discuss it.

You can use this tool in a variety of ways depending on your requirements and preferences. For example, you might include factors in addition to those we've provided. You might use a different scoring system. We've added a column for factoring in the weight of a feature, so that you get weighted scores based on the importance of that feature to you. We also believe that this tool will give you a good outline for doing your research, asking the right questions, and evaluating demos of products and services. It might even serve as a template for preparing a request for proposal (RFP) when you're selecting a vendor or service provider.

VENDOR/PRODUCT COMPARISON CALCULATOR

Feature	Vendor 1			Vendor 2		
	Score (1–5)	Weight (0.1–1.0)	Weighted Score	Score (1–5)	Weight (0.1–1.0)	Weighted Score
Barriers to Entry						
Reducing Silos						
Common Platform						
Leverage Existing Tools						
Getting Data In						
Getting Data Out						
Integration with Other Tools						
Accessibility						
Portability						
Security Issues						
Ease of Learning						
Ease of Use						
Legal-Specific Features						
Other Collaborators Use						
Long-Term Prospects						
Other Factors						
Total						
	Raw Score		Weighted Score	Raw Score		Weighted Score

Collaboration Tools: Free vs. Pay 24

People are often surprised when we tell them that many of the collaboration tools we discuss in this book are free. And by free, we mean free, as in no cost, nada, zip, bupkis—really! Most of the collaboration we undertook while writing this book was accomplished with Google Docs, a free tool. We discussed our plans for the book and instant messaged each other about it using Skype, a free tool. We shared bookmarks of useful web pages using Yahoo's shared bookmarking feature, a free tool. We transferred large files back and forth using YouSendIt.com, a free tool. We record and edit our podcasts with Audacity, a free tool. Do you see a pattern?

It is amazing how much collaboration can be done for free. This is primarily due to the explosion of Web 2.0 tools on the Internet. But if you include in this mix the collaboration features existing in tools that you already own, then you have another large set of tools that can be used at no additional cost.

In this chapter we consider whether free tools are really an option for lawyers. If they are, under what circumstances will you choose a free tool over a fee-based alternative? Is there an approach to free and pay that will work for you?

Free tools come in several varieties. The Internet-based and Web 2.0 tools are often free because they are supported by advertising. For the people who use these tools, having to view a few ads is a small burden to endure in exchange for a good collaboration tool. On the other hand, working with a client using a service or tool that serves up advertising probably does not give you the professional appearance you might prefer. Free services may also track behaviors of site visitors or gather other user information for demographic or marketing purposes. If these practices make you wary, that's understandable—they should. Before you start putting confidential client information into free applications, you owe it to your clients to read the terms of use and other **click-wrap agreements** of the service.

In addition to Internet-based tools, you may find that free software programs have collaboration features. Today, free software comes in two flavors: freeware and Open Source software. **Freeware** is software with a standard commercial license developed by an individual or company and offered to the world at no cost, although usually with a request for a donation. You can find freeware on sites like Download.com, where it's a snap to simply download and install them on your computer. Freeware programs are compact and tend to focus on certain tasks typically suited to individuals and small projects, although some are more complicated and versatile. What you usually will not find is dedicated, round-the-clock support from the developer. Further, development on the software will often stop abruptly and with little to no warning (not that commercial software is immune to that problem). Some freeware providers do offer "professional" versions for a fee, with additional features and support. A solo or small firm lawyer can do quite well with freeware tools; and for certain, infrequent tasks or special situations, a freeware utility can quickly and easily resolve your problem.

The second, more interesting, and possibly world-changing type of free software is Open Source or free software, sometimes referred to by the acronym FOSS (Free and Open Source Software). **Open Source software** is one part philosophical movement and one part software license. Famously, the "free" in Open Source software has been described as "free as in freedom, not free as in beer." The philosophy of Open Source is to make the source code of software freely available and to give users who are able the freedom to modify the software in ways most helpful to them. If they choose, the users can then contribute their changes and improvements back to the software community. It's an approach taken by Linux, Firefox, Apache, and other widely used software programs that are often seen today as leading competitors to Microsoft and other dominant software products.

Unlike commercial software, Open Source software typically has no vendors to distribute the product. In fact, Open Source programs are usually maintained by an ad hoc, loosely organized community of programmers who post material and edit source code using collaborative websites for their projects. If you find it difficult to believe that this system produces software that actually works, you are not alone. However, the history of

Open Source proves that this approach works quite well, and it has even been said that the Internet runs on open source software.

There are three aspects of Open Source software that should be mentioned here. First, Open Source software is often called "free as in beer" as well as "free as in freedom." Indeed, you can find many excellent Open Source programs at no cost. In fact, major corporations are now routinely evaluating Open Source software as an alternative to commercial software purchases. Second, when you consider that Open Source depends on the collaboration of widely scattered, part-time programmers in many geographic locations, it makes sense that these projects use very good, very powerful Open Source collaboration tools. For example, programmers routinely use Open Source wikis to post code, new releases, and other information. Third, Open Source programs are available in many categories. A visit to SourceForge.Net will show you how many Open Source projects are active. However, legal-specific Open Source programs are still rare.

Lawyers using Open Source programs are likely to use them as alternatives to Microsoft products or for specific tasks, such as the Firefox browser, Thunderbird email program, or other utilities. Otherwise, they adapt general Open Source tools to fit their legal practices. We expect to see a growing interest in Open Source from the legal technology community.

Lawyers may also take advantage of the "practically free" category of tools. We define this category loosely as using programs you already own but don't use at all or to their potential, or as features of programs that you weren't aware of. You have already paid for the product, so you don't have to pay any more to use it. Simple examples include the reviewing tools in Microsoft Office and Adobe Acrobat. You might also find that you or your company already owns Windows SharePoint Services or Groove as part of your Windows and Office installation.

Other legal-specific programs, from case management to document management to litigation software, also have collaboration tools built into them. For example, to avoid purchasing an extranet platform, a mid-sized firm using Worldox for document management might use its collaboration features to create an extranet that makes documents available for clients. Our best recommendation to anyone looking into collaboration tools is to start by taking a good look at what you already have.

Also in the no- or low-cost category are plug-ins, updates, or upgrades that provide collaboration tools to your existing programs. Software vendors are continuously adding new collaboration features to their products, which are often available as free upgrades. Some programs require an expensive upgrade to a new version, but you might find that for other applications a free plug-in or update might give you just the functionality you need.

Free software can be installed on your computer or used via a hosted service, as with Google Docs. Vendors also use Open Source software to offer low-priced hosted services, such as the project management platform Basecamp.

The bottom line is that free software should be a collaboration option for your practice. However, there are consequences to using free tools, and you must weigh carefully the risks and rewards before proceeding with them. At a minimum, though, free tools provide an excellent way to experiment with collaboration technologies and determine whether they might work for you.

Skype provides an excellent example of the promise and pitfalls of free collaboration tools. As we've discussed, Skype is a free software program that provides a platform for people to make free computer-to-computer voice calls and instant message each other. The basic calling features are free, it's amazingly popular, and it's very reliable—with a surprisingly high level of quality service. Skype calls often sound better than calls from cell phones, and podcasters who have guests or multiple hosts often record their calls over Skype.

Because Skype is free (at least when calling other computer users) and reliable, many small businesses have adopted it as their primary telephone service for nationwide and even international calling, saving thousands of dollars in phone expenses. Skype just works.

At least it did until a few days during the summer of 2007, when a software glitch made the service inaccessible to many users. Skype is well supported and was back online within a few days, but the downtime illustrated the concerns you must weigh when considering free software and services. What happens when a service goes down? How will you be supported when there is a problem? Most important, can you reasonably operate certain parts of your law practice on a free service if the services supporting you are unreliable? The answers to these questions will vary depending on the tool you're considering.

Due diligence is also important when using free services. Using a free tool from Google is one thing; we have grown comfortable using Google's free services because it is a highly visible, well-regarded company worth a zillion dollars. We know that Google has state-of-the-art servers and technology, and the company hires good people. On the other hand, a freeware program created by single developer in a foreign country or as an Open Source project probably will not give you the same level of comfort. Doing your homework on them and determining where they best fit into your efforts will help you grow more comfortable with these companies.

It's also worth mentioning again that just because the software or service is free does not mean you will not have other costs in implementing or using it. The cost of additional hardware, software, personnel, consultants, training, and the like might be significant, even though the lure of free software can be quite attractive. Consider *all* of the costs.

When do free collaboration tools make sense? First and foremost, when budget is an issue and time is of the essence. Solos and small firms have become the innovators in using free collaboration tools simply because in many cases it was the only affordable option available. In fact, we hear about new collaboration tools with far greater frequency from our friends in small firms than we do from those in large firms. Free tools make sense if you want to experiment with different types of tools. If you want to try out a wiki, grab a free Open Source tool and give it a test drive. Free tools also make sense when you want to develop a fast prototype for a collaboration project. Finally, free tools make sense any time they meet all of your requirements and get your job done, especially if you have backup systems in place.

When do free tools *not* make sense? Simply put, any other time. Law firm technology systems have strict requirements—among the highest in any industry—for security, uptime, backup, reliability, and performance. Immediate, round-the-clock support may be a requirement for some firms, and it is not always available with free tools. While the voice quality on Skype is good, it may not be consistently be good enough for your requirements.

Many factors will drive your decision on when to use free tools. The better you understand your needs and requirements, the better your decision. The best "free" approach might well be activating and using different parts of commercial tools you already own. However you choose to use them, free tools clearly should be an option that you consider when putting together your collaboration toolbox—as long as you exercise due diligence and understand the risks. Remember that the book you are now reading was written using free collaboration tools.

Involving Clients in Your Decisions and Choices 25

To introduce this chapter, let's take a look at what we believe is the biggest sea change in the history of legal technology. Throughout the 1990s, some estimated that more than 80 percent of law firms used WordPerfect for word processing. In fact, WordPerfect dominated the legal market. At that point, however, the tables turned—and in a dramatic way. Over the next few years, Microsoft Word caught up with and passed WordPerfect in market share; and Word now holds a greater share of the legal market than WordPerfect ever experienced.

It is instructive to think about the reasons for that change. Lawyers will, and do, continue to debate the relative merits of both products. Corel certainly made some missteps with WordPerfect, and its initial move to Windows was something of a disaster. Further, Microsoft certainly benefited from the dominance of Windows and bundling arrangements with manufacturers of new PCs. The biggest factor in the change, however, had little to do with technology markets. It had everything to do with the demands of the clients, who were moving to Word in droves. As statistics showed that the vast majority of businesses (i.e., clients and potential clients of law firms) used Microsoft Word, and lawyers and their clients began to exchange electronic documents by email, the writing was on the wall for WordPerfect. In retrospect, what first appeared to be an unexpected sea change in technology now seems quite predictable and expected.

The Word versus WordPerfect story is important when considering collaboration tools, simply because lawyers and law firms tend to be followers rather than leaders with technology. With WordPerfect, lawyers were surprised when their clients began demanding that documents be delivered in Word format, and law firms did not do a good job of creating a middle ground (such as standardizing on the Rich Text File format) or providing workable alternatives.

There are other examples of clients waiting patiently for lawyers to lead the way on technology, only to be disappointed with the lack of leadership from their law firms. Encryption and electronic billing are notable examples. Although more firms are moving to these technologies, they are slowly and grudgingly making the change. As a result, clients are making their own decisions and imposing those decisions on their law firms, sometimes with less than ideal results. If law firms had taken the initiative several years ago in electronic billing systems and offered a standard billing program, it probably would have been acceptable to many of their clients. Instead, many law firms today lament that they must deal with several different electronic billing formats chosen for them by their clients.

How will clients affect our choices of collaboration tools? A continuing theme of this book is that innovative and successful lawyers should become leaders and take action on using collaboration tools rather than simply following and reacting to the demands of their clients.

To alleviate this problem, the best advice we can give here is to involve your collaborators in your decisions and efforts from the beginning. Ask for their input, take advantage of their expertise and experience, and obtain their involvement and buy-in for the process and the tools you select. The most important of your collaborators to consider are obviously your clients.

The term "client-driven technology" applies here, and it can mean one of two things. First, technology is client driven when the client forces, implicitly or explicitly, the lawyer or firm to adopt certain tools to be used in representing the client. Often the law firm is dragged kicking and screaming to use the technology preferred by the client. In this chapter, we want to focus on the other type of client-driven technology: where the lawyer or firm anticipates the needs of the client, and actively proposes the use of certain technology tools to enhance the working relationship. This is a reasonable and arguably quite beneficial approach to take when determining your technology strategy in general, and with collaboration tools in particular. How, then, do you move into the world of client-driven technologies?

For many years, the best starting point for lawyers considering new ways to collaborate with clients has been what's known as the DuPont Legal Model. In 1992, chemical giant DuPont wanted to find a way to reduce drastically the number of its outside counsel. It was successful in this goal, reducing its outside counsel from more than 300 to approximately 35 firms. Secondarily, but more importantly, DuPont wanted to change the working relationship with the firms it continued to use. The DuPont Legal Model is constantly evolving, with other clients and law firms evaluating and adopting parts of it over the years.

The core elements of the DuPont Legal Model are (1) a business focus on DuPont's legal issues, (2) an ongoing work process reengineering, (3) a commitment to cutting-edge technology, and (4) a shared culture of efficiency and cost control. (See http://www.dupontlegalmodel.com/files/onlinelibrary_detail.aspibid=14.) The approach we have taken to collaboration tools in this book shares important similarities with these four principles.

Among other things, the DuPont Legal Model resulted in creation of the DuPont Primary Law Firm Network, an early version of the "virtual law firm," a collaborative team of law firms and service providers who work together on matters for DuPont. DuPont believes the next phase of the process is the evolution of the model toward collaborative work teams using sophisticated technology. DuPont's description of the virtual law firm envisioned at the core of the model is also instructive when considering the role of collaboration tools in your practice:

> The virtual law firm connects lawyers electronically and culturally. Through the use of applied technology, such as extranets, integrated case management software, computerized databases, electronic invoicing software, document imaging, cell phones, personal digital assistants, and trial presentation software, team members in different geographical locations can perform legal work efficiently and cost-effectively in a shared environment. But this technology still depends on the human element and on the willingness of committed participants to implement and use it constructively in furtherance of an articulated vision and clear goals. In a virtual law firm, participants must share a common culture.

We do not expect anyone reading this book to jump directly into the virtual law firm model described here, but you might use it to help set your strategic goals. When you take advantage of opportunities to collaborate with clients, you also begin laying the technological underpinnings that can lead you to such a model. Starting down this path will provide significant benefits for both you and your clients. Law departments can also use the model as a way to streamline and improve their work with outside counsel.

Most of your clients will be willing to respond to your inquiries about how you can serve them better, especially if you are asking about ways to make working with you more efficient and economical, eliminate annoyances, reduce costs, and receive better legal service in general.

The first steps are the most obvious and easiest to undertake. Start asking your clients what they want. Listen carefully to what they are already telling you. Learn about the ways they use technology in their businesses. Don't assume, ask.

The simplest tool for accomplishing this task is the client technology survey. Consider the sample survey in Chapter 5 as a starting point that can be tailored to address your client's specific situation. We recommend you keep it simple and short, ideally just a few pages. After you send the survey, follow up with a conversation where your goal is to do most of the listening and not much of the talking.

As part of your survey, you will want to get a good sense of the technologies your clients actually use. It is also important to understand the specific technologies they would prefer to use when working with you. In firms of sufficient size, you might involve your technology committee or IT department in this process. In large firms and for certain clients, you might even put your IT people together with your client's IT people, so that both sides have a good view of the playing field. The purpose of this effort is to gather data you can use to make good choices about collaborating with your clients.

During this process, you will want to learn as much as you can about the ways your clients collaborate and use collaboration technologies. For example, instant messaging is far more prevalent in businesses today than many lawyers are prepared to accept. Your survey may reveal ahead of time that your firm's policy prohibiting lawyers and staff from using instant messaging is going to cause issues for your clients, allowing you to deal with the potential problem in advance.

Finally, you should definitely determine your client's pain points, and where they exist. Are your clients frustrated with you because of technologies you have or do not have? Listening to their criticisms rather than arguing or trying to explain away the problem is an important part of the process.

We recommend conducting the survey with a good cross section of your clients. A large enough sample will help you spot trends and patterns in how you use technology with your clients. You may also learn where to target your efforts, set priorities, or deal with easy-to-solve conflicts. It will also help you avoid the rush to address the unique concerns of a single client or small number of clients in ways that will later cause problems with your other clients.

With these efforts, you will have a solid factual basis for making your decisions on collaboration technologies. The information you receive in these surveys may also help you identify "low-hanging fruit," or those simple, inexpensive, quickly implemented efforts that your clients will greatly appreciate. As we discuss in Chapter 26, using the **80/20 rule** and looking for ways to get good results will likely produce immediate benefits.

As you begin to formulate your collaboration strategy, follow up with your clients and try to learn from their experiences and expertise. Share your thinking and your research with them if appropriate, and identify clients willing to test tools or try pilot projects. In fact, we are seeing that both clients and law firms are not approaching each other with collaboration initiatives. These are excellent opportunities to share costs, piggyback on efforts made by others, and otherwise streamline the collaboration process.

A good collaboration strategy can succeed only when the input of other collaborators is requested and acted upon. Your clients are likely a rich source of information and experience you can use to help develop and implement your plan. The simple act of reaching out, especially if you follow it up with a meaningful response, will keep you out of a reactive mode in responding to client demands. It will also identify you as leader rather than a follower when it comes to finding ways to improve the working relationship between clients and their lawyers.

Determining Which Factors Will Drive Your Strategic Planning | **26**

Now that you are familiar with the different types of collaboration tools, we conclude Part VI with a look into the factors that will drive your planning and implementing them into your practice. Your best approach is to develop some kind of a strategic plan—one that is thoroughly researched, well thought out, and clearly written. It should also be revisited and revised on a regular basis.

We recognize that most of you will not reach this ideal situation, but in recommending a consistent strategic approach we hope to encourage you to move away from the ad hoc, reactive approach to collaboration. If you work through the following questions to focus your thoughts, you'll be well on your way to a strategic plan, and a foundation for making good choices about collaboration tools. This chapter serves as a review and summary of the key points presented in this part and gives you practical pointers for developing your own plan.

Locating Point A and Point B

Good strategic planning focuses on the basics. As we have mentioned before, it does not get any more basic than finding a good way to get from point A—where you are—to point B—where you want to be. If you do not get that right, your strategic plan will be built on a shaky foundation and probably will not stand the test of time, even if it's only a short time. However, locating both point A and point B can be more difficult than people expect. The more thoroughly you understand where you are and the better you define where you want to be, the better your chances of success. This is not rocket science; but as they say, the devil is in the details.

Thanks to the IRS, accounting firms, and Sarbanes-Oxley, the very word "audit" makes most people uncomfortable. But it's a necessary step if you're serious about strategic planning. The best way to understand your point A is to undertake some form of formal or informal collaboration technology audit in as much detail as you can stand. The sample Collaboration Technology Audit Questionnaire in Chapter 5 can serve as a starting point to help you know where you are today.

Defining point B can also be a formal or informal process that helps you identify short- and long-term goals with collaboration tools. What do you want to be able to accomplish both inside and outside your firm? What will you be required to do by your clients or others? What role will collaboration play in your technology or business strategic plans?

Existing Platforms

As we have discussed in previous chapters, there are many benefits to using software and hardware you already own for your collaboration efforts. However, you might also find limitations with your existing platforms and decide to take off in new directions. Before you do this, evaluate and understand what use can be made of your existing platforms and whether they will move you closer to point B. The increasing use of Microsoft SharePoint and Office by large law firms for collaboration comes in no small part from the belief that these existing platforms can serve as a logical path to achieving the firm's strategic goals in an economical and evolutionary way.

Sequencing and Timetables

Whether you are a solo practitioner looking for an inexpensive way to handle conference calls or a large law firm wanting to roll out extranets for every client, the first step is often the hardest one to take. Start out with a small step. Then take a series of steps to get where you want to go. You should have a timetable, hopefully with deadlines and even phases for implementation. Along the way there may be demos, testing, prototypes, a "soft" launch, and then the final launch of your new tool. The size and scope will vary, but the process remains the same. If you need to find a conference call service by tomorrow, your plan and the sequencing necessarily will compress. Your strategic plan will change depending on the timetable you develop and the phases and stages needed to complete your project.

Client Needs

Collaboration tools are an excellent example of client-driven technologies. Your clients' needs, spoken or unspoken, are likely to be the primary drivers in implementing collaboration tools. We encourage you to learn what your key clients need, expect, and want in their collaborations with you. Informal questioning or a formal survey can provide the necessary information. The sample Client Collaboration Survey in Chapter 5 can be used as a starting point. You ultimately may decide not to implement tools according to your clients' wishes, but it is important to understand those wishes and determine if and how you can accommodate them when formulating your strategic plan.

Needs of Other Collaborators—Internal and External

Many lawyers begin using collaboration tools in reaction to what other collaborators are doing. You may not have planned to use the Track Changes feature in Microsoft Word, but when you receive a document from your client with Track Changes activated and directions to send back your marked-up copy by e-mail, you will suddenly become a user of Track Changes for document collaboration—whether you want to or not. Part of your strategic planning should be based on your understanding of what your likely collaborators—internal and external, on your side and on the other side—are using and may use in the future. You also may want to determine when you can push your preferred solutions onto collaborators, and when you will accept their choice of collaboration tools.

Cultural Issues

It takes two to collaborate—at least. There always will be some give-and-take between people who are working with each other. The success of knowledge management, social networking, and other collaborative projects largely depend on the culture of an organization and whether it will support or reject the proposed tool. To the extent you can work within your organization's culture, you improve your chances for success. Perhaps the most important cultural element to consider when implementing new technology is tolerance for change.

Budget

Money matters. Financial limitations may place constraints on what you can realistically plan for and accomplish. But keep in mind that early successes also can pave the way for future funding. Your budget might dictate the phases of your project or even the tools that you will consider, especially to the extent you might use free tools.

Hosted versus Internal

Can you implement the tools internally? Will you need additional hardware, software, or personnel to implement and maintain the tools? Are there other demands on your infrastructure? Under certain circumstances it makes sense to outsource tools or used hosted services. There are philosophical as well as financial aspects to these issues. Determining your approach to this basic issue will have a major influence on your strategic planning.

Security and Special Concerns

Once you begin to share documents outside of your firewall, security becomes a primary concern. Although all lawyers must meet high ethical standards, certain practices may have higher standards or security issues. For example, firms handling highly confidential mergers and acquisitions or solos handling medical information will have special concerns about security. How do you expect to handle the security of your confidential client information? What are your security obligations? Your ability to respond to these questions responsibly and ethically is likely to shape your strategic planning.

Return on Investment

In any firm project, value for services purchased is a critical issue. To make sure your investments in collaboration technology pay off, you'll want to be thoughtful and deliberate about how you spend your money. How will you measure the economic benefits of collaboration technology? Can you determine whether the investment is reasonable, will pay for itself over a period of time, or actually makes money? If you can calculate the predicted return on investment (ROI) or, better yet, measure ROI on the collaboration projects you have implemented, you can direct your planning toward better projects and gain support from decision makers for future projects.

SWOT and Other Strategic Approaches

Businesses use a variety of strategic planning approaches. It's always a good idea to keep up with some of the classic strategic planning approaches. Our list of resources in Appendix 2 contains several sources of discussion on strategic planning approaches. The SWOT (Strengths, Weaknesses, Opportunities, and Threats) approach is one commonly used by law firms. Using the SWOT analysis, you can assess each of the four categories while focusing on collaboration and then use the results to shape your strategic planning on collaboration to fit the overall business strategic plan. There is no magic formula, but trying one or more of the classic approaches will help you put together your own plan. Any of these approaches can be done formally or informally, and they could be as simple as applying the SWOT analysis to the back of a napkin while having lunch.

The Portfolio Approach

In economics, modern portfolio theory is a Nobel Prize–winning idea for making prudent investments. The theory states that you can minimize risk and optimize long-term results by compiling a diversified mix of investments that include a balanced set of high-risk and low-risk assets best suited to your investment goals, philosophies, and tolerance to risk. Paradoxically, the theory states that investing only in classically low-risk assets is one of the riskier approaches you can take over the long haul. The same principles apply to strategic technology planning. As you develop your strategic plan, you will want to consider your efforts as a "portfolio." Are you diversifying your portfolio of technology tools? Have you included some higher-risk, higher-return projects in the mix with your "safe" projects? Have you put all your eggs in one basket? Portfolio theory suggests that you test several projects in order to minimize the impact of one that does not work.

The 80/20 Rule

The **80/20 rule**, or **Pareto Principle**, is a popular planning approach, and it's based on the observation that we get 80 percent of our results from 20 percent of our efforts. Other formulations suggest that getting 80 percent of the way to our results is the easy part, but getting the final 20 percent is much more difficult. We see the 80/20 rule as more of a rule of thumb than a scientific law. There are two important roles the 80/20 rule can play in your strategic planning. First, it helps you focus on projects that take you farthest toward your goal for the smallest amount of effort. Second, it helps you break away from dwelling on the fact that a project may not take you 100 percent of the way to your goal and, therefore, is not worth the attempt. The best often is the enemy of the good. "Good enough" projects and "good enough" plans that result in action and improvement are far preferable to perfect plans that never get off the ground.

Who Makes the Decisions?

Determining the final decision maker and making sure that he or she is involved in the planning process and in approving the plan are key components of any successful strategic plan. Who signs the checks? Who gets to determine when the project is completed, and whether it was successful? Are they in the room when decisions are made?

The Written Plan

Committing your plan to writing gives it a much better chance of being successful. A written plan requires review, organization, and dedication. All of these elements are vital to success. A written plan also provides you something concrete you can review and evaluate in the future. It can be one page of bulleted items or a 100-page report, but having it in writing will make a big difference.

Every strategic plan for collaboration technologies will be different. The size of the firm or company, type of collaboration tools involved, or budget available to the collaborators—all can combine to create varying strategic plans. But even if you have no strategic plan, you still have a strategy (whether you like it or not)—to be reactive rather than active, to make ad hoc decisions, and to move forward with no direction in mind. It might work out for you, but the odds are against it. If you work through the factors listed in this chapter while working on your plan, your chances for success will dramatically increase.

Practical Issues, Tips, and Techniques

Getting the Word Out to Your Collaborators 27

Here's a question for you: what happens if you make a change to a document in a collaboration tool and no one knows you did it? More simply put, what is the sound of one collaborator collaborating?

A collaboration tool works only if your collaborators actually use it, either routinely or as it is needed. The simple failure of people to use those tools is what dooms most collaborative projects. For example, in our experience the messaging tools of Internet social networking sites began to take the place of scattered email discussions as people migrated to those services. However, some people eventually abandoned social networking tools and reverted to their earlier emailing habits. Understanding the reasons for this phenomenon and designing and building tools that address these issues will help to ensure that your collaborative technologies are properly utilized.

The main villain causing people to abandon collaboration tools is something we discussed in Chapter 22—the multiplication of information silos. We keep our information in a number of separate locations—email, documents, and financial information, for example—that we must visit separately to use. A collaboration tool that either reduces (or at least does not increase) the number of information silos, offers a bridge between them, or provides an entry point to several silos will have a greater chance for success than a tool that creates an additional silo you and your collaborators must remember to visit.

As a general rule, most people do not want or need an additional silo to hold new pieces of information. It's confusing, time-consuming, and only adds to the general sense of information overload. An exception to this rule is that under the right circumstances people will add one more silo if it is sufficiently attractive, provides additional benefits, and is easy to access. For example, a social networking site like Facebook creates another silo for information—another site you must visit every day. However, it also offers access to your friends, updates on certain types of shared information, and a channel to exchange information with friends that might make it attractive enough for you to add it as another silo. The Facebook site is very easy to access—you can just create a bookmark to remember it, and entering the site requires only your email address and a password. While many people use Facebook, however, there is no guarantee that it or any other collaboration tool that resides in its own silo will be sufficiently appealing to attract users on a daily or other regular basis. There are too many other sites and silos competing for the user's attention.

The Feed Concept

Because you cannot rely on a collaboration tool whose effectiveness depends on people visiting every day to check for new information, you must consider other alternatives. These alternatives must provide your collaborators with information about changes and updates inside collaboration tools without actually requiring them to return to the tool to read the information. These alert tools can either provide notice and a mechanism for the recipient to easily visit the collaboration tool to review the new information, or they can provide notice along with the actual changed materials.

When it comes to getting information out to your collaborators, we believe the idea of the "feed" is the most effective method. Think of the news ticker, the "crawl line" at the bottom of a TV screen, email alerts, and especially the RSS feed, which we'll discuss in greater detail later in this chapter. Each of these feeds is designed to provide you with timely notice in headline (or more detailed) format that something of interest has occurred and indicate where to go if you want more information on the subject. Other terms for this process include "newsfeeds," "alerts," and "current awareness." No matter what you call it, the idea is the same—alerting your collaborators to new or updated information without requiring them to go back into the tool to get that information. The concept is quite simple and exceedingly important, but implementing it successfully is harder than you might expect.

Feed Mechanisms

Most collaboration between lawyers and their clients occurs through the medium of email. Lawyers and BlackBerrys are like bacon and eggs—you always see them together. It should be no surprise that one way to get the word out from your collaboration tools is simply to piggyback them on email.

Many collaboration tools, especially those found online, incorporate email as an alert mechanism. If changes are made within the site or tool, an email is sent to collaborators notifying them that activity has occurred. The email might just give notice of the change, summarize it, or perhaps deliver a complete copy of the change or addition. The email might be sent immediately after the change is made, or it might be sent out with a single daily summary of all activity. Collaboration tools can also make use of email in the opposite direction. Rather than having to enter the collaboration tool to leave a message, users of many products can send an email to a specified address and have that email or its content published directly at the collaboration site.

Email is an appealing way to handle alerts. Everyone uses email. You can take advantage of email tools such as Outlook to create folders and rules that will manage alerts and keep them in one place. Your collaborators also invariably have and use email. With Blackberries and other devices now becoming ubiquitous, email is available anytime, anywhere.

However, there are disadvantages to using email as an alert mechanism. Perhaps 80 percent of the email we receive these days is spam. Most lawyers receive hundreds of emails a day, and adding more to that load is not an inviting prospect. With the sheer volume of email we receive, alerts can get lost or overlooked. As spam filters become more aggressive, alert messages could be identified as spam and never reach the intended recipient. Further, people who do not use rules, folders, or other forms of email management can easily be overwhelmed, especially if they receive email updates for each matter or change.

Another form of alert mechanism, and the one we prefer by far, is RSS. **RSS feeds** have become an interesting alternative to email for collaboration alerts and notices. J. D. Lasica defined RSS as "news that comes to you," which is exactly what we want to find in an alert mechanism. Technically, RSS stands for Really Simple Syndication, and it is an **XML** (Extensible Markup Language) file format used to publish frequently updated content such as blog entries, news headlines, or podcasts. RSS content can be read using software known as a newsreader, news aggregator, or RSS reader. Newsreaders can be stand-alone programs like FeedDemon or online services like Google Reader, and they are built into the current versions of Internet browsers like Internet Explorer and Firefox.

Blogging software, many Web 2.0 applications, and other customized collaboration tools allow you to easily set up and generate RSS feeds that deliver information to you whenever new items are added. An RSS feed has its own URL, and a collaborator with a newsreader can take the URL and "subscribe" to the RSS feed. We use the term "RSS feed" generically, because there are several flavors of XML-based feeds, including RSS, Atom, and RDF. It is not important to understand the differences between these types of feeds, or even how they work. All you need to know is how RSS can help deliver information to you.

With RSS feeds and a newsreader, we can have all the benefits of email alerts while eliminating most of the disadvantages. When a change or other actionable event occurs, a new item is generated and automatically shows up in our newsreader. All of the feed items are kept for us in a separate folder for that feed, which we can read at our convenience. As a result, you don't need to set up email rules, as in your email program. RSS feeds also have no issues with spam. We receive only the information we have requested, from the feeds to which we subscribe. There's no need for spam filters, so all the information we request gets through to us. Because we decide which RSS subscriptions we want, we have control over newsreaders where we lack control over our email inbox. Alerts are not likely to be lost or overlooked, as they might in the daily deluge of email.

One concern you might have with RSS feeds is security. Indeed, ensuring that only intended users can subscribe to the feed, and not just anyone who has the feed URL, is an important consideration. There are ways to provide security for RSS feeds, but doing so will take some research. In the case of tools with integrated RSS feeds, which are becoming more common, you will want to find out how access control and security are maintained.

Because RSS feeds are based on the flexible XML standard, they can be repurposed in many different ways. XML is a technical subject outside the scope of this book. However, one key feature of XML you should know about is that it allows an author to separate content from display. Using XML coding tags, you can keep the same content, but display it in the format best suited for the device used by the reader. The same content might appear as a web page, a document, a database record, a text message on a cell phone, or even as audio by a text-to-speech application. In fact, many of the major news sites or other websites that provide news headlines actually incorporate RSS feeds to update those items.

Another way to provide alerts is to take advantage of RSS feeds and create your own newsreader, aggregating alerts on pages your collaborators regularly visit. There are several free tools on the Internet that will aggregate feeds and display them on a web page for you. These pages, or small applications on those pages (called applets or widgets) are typically referred to as portals or dashboards. Again, the underlying idea is to have the alerts appear in such a way that your collaborators will see and use them.

A portal or dashboard will generally be incorporated into an intranet or extranet, in a place that its users visit daily. It might also be built into other programs, like Outlook or SharePoint, that are opened and used every day by collaborators. The alerts should appear in places where they will be noticed and can be acted upon. The alert generally will appear as a hyperlink that the user can click to go either to the notice or the actual site of the change or new information. The advantage of a portal is that the notices appear where someone is most likely to see them. Because these alerts are built into a web page, portal designers can organize them or let users personalize them to suit their tastes.

It's a small step to move from RSS feeds to other ways people can receive alerts, and to incorporate those mechanisms into collaboration tools. Short Message Service (SMS), text messages, instant messages, and other short text-based communication tools can also become vehicles for distributing alerts. As audio and video use becomes more common and accepted, it's possible we will see alerts distributed by voice mail or podcast.

Some companies now use instant messaging as an ad hoc alert system on its own. For example, once a meeting organizer sees people are available for instant messaging, he or she can assemble the available group on the fly for a group instant messaging session, all with a simple IM alert.

Another factor to consider in using messaging, feeds, and alerts is that of keeping a permanent record. Is there a central storage point or archive of all the alerts? Can you trace where and when the alerts were sent? Can you use the archives to reconstruct deal points or determine how decisions or changes were made? Some tools offer these options, which might be important in your setting.

The Multiple-Channel Approach

If we have done our job in this chapter, you'll understand by now that the ability to alert your collaborators is vital to successfully implementing any collaboration tool. Users must know when changes are made or that actions are required. If users fail to receive sufficient notice, a collaboration platform is likely to fall short of expectations or even fail. Fortunately, most tools offer one or more avenues for notifying users. We think of these as communication channels. Consider your users and the channels they already use, then adopt an appropriate feed strategy. In most cases, you will want to use several communication channels simultaneously, to make sure you cover all of your user needs and preferences. This approach will bring the best results.

Ethics, Metadata, and Other Practical Issues 28

Collaboration tools take lawyers into uncharted waters in many ways. In this chapter, we discuss some of the issues that collaboration tools raise in areas of particular concern to lawyers—ethics, confidentiality, and privilege in the practice of law. Lawyers are still relatively new to using collaboration tools, so we will attempt to reason from analogies with practices and examples that already exist. If bar regulators can understand collaboration tools as evolutionary rather than revolutionary changes and as extensions of processes lawyers already use and know well, they may decide that new types of regulation are not necessary. However, if, as recent history has shown, bar regulators treat these tools as presenting completely new issues requiring completely different approaches, we all could be in for a wild ride.

Lawyers have not yet systematically addressed the ethical and related issues raised by the use of email, the Internet, data storage, and computer technology in general. ABA Formal Opinion 99-413, which states that unencrypted email between lawyer and client does not lose its confidential nature, has been accepted as approving the nonuse of encryption for routine email. This interpretation is probably broader than the intent and language of the opinion, which was issued in the twentieth century and reflects the state of technology at that time. Much has changed.

Unfortunately, if you search through the applicable ethical rules and comments you will not find any references to wikis, service-level agreements, or strong passwords. And it's a good bet that clear guidance on the ethical implication of using collaboration tools probably will not come for some time (if ever), while technology continues to change at a rapid pace. As a result, when dealing with the ethical issues involved with collaboration tools, you should work from a clear understanding of basic legal ethics principles, take reasonable steps, monitor developments, and look to the technology itself for answers.

In the past, ethical questions involving the use of technology tended to arise and be addressed in the context of marketing, especially on the Internet. Lately, attention is being paid to the area of electronic discovery, particularly the use of metadata. ABA Formal Opinion 06-422 offers some advice in this area. We have also seen activity, largely driven by malpractice insurance carriers and state bar practice management advisors, in the areas of conflict checking, case management, and billing and accounting. Collaboration tools, especially those found online, can raise similar questions.

In this chapter, we want to discuss other areas where collaboration tools inevitably will have a large impact—confidentiality, lawyer-client privilege, multi-jurisdictional practice, unauthorized practice of law, and what it means to represent a client in the Internet era. Collaboration tools raise difficult issues, but they also often contain the means to address them. If reasonable practices and procedures will be the test of how lawyers handle these problems, how can we start to determine what is reasonable?

Confidentiality

Confidences are easy to keep when few people have access to the information. They are easy to manage when they exist within a physical document that can be locked away in a safe deposit box. Once information is stored in digital form, it becomes easy to copy and move, and much more difficult to secure, especially when it is stored on or accessible via the Internet.

Over the years, terms like **hacking**, **cracking**, and **phishing** have entered our lexicon, along with **social engineering**, **spoofing**, and **identity theft**. Microsoft and other software vendors routinely release patches for security flaws that would permit someone to access and control a computer. **Spyware**, **keystroke loggers**, **Trojan horses**, and other **malware** create a perilous environment for any computer connected to the Internet, even with appropriate protection. Outsiders can access unsecure wireless networks, and **packet sniffers**, **password crackers**, and **hacking** toolkits comprise the arsenal of today's wrongdoer, increasingly a professional data thief or someone involved in organized crime. Computer security is an ongoing chore and a never-ending battle.

It's a fact that the game today is drastically different from when we dealt only with paper. Further, we are not likely to go backward. If you use collaboration technologies in your practice, especially tools that potentially expose your data to outside parties by means of the Internet, you must consider the impact on your ethical obligations of confidentiality. At the same time, this obligation must be interpreted within the context of the real world of computer security.

Security is the technology analogue of confidentiality. To be successful and ensure your collaboration tool gets used, the security around the tool must involve a balancing between protection and convenience. To protect something perfectly will all but guarantee that it will be inaccessible and unusable to the collaborator. Consider cartoons where characters lock the door and throw away the key. If your collaboration tools are behind that door, they aren't of much use to you. On the other hand, maximizing user convenience and access (no passwords or other barriers) effectively will eliminate any protection of the data. Security, and therefore confidentiality, requires finding the right balance.

Security requires a multifaceted approach. Authentication, authorization, encryption, and other security technologies all play a key role. You also will need to augment these security features with procedures and processes designed to maintain security. In addition, you should also address the personal dimension of security—strong passwords, user training, and good practices.

As we discussed in Chapter 15, the security of most collaboration tools combines some level of authentication and authorization. You need to be certain the person using the tool is actually the person with permission to do so; this is the authentication component, with user names and passwords its primary tools. Once someone is authenticated, their access and rights must be limited to only those areas to which they are actually allowed. Users are walled off from data they do not have permission to see, and they are not allowed to access, copy, or change data for which they have no permission. That is where authorization comes into play. It is usually handled by setting network permissions, designating user rights, and placing certain users into groups with defined roles.

Identity management combines authentication and authorization into one seamless process. Once the system verifies your identity, your rights adjust automatically as you move within a tool or from one tool to another. Because lawyers and others work on many different matters and may have different roles in each of those matters, identity management can invisibly tailor a user's experience so they can access and work on all of their matters, without requiring multiple logins or other annoying procedures. These security measures will help you manage confidential information, maintain ethical boundaries, and log and track access to materials.

It is also important to ensure your online activities are secure. The most common standard for securing a websites involves the use of the Secure Sockets Layer (SSL). You'll know you're visiting a site with SSL when the URL starts with an https:// rather than an http://. Sites with SSL security should be a requirement for your online collaboration tools, whether you host them or use someone else's service. Online collaboration tools also often use encryption during transmittal of data. As use of collaboration tools increases, expect all forms of encryption to become more common, including the use of digital certificates.

Finally, your security scenario should have an emphasis on strong passwords. Because longer passwords are harder to crack, a **strong password** consists of combinations of seven or more letters, numbers, and symbols (for example, b5@2057*JMS). Some online tools show you the strength of your password when you register, and they encourage you to create stronger passwords. Your organization can also enhance security by enforcing strong password requirements. There is a move in some organizations toward using randomly generated passwords created by a **fob**—a small hardware device that is synchronized with a network's password on a minute-by-minute basis. Biometric forms of "passwords," like fingerprint or even retina scanners, might also come into wider use, partly because of people's tendency to use weak passwords. Surveys show that the most commonly used password is still "password"—which only reinforces the need for greater security measures.

Privilege

Some feel the attorney-client privilege is under attack in the United States. That view may be open for debate, but it is fair to say that the privilege seems to be shrinking and its limits are harder to discern. Use of collaboration tools may only add to the confusion regarding the scope of the attorney-client privilege, but such tools do have the potential to help.

Collaboration tools allow lawyers to label privileged material and protect it electronically, limiting access, tracking use, and providing ways to validate that the material was properly handled. For example, on a litigation extranet, privileged material can be segregated to a certain area of the site, with access tightly controlled. Comments, labels, and access mechanisms can all help in identifying and working with this material.

A related issue is the inadvertent waiver of privilege. Lawyers' use of technology is fraught with danger and risk, and not just in the area of collaboration tools. Consultants and vendors increasingly have unrestricted access to our computer systems. Further, various types of IT services, hosting, and even license agreements may contain provisions allowing third-party access to data, which can raise privilege and confidentiality issues. Lawyers must pay close attention to these agreements and adequately address any specific concerns they may have.

Other Practical Issues to Watch For

As lawyers use hosted collaboration services more and more often, they will need to keep a watchful eye on potential security issues that arise in hosted environments. Security, disaster recovery, backup, archiving, and redundancy are among the big concerns. Other important issues include loss of data, support levels, response times, warranties, limits on liability, error handling, uptime, and bandwidth requirements. In addition, if you experience problems with your online tools, you will want to have clearly defined escalation procedures, termination and other exit strategies, and requirements for the safe return of your documents and data in a timely manner. You'll also want to formulate procedures for easing transition to a replacement provider if moving to a new service becomes necessary. Software licenses and hosting agreements in the IT industry are notoriously one-sided in favor of vendors, so you cannot expect the "standard contract" to be adequate. It's important to note that many of the same issues arise when lawyers host tools on their own computers.

Further, because some online collaboration tools offer a communications channel to non-clients, you run the risk that communications to these individuals may run afoul of your state's advertising and solicitation rules. These rules might affect what you can say online and whether you need to retain your online materials, apply for preapproval, or comply with other rules that typically apply to advertising or communications directed to non-clients on the Internet.

We've only looked at the tip of the iceberg on practical security issues that might arise when developing a collaboration strategy. Many other questions remain. How do the new electronic discovery rules apply to documents stored in collaboration tools? Will you be obligated to produce materials held in document repositories? How will the question about handling metadata be resolved? What are a lawyer's obligations for maintaining data in online tools after the project or matter is completed? What happens when vendors offering hosted sites go out of business or lose data? Who is responsible if payments for online services are not made, and the service is suspended?

You'll also have to deal with maintenance and supervision issues whether you host your collaboration tools internally or use a third-party provider. Who sets and manages user access and permissions? How are updates handled? Who fixes broken links? How long are you required to keep a collaboration site active after the project or matter is completed? And what if clients or lawyers switch firms—how do you transfer the data in your tools to them? We expect the answers to these questions will develop in the coming years.

All of these practical issues are manageable, especially if you think about them and plan for them in advance. Your best approach is to treat collaboration tools as something you will be using over the long haul and to start addressing these issues from the outset. You will also need to monitor developments constantly and watch for advice from malpractice carriers as well as opinions and rule changes from bar regulators. With careful planning, you'll be able to navigate the uncharted waters of collaboration tools with greater confidence.

Ownership, Control, and Other Legal Issues **29**

Collaboration tools bring to the forefront a variety of issues that generally were not given much thought in the days of paper-only practice of law. Ownership, intellectual property, and right to use issues traditionally arose only when lawyers left a firm and took files, copies of forms, or other materials with them. The maxim that "the client owns the file" resolved most issues or disputes over who owned or had control over paper files. Even the question of "who owns the draft" in a negotiation often turned on actual physical possession of the draft document. Locked doors, drawers, file cabinets, or even tying the strings on a Redweld folder were used to handle many security issues. Shredders disposed of paper documents. The onslaught of electronic documents and their attendant issues now make the days of paper seem like much simpler times.

The ability to easily create copies of digital files of any type and electronically move them around may well be seen as one of the most important advances of our computer and Internet era. The copying of data has raised different, and well-litigated, issues in the music, movie, and other content-based industries; but to date there have been no happy or effective solutions. We have moved from buying physical objects—books, tapes, CDs—to licensing intellectual property rights wrapped in the form of digital files. Nicholas Negroponte famously referred to this as the movement from "atoms" (stuff) to "bits" (electrons).

It should be no surprise that the legal profession has started to experience many of these same issues. Are legal strategies, tax shelter formats, appellate arguments, or methods of delivering legal services patentable? Does a lawyer or the law firm own the copyright on their forms, articles, presentations, blogs, or other materials created by those who work at the firm? Can a firm use copyright laws to keep a lawyer who has left the firm from using forms the lawyer himself created?

In this chapter, we will discuss some of the intriguing legal issues collaboration tools present for the lawyers who use them. We are still early enough in the evolutionary process of collaboration technologies that there are far more questions than answers, but it is important that we start to see the issues that are coming up and identify the concerns you may need to address in the future. We will cover three areas—control, ownership, and the new emphasis on intellectual property rights and licensing—as they apply to new collaboration technologies.

Control

One of the first pieces of advice a new transactional lawyer learns is how important it is to control the draft. Creating the first draft of a document based on your "paper" or your forms generally gives you a significant advantage in negotiations and tends to result in a more favorable document at the end. Similarly, if you can set depositions or meetings at favorable times on your home turf, you tend to have some advantage and more control over the deposition than if you travel to an unfamiliar setting that is the other side's home turf.

With collaboration tools, we again see the evolution and expansion of traditional elements that have always been present in the practice of law. The questions we ask now are ones we have asked before, but now they are much more complex and difficult to resolve. The question of "shall we start from your form or mine?" has moved logically to "shall we use your deal room or ours?"

The question of control can be addressed from the outset and resolved in a mutually satisfactory way—as long as you know that the issue exists. Otherwise, the advantage goes to the first mover or the party with the most leverage. If your client or a vendor sends you a contract in Microsoft Word with Track Changes activated, it becomes difficult to demand or make the transition to a process of sending drafts using your redlining tool, no matter your standard internal policies or practices. At that point, you must either try to make a strong case for your document tools or be prepared to use Track Changes, with full awareness of the difficulties you face with metadata and other issues.

From electronic discovery to extranets to other aspects of collaboration, lawyers must address at the earliest possible moment who will have control of the process and understand the implications of losing that control. How easily or quickly can you add new users to someone else's extranet? How do you get technical support if problems arise using someone else's hosted collaboration tools? Who makes decisions about how files are organized, how user rights are granted, and the other aspects of operating sophisticated, shared tools? Ultimately, who is in charge?

Wikis, blogs, and Web 2.0 tools raise other control issues, especially if they contain user-generated content or the ability to make comments. If you allow comments or edits within a particular tool, how will inappropriate, infringing, or even obscene materials be handled? Who is responsible for quality control and content management issues? How will sites be updated, backed up, redesigned, and archived?

Security, privacy, and other management issues also raise questions of control. Who is responsible for security matters, software updates, and security testing? Securely setting up new employees as computer users on your internal networks is hard enough; but those issues, especially timeliness, can be larger problems on an external site. If you are up against a deadline or desperately need access to materials and do not have rights to them, what can you do and to whom do you go?

Confidential material also must be treated differently from other data, and in ways that can be enforced. If you create the appropriate permissions, collaboration tools can definitely maintain confidentiality; but you must ensure the job is correctly done. Worse, if you focus only on the "real world" and the paper world when thinking about these issues, granting access to an extranet without appropriate care and attention might undo all of your other efforts.

Collaboration tools offer excellent ways to control information and how it is used. You can secure individual documents from being copied, printed, or moved. You can "hide" and encrypt materials so no one without authorization will even know they exist, let alone be able to read them. Some tools can prevent email from being forwarded. However it is done, someone must take charge early in the process and determine how information will be controlled.

Ownership

Lawyers traditionally take a cavalier and easygoing approach to the ownership of their data, and accompanying intellectual property rights. Check your firm's partnership agreement to see if intellectual property rights are addressed. If they are, the agreement was probably recently amended in response to a specific issue raised when a partner left the firm.

When lawyers leave a firm, they usually take their forms, sample agreements, and documents with them. In the past there were usually no questions about the ownership of intellectual property rights in articles, presentations, and other materials of the departing lawyer. Even if a lawyer wrote a book or treatise, the only issue that concerned the firm would be the split of royalties, not ownership of the copyright.

Today lawyers create websites, blogs, podcasts, audio, video, and many other types of content. Some of these efforts can be quite valuable. We are beginning to see ownership of this content becoming a source of contention upon the departure of a lawyer from a firm or legal department. Sometimes the issues arise even before departure.

With collaborative tools, the questions of ownership become even more difficult. If the client "owns the file" for a matter, as the traditional rule states, does the client also own everything contained in an extranet for that matter? If not, why not? What does it mean to own the file, when data for a client can be scattered among several tools? Since the material is digital, can we simply make a copy for everyone and move on? In sophisticated collaboration tools, can you even pull the client's data out in a usable format, or do you have to create a duplicate system?

In the case of collaborative efforts like wikis, the "work product" is a team effort prepared by different constituents—lawyers, clients, vendors, and potentially opposing counsel, among others. Who owns that product? An agreement today might begin with one party's form, be modified by both parties' lawyers, include language from vendors and other parties, and end up looking far different than when it was created. Who can later use that agreement as their own form? Similarly, a collaboratively written brief may involve many hands. Who owns the brief and the arguments in it? Can you take parts of the brief you collaborated on but did not write and use them in another case where you are working with different collaborators? Can clients keep you from using research, briefs, agreements, or other legal deliverables for other clients because they own it, especially if they have contributed to the effort through collaborative tools?

These questions have always existed. The use of collaboration tools will simply bring them out into the open and make them more visible than ever.

Licensing

As we move into an era where the licensing of intellectual property becomes enormously important, it should be no surprise that licensing issues will begin to play a larger role in the practice of law. Although we may never need to obtain patent licenses to use a new estate planning strategy patented by another lawyer, expect lawyers to increasingly address the issues of permissions and intellectual property rights as well as what can be done with materials prepared in collaborative ways.

Ideally, you will want to address licensing issues, to the extent they will exist, up front and before collaborative materials are created. Ethical rules might have some impact on this area, but they tend to lag behind the pace of technology and do not often show an appreciation of how technologies work. For example, Florida and other states trying to address the issue of metadata in documents have demonstrated a lack of understanding of how metadata works, especially in a collaborative setting. As a result, they are establishing rules that make it difficult to use normal collaboration tools, like Track Changes and comments, in the usual way. Setting out the ground rules in advance with your collaborators and agreeing to them from the beginning hopefully will avoid difficult issues later.

In the near future we expect to see collaborators starting to agree specifically about how materials and deliverables can be used and repurposed, how intellectual property ownership issues will be determined, and how licenses will be granted for the use of our materials. And these issues work both ways. For example, a law firm that uses an extranet to deliver training tools to one client will want to be able to use those tools for other clients while ensuring that a client cannot offer those same materials to others for a fee.

The Role of Contracts for Collaboration Tools

Collaboration tools often are provided by third parties through hosting arrangements. With these services you don't have to buy a box of software or install something on your computer. Instead, you're obtaining a set of services delivered over the Internet. If you have ever negotiated an agreement for a hosted service, application service provider, or software as a service relationship, you know how complicated these agreements can be. At the other extreme are Web 2.0 and other Internet services that utilize non-negotiated, highly one-sided click-through or click-wrap agreements that typically are inadequate to provide the level of protection lawyers need to satisfy their ethical obligations to their clients.

Hosted collaboration tools in particular require a high level of certainty before lawyers can commit to them. It is critical to avoid agreements that would allow the actions of a vendor to cause a breach of confidentiality. Do you have a Service-Level Agreement (SLA) that covers uptime, response time, support coverage, and escalation of issues? Is there a way to get out of a service that is not working for you? Can you retrieve your data in a format you can use? How is your data backed up, and what security and disaster recovery procedures are in place? These are just a few of the major issues you will want to address when entering into a hosted services arrangement.

Is it any easier to host the collaboration tool yourself? Not really. You still have to answer most of the questions just described, no matter who provides the services.

Moving Toward Different Models of Delivering Legal Services

The use of collaboration tools is likely to cause lawyers to rethink the nature of the deliverables of legal services. Do lawyers deliver advice, documents, or something else? Does the answer vary for different firms? What deliverables do law departments receive or create? In collaborative efforts, is some form of joint deliverable created? How do we think about these things in a way that helps us to move forward?

We are just beginning to feel the impact of how digitization of the legal practice, the Internet, and electronic collaboration affect the practice of law. As a result, right now there are more questions than clear answers. We can learn and work together to find the answers, or others will decide the answers for us—as the music, movie, and encyclopedia industries, to give a few examples, have discovered.

As we ask these questions, however, one thing is clear: collaboration technologies are allowing new forms of legal services and new sources of revenue to be created. In a licensing economy, the ability to license intellectual property to generate revenue not based on billable hours becomes an area of opportunity. To do that in collaborative ways raises potential problems as well as potential revenues, which we will explore further in Chapter 34.

It's not so much that collaboration tools raise so many new issues. It's that they bring to the surface issues lawyers preferred to gloss over in the past. Many of the questions raised in this chapter have long been asked in the paper-based practice of law. Technology is bringing these questions into sharp focus. In many cases, there are no easy answers. But there are no places to hide as these issues increasingly come into play. The earlier and more directly you can begin to address them, the better off you will be.

Potential Pitfalls of Collaboration: Where to Be Wary 30

In this book, we want to paint a realistic picture of collaboration tools. Without question, the promise of collaboration using technology is great. Excellent tools already exist, and new and better tools are likely just around the corner. Web 2.0, social networking, and other online phenomena are the buzzwords of our time. However, we do not see collaboration tools only through rose-tinted glasses.

The truth is, the history of using advanced technologies in the practice of law is the story of more failures and so-so results than it is a list of resounding successes that people try to imitate. Many technology projects are overhyped and, in a classic recipe for failure, overpromised and under-delivered. Firms sometimes boast of modest successes, but nothing compared to what was promised. Will this new generation of collaboration tools and platforms be any different?

In our view, yes. In large part, that is because the underlying systems and collaborative processes are already in place. People in different geographic areas are accustomed to working together on documents. Track Changes is routinely used in documents exchanged by email. The focus on practical tools that reflect the ways lawyers already work, combined with the industry's experience and learning in knowledge management, will benefit vendors and lawyers and find their way into products and services. Perhaps most important, we will also see successes because the past has trained lawyers to take a realistic and critical look at technology tools and understand what they can actually accomplish. Collaboration planning works better when focused on building on small successes, rather than on swinging for the fences and trying to hit a home run.

In this chapter, we survey some areas where you need to be watchful when considering collaboration tools and the potential pitfalls that may await you.

Losing Control of Documents and Data

Document and data control has many important elements, and the failure of any of them can lead to disastrous consequences. Lawyers have obligations of confidentiality and privilege, and they may be required to keep data private and secure pursuant to regulation or contractual agreement. A fundamental tension occurs when lawyers open up and share, even in the most controlled way, as compared to when they keep communications closed and under tight control. Part of that is natural—the odds of keeping a secret decrease as the number of people who know it increase. When using collaboration tools, we take the chance that the benefits of having several people working together on a project will outweigh the risks of bringing more people into the project. In simplest terms, collaboration tools may work well for certain projects and types of data, and not work at all for others. You still need to think carefully about what is actually happening and what security will best protect the confidential information in your care.

Although we don't want to focus on the gloom-and-doom aspects of security failures, the potential dangers are hard to ignore: inadvertent disclosure of confidential information, accidental waiver of privilege, exposure of metadata and other hidden data in documents, violations of ethical rules, data loss, downtime of tools when they are needed, and other bad consequences we seem to read about in newspapers, magazines, and blogs on a regular basis. However, each of these consequences can also happen without using technology or with only the most basic technology. Let's face it: if you think about it long enough, you might see the security problems inherent in briefcases, and to avoid the danger of data theft or loss, want to prohibit lawyers from carrying one that is full of documents around town. Lawyers have accepted those risks in a paper-based world and live with them every day. You want to be cautious and thoughtful, weigh the risks and benefits carefully, and make solid decisions based on the facts at hand.

Introducing Friction into Processes That Work Well

The best collaboration tools make it easier for people to work together than with existing processes and tools. It's easy to fall in love with a cool tool and not notice that, despite its coolness, it actually makes it harder for people to work together than before. Friction comes in many forms. Understanding how your current systems and processes actually work is a must when selecting collaboration tools. Simply put, tools that make it harder to complete standard tasks will not be successful over the long haul.

Disrupting Existing Patterns and Types of Collaboration

Picture this: a firm might find some of its younger lawyers communicating regularly with clients on projects using instant messaging. The clients are happy and work is getting done, but the firm's management freaks out because they have read alarmist articles about the dangers of instant messaging. As a result, the firm institutes a new rule prohibiting instant messaging and requiring communication with clients only by email. In a surprisingly short time, complaints arise from clients; and soon thereafter, both young lawyers and major clients leave the firm.

There is a cultural and personal aspect to collaboration. You want to find the tools and processes that best fit your culture, environment, and processes—and those of your clients as well. The better you match your tools with firm culture, the better your results. Introducing friction is one concern, but disrupting a collaboration culture can be an even more serious problem. Focusing on the tools alone without considering and understanding your culture and systems is a trap for the unwary.

Creating More Silos

One of the reasons knowledge management projects fail is that they create a new knowledge management silo that either is or seems to be separate from other places where information is stored. In these days of information overload, collaboration tools or platforms that give people one more information silo to worry about are likely to be met with resistance and fall out of use. We have discussed the silo factor throughout this book, but we cannot overemphasize the importance of understanding the nature of information silos and how people react to using more silos than they need or want.

Using Nonstandard Platforms

Compatibility with and conversion to other platforms can become serious issues when sharing documents and data. Connecting your data and systems to other systems, while much easier these days, can still cause significant problems. For good reasons, large corporations standardize on popular platforms and use tools like Gartner's Magic Quadrant to identify highly rated vendors in a given category. Using the Internet as a platform helps deal with the standardization issue, but you don't want to wander too far from the beaten path unless you are prepared to look for dangers, think carefully, and worry about not getting lost.

Requiring Installation of New Programs for Each Collaborator

It's one thing to require your firm's employees to install a new piece of software. The IT department can easily deploy new tools across the network, even overnight. However, it's another thing entirely to expect clients, co-counsel, and others outside your office to install new software merely so you can work together. Policies and procedures of their respective companies may make that impossible. Many companies require extensive testing before installing new software. We like WebEx and other conferencing tools, but we do not like the fact that they require you to install a new version of the software every time you want to hold a meeting. Some employers do not allow employees to install new software on their own, or the employee may have insufficient user rights to do so. These factors should make you think carefully when implementing collaboration tools—especially when compared to the pure web-based approach, which usually requires only a browser and maybe a simple browser plug-in to use. Remember, too, that some people still use dial-up connections or have slow access to the Internet, and requiring a download and installation might take some time.

Locking in with Proprietary Tools and Formats

The beauty of the Internet is its openness. HTML and other standard formats are the lingua franca of the Internet. For the most part, data moves quickly, easily, and without burdens or lock-in. As a general rule, the more proprietary your collaboration tool, the more difficult it will be to share data with people using other tools and formats. There will be some exceptions to this rule, but you always want to be careful before choosing tools with proprietary formats or other features that will make it difficult to make the transition to a replacement platform.

Experiencing Lack of Data Mobility

Ideally, you want collaboration tools that make it easy for you to move data in and out, especially in a hosted environment. If something goes wrong, you need to be able to pull data out of an application or service and put it into another format or service. If you have not planned for these contingencies, you could have a nasty surprise in the future when you expect it least and need your information the most.

Dealing with Inadequate Training

The best tools are of little use if your collaborators do not know how to use them. The need for more training is a frequent complaint in legal technology in general, not just with collaboration technologies. But because collaboration tools involve the participation of different individuals, organizations, and systems, scrimping on training is likely to have negative consequences for the success of a collaboration project. If you do not have much of a training budget, focus on small projects using existing, familiar tools.

Making Poor Decisions about Hosting Yourself or with a Third Party

Many collaboration tools and platforms offer you the choice of using them as hosted services or installing them yourself as part of your technology infrastructure. In the hosted setting, you pay a subscription or other usage fee to use the tool. The vendor gives you access to its servers over the Internet, hosts and maintains the software, and makes the service available to your users on a secure, round-the-clock basis. Unlike with your local applications, you don't install the software yourself or have it physically reside on a computer at your location.

There are pros and cons to each approach. The costs can be greatly different, and larger firms often enjoy cost savings when hosting an application on their own servers. However, hosted services allow smaller firms and others to use advanced technologies in cases where they simply cannot afford the capital expense to install and maintain it themselves. The biggest disadvantage to using a hosted service is the risk of losing your data, which of course resides on someone else's computer. We are both more comfortable with a hosted services approach than most lawyers, but we also can vouch that it is no picnic when a hosted service has performance problems, loses data, or goes out of business.

Dealing with Inadequate Contracts and SLAs

It's no secret that software license and information technology contracts tend to be one-sided in favor of the vendor. These agreements can and should be negotiated to include better terms and cover your specific situation. Lawyers have definite confidentiality and other ethical considerations that simply are not addressed in standard contracts. Twenty-four-hour response or 99 percent uptime might seem adequate in the abstract, but they will prove to be woefully inadequate on the morning of a trial or the afternoon of a filing deadline. The magic acronym in this area is SLA, or Service-Level Agreement. SLAs allow you to set out in specific detail the performance, support, and response time you require from a vendor. Signing a software license or IT contract without careful review and negotiation is as big a mistake for you as it would be if you allowed your client to do the same without first carefully considering the terms of such a contract.

Paying Insufficient Attention to Security Issues

Simply put, shared documents and data require that security issues be analyzed and properly addressed. If you fail to do this, you invite substantial risk and exposure, potential loss of money and clients, bad publicity, and worse.

We like collaboration tools that are inexpensive and directed toward specific tasks. We also like technologies that work right at our fingertips and are simple tools rather than elaborate systems. As a result, we often recommend free or low-cost tools. Still, there are many excellent, high-end collaboration tools that cost a lot of money to install and maintain and might also provide excellent benefits and return on investment. On the other hand, free software might have substantial hidden hardware, infrastructure, or other costs. Failing to allocate money for training can increase long-term costs in terms of efficiency and lost productivity. As with any technology project, budgets can be blown, and "cost creep" may occur. Keeping financial control of collaboration projects, setting a reasonable budget, and staying within that budget are necessities for successful projects.

We encourage you to focus on the positive benefits of collaboration tools, because we believe there are many. However, you must be realistic about the potential dangers involved in using these tools and understand where problems can occur. If you do, you enhance your chances for a successful project and pave the way for future projects.

Implementing Collaboration Tools | **31**

We've done a lot of talking about selecting collaboration tools. You've done your research, considered your options, worked through your checklists, and developed your strategic plan. In this chapter, we discuss some practical pointers to help you implement and roll out your collaboration tools. It's time to roll up your sleeves and get to work.

To do that, let's first take a step back and consider how the most commonly used collaboration tool—email—was implemented in many law firms in the early 1990s. While most of us would like to believe that forward-looking lawyers jumped on board the email train to provide better service to clients, or that client needs pushed lawyers to use external email, in many firms that was not the case. What was the actual driving factor? Managing partners of law firms found that external email was an easy way to communicate with their children in college. Suddenly, the objections to email, the slow decision-making process, and the many concerns disappeared. The mandate went out to implement email systems for communicating with clients. As a result, lawyers who learned to exchange email with their children became comfortable with the technology, and the transition to using email with clients was easy and all but seamless.

Will the same pattern repeat itself with instant messaging, social networking tools like Facebook, and other collaboration technologies? Don't bet against it.

The lesson here is that when you place collaboration tools in the hands of motivated users who want to accomplish something meaningful to them, you dramatically improve the chances for successful results. You can talk about platforms and channels all you want, but if you look for ways to introduce collaboration tools for purposes that matter to your employees, you'll better help them to get things done.

With that in mind, here are some tips and techniques for implementing your collaboration strategy.

Break Out of the Reaction Mode

An important theme of this book is to push you to prepare and plan for collaboration and to have tools in place before they are needed. Otherwise, you will always find yourself reacting to the demands of other people and using the tools that work best for them rather than the tools that work for you.

Standardize and Minimize

Before the computer era, an associate who worked for many partners might have to adapt his or her writing style and work product to the needs (or whims) of the partners. Today, the associate might have to use different collaboration tools for each partner as well. There are many ways to collaborate and many tools you can use. As much as possible, you must reduce and standardize the number of tools used by you and your firm or organization.

Understand the Collaboration Tools Landscape

This book gives you an overview of most types of collaboration tools and their potential uses, but it is not exhaustive. Expect these tools to change over time and new tools to be introduced. Keeping current on collaboration technologies and having a good idea of what is available will help you in any implementation. You'll have other options to consider if anything goes wrong, as well as other paths to take as opportunities become available or limitations of certain tools appear. The resources in Appendices 2 and 3, as well as the companion website for this book (http://www.lawyersguideto collaboration.com to be launched later in 2008), will help you keep current and continue the exploration for collaboration tools.

Provide Demos and Training

Many collaboration tools are difficult to describe, or their description does little justice to their capabilities. As you make selections and roll out projects, you will want to provide good demonstrations and hands-on opportunities for people to learn about the features of these tools. Demos also help you work the bugs out and identify problems or difficulties with the tools before you roll them out.

Lead by Example

Training on these tools is a great thing, but it often is the first budget item to be cut. Why? Because getting lawyers to attend training sessions, even if you provide free food, can be quite difficult. However, there's no doubt that showing people how the tools benefit them in the real world will help move a project forward. Short videos and screencasts of a few minutes in length often work better than long training sessions. Building a library of computer-based videos covering specific tasks will let you provide just-in-time training when someone needs it.

Eat Your Own Dog Food

Microsoft refers to the practice of using its own programs before they are released to the public as "eating its own dog food." If you are not using the collaboration tools you expect others to use, we can confidently predict that your chances for a successful project are not good. Lead by example, and show people how the tools actually work for you and why you use them.

Take a Team Approach

Collaboration is a team game. Create teams to work on your implementation of collaboration tools. Enough said.

Go Where the Action Is

Successful technology projects often start by rolling out the tools to a small group of people who are most willing to use them. Today, that often means younger lawyers. Start in places where you are likely to succeed.

Get the Tools in the Hands of Evangelists and Influencers

Parents and teachers told us that eating broccoli was good for us, to no avail. Our friends and peers convinced some of us (except Tom) to eat broccoli because it tastes good or that it was cool or valuable to eat it. Experience in most legal technology projects indicates that top-down mandated rollouts are less likely to succeed than bottom-up flexible approaches where people learn from their peers.

Build on Small Successes

Talk to any lawyer and you're likely to hear about a grandiose technology project that turned into a disaster. Collaboration projects need not be large or expensive. Focus on the immediate needs, win small battles, and amass the goodwill and budget to move forward with larger projects. Small, successful projects build momentum. Take small bites.

Be Guided by the 80/20 Rule

Use the 80/20 rule of thumb. Look for projects or portions of projects that bring the biggest results for the least effort. What can you do for people that gets them most of what they need? Get that done first.

Expect Fast Prototyping and Beta Releases

New Web 2.0 tools come online every day. Some work well and some do not, but all of them make adjustments. No collaboration tool survives first contact with the people who are using it. Expect changes. Let people know that the technology is not fixed in stone, and they will help you improve it. Google's Gmail was in a "beta" or test version for years. Google is now worth a zillion dollars. There might be a lesson there.

Build in Feedback Loops

Former New York City mayor Ed Koch was known for asking, "How am I doing?" You won't know whether your project is succeeding unless you ask. Surveys and questionnaires help, but nothing beats asking people directly how the tools are working for them. Don't ask simply for the sake of asking; feedback should be used to improve the project. People tend to give more, and more valuable, feedback when they know that you are listening to them and actually paying attention.

Take a Portfolio Approach

Diversify your projects. Focusing only on low-risk, low-reward, "safe" projects is not always wise. Take some chances. Start with several different efforts to help guarantee that winners more than balance out losers. Not every project or every aspect of a project will be a winner. The very nature of collaboration tools is that they evolve, and we expect them to change as different people use them in different ways.

Know Who Is in Charge

The best question you can ask about any project is, "Who gets to decide when it's done?" If that person is not engaged in the project, you need to fix that, and fast. Typically, technology projects in larger firms are handled by the technology committee and IT department. That might be appropriate, but no matter who is in charge, you always want to ensure that person has a presence in the project, ideally as one of its first users.

Learn from Others

Talk to others who have been there before you. Learn what works and what does not. Get practical advice from those you trust. Most important, find out why projects succeed or fail in other places.

Your organization's history with technology projects will play a big role in the success of your collaboration strategy. To be prepared, you will want to learn and understand that history. Implementing technology for lawyers is difficult. Everything that you can do to increase your odds for success will help you in the long run, and it will be worth your time and effort.

Recommended Choices for Common Scenarios: From Solos to Large Firms 32

In this chapter, we make some recommendations on suggested choices for collaboration tools in a variety of law practice scenarios. We offer these only as guidelines and to help you start a discussion with your collaborators. One clear lesson you should learn from this book is that collaboration technology choices should be based on your unique situation, requirements, and assessment of your current and future projects. However, the following list will illustrate our way of looking at collaboration tools in various settings.

Keep in mind a few assumptions as you read this chapter:

- Specific client needs or requests might change recommendations.
- Making use of collaboration features in existing tools should be considered first rather than moving to new programs.
- Specific concerns about issues like security, external hosting, and the like will change your results.

Solo Lawyers

Solo lawyers, especially those just starting out, have been among the pioneers in the use of collaboration tools, especially Web 2.0 and other online tools. For most solo lawyers, simple economic concerns make free and low-cost tools attractive. Despite their low cost, collaboration tools also provide ways for solos to create a professional presence well beyond their actual size. Collaboration tools and technologies make it easier for solos to take on legal matters of large corporate clients, earning them a place at the conference table they might not have had in earlier times. In litigation matters, these tools can help solos participate in large, complex litigation matters and come very close to leveling the playing field. Even in the most traditional solo practice, however, collaboration technologies let solos work out of their homes, provide better client service, and compete with larger firms.

We recommend that solos start with two basic collaboration tools. First, a conference call service will allow solos to present a professional appearance and manage routine or larger conference calls. Second, Adobe Acrobat provides a versatile way to handle the creation, sharing, and review of documents, and it aids in electronic filing with the courts.

Solos who routinely share documents should consider an online office suite like Google Docs. We have also been impressed by the way solos have used Basecamp to create simple extranets that provide basic information, calendars, task lists, and documents to their clients. Solos in rural areas especially should investigate the online meeting tools mentioned in this book, to cut down on time spent traveling.

Solo trial lawyers would do well to invest in CaseMap, online electronic discovery review tools, online document storage and sharing services for large documents, and online meeting tools. Solos with transactional practices should consider redlining and metadata removal tools; case or project management applications; and, depending on their clients, instant messaging programs. And it goes without saying that all solos should learn more about the advanced features of their email systems.

Small Firms

In small firms, lawyers should look first to the tools recommended for solos, and then specifically consider tools that will improve internal collaboration. Case management and project management tools often make sense for small firms where several people are working on the same projects. Even in a small firm, a collaboration platform like SharePoint might make sense, especially where a Windows Server infrastructure is already in place. Alternatively, small firms could utilize a hosted SharePoint portal. Exploring the collaboration features of Microsoft Office, including OneNote, is another good approach. Online meeting tools also should get more emphasis as firms increase in size or have more than one office.

Mid-sized Firm

As firm size increases to 15 or so lawyers, you start to see a change in thinking about collaboration. The focus on tools for individual lawyers continues, but firm-wide collaboration tools also come into play.

For individual lawyers and staff, start with the recommendations we make for solos and small firms. Then look more closely at taking greater advantage of advanced collaboration tools built into the software that the firm already owns. In mid-sized firms, we would expect to see greater use of collaboration tools in the Microsoft Office suite (including shared calendars) and in email programs in particular. Almost every type of tool mentioned in this book makes sense for lawyers in mid-sized firms, so focus on what matters most and works best for your practice. Practice areas and client needs will also drive your choices in this area. We suggest picking a few collaboration technologies and trying to use them well as our preferred approach for lawyers in mid-sized firms.

At the firm level, it makes sense to consider a few platforms and standardize on tools. Using SharePoint as a collaboration platform (intranet, project management, document management, and communications) definitely comes into play. Google Apps might be a way to save money on software for staff and provide document-sharing capabilities. Online meeting tools and conference-calling services are all but essential. Mid-sized litigation firms will also need to move into using electronic discovery tools, and extranets begin to make sense at the mid-sized firm level. Firms with several offices must focus on tools that will connect them, including meeting tools, extranets, and others.

Mid-sized firms are in an exciting place for implementing collaboration tools. Even though narrowing down your choices to the right tools can be difficult, the potential benefits of small investments can be great—even practice-transforming—for mid-sized firms in today's competitive environment.

Large Firms

Firms at or near the AmLaw 200 level tend to consider many different collaboration platforms rather than individual tools. The choices of individual lawyers will be driven almost completely by what the firm already owns or has installed. There's an important point in the last sentence; large firms occasionally own software and other tools that have not been installed or are not in use. We like to recommend that large firms start with an inventory of the collaboration capabilities of software they already have, with an eye toward making better use of existing products and services rather than starting fresh with new tools.

Almost by definition today, large firms have multiple offices in several locations. Even in the same office, a big firm will stretch over several floors. Information sharing is one of the biggest collaboration concerns in firms of this size. As we've mentioned, SharePoint might be the hottest topic in legal technology for large law firms, but intranets and knowledge management projects are all part of the emphasis on information sharing. Large firms will also take bigger steps (or more likely be pushed by their clients) into the area of electronic discovery, where document review, document repositories, and project management take on greater importance. On the transactional side, document markup (redlining and metadata removal), document sharing, online meetings, and advanced videoconferencing (often across many time zones and borders) will be a priority and are considered table stakes for these types of practices. Alert and notification tools like RSS also make good sense at the large firm level.

More so than solo and small firms, large firm choices will be driven by client needs and constrained by existing technology infrastructure. Being fast and nimble will become important for large firms in the area of collaboration because small firms can and will use inexpensive tools to create a level of presence and service that rivals or equals what large law firms are doing now.

Corporate Legal Departments

The unique constraint for corporate legal departments is that often their choices are driven by company-wide technology policies made without the legal department specifically in mind. For example, a legal department might be required to use a project management tool that is part of the company's high-end enterprise software system. It would probably not be the lawyer's first choice for a project management tool, but it's the only available option. Other policies might also restrict collaboration. For example, external instant messaging with outside counsel or others might not be permitted.

After considering their specific needs, corporate legal departments should focus on a few key areas of collaboration:

- Management of and communication with outside counsel—communication tools, online meeting tools, project management, extranets
- Contract management (preparation, negotiation, records)—document collaboration tools (redlining, metadata removal, Adobe Acro-

bat, advanced review and markup tools), online meeting tools, calendaring, project management and workflow tools

- Electronic discovery—CaseMap, electronic discovery and document review tools, document repositories, project management tools
- Information sharing—intranets and extranets, SharePoint, case management tools, knowledge management programs

The size of departments, areas of practice, existing infrastructure, and budgetary issues all will play key roles in the corporate setting. Like mid-sized firms, corporate legal departments will want to focus on a few areas and do them well, rather than trying to cover all possible areas of collaboration.

Government Law Department

As a general rule, government law departments will have tight restrictions—budget, policy, and infrastructure—that will make significant collaboration technology initiatives difficult at best and impossible at worst. Some of the collaboration options simply will not be in play. In the government setting, we recommend trying to get a good understanding of all the tools that are available to you and then focusing on a small number that are workable and provide the biggest bang for the buck. Document collaboration tools—especially metadata removal tools (because of past metadata issues in government documents), redlining, and Adobe Acrobat—might be one area to target. Inexpensive litigation collaboration tools like CaseMap might be another; the litigation divisions of many governmental agencies currently use CaseMap. We also suspect that because they are available at no cost, Open Source collaboration tools might make inroads in government legal departments over the next few years.

Legal Services Organizations

Legal services organizations (and we include public defender offices and similar groups of lawyers in this category), like government legal departments, often operate under tremendous budgetary limitations. Our recommendations are similar to those just discussed for government law departments. You must be creative and focus on determining which tools will provide the most help to you and your clients, at the same time identifying the tools that are actually possible to implement. Open Source tools and online or Web 2.0 services might become very interesting in this context.

Recommendations Based on Budget Considerations

Budget is always an issue with technology. Here are a few tips on what to consider according to the budget you have.

No or Little Money Available

- Use collaboration features of software and services you already own.
- Consider Open Source or Web 2.0 tools.
- Focus on simple improvements that address major pains or provide significant benefit.
- Learn better ways to use what you have.

Modest Budget Available

- Focus on just one or two areas, such as electronic discovery, Share-Point, or Adobe Acrobat.
- Consider hosted applications and services.
- Upgrade current software to "professional" or "enterprise" versions, or move to the most current version of the software.
- Seek the recommendations of clients.

Significant Budget Available

- Consider collaboration in terms of building platforms.
- Standardize tools with a focus on integration.
- Invest in both client-facing (extranet) and information-sharing (intranet) efforts.
- Make it easy to communicate with you and hear from you (online meetings, alerts and notices, extranets).
- Seek the recommendations of clients.

Consider these recommendations as starting points for your discussions or as a checklist of tools you should consider. Before making your final decision, however, be sure to take into account the most important factor of all in collaboration technology efforts—creating a culture of collaboration, which we discuss in the following chapter.

Creating a Culture of Collaboration **33**

While this book has emphasized the technologies and tools that lawyers and those who work with lawyers can use to collaborate, selecting the right tools alone does not guarantee that a collaboration effort will be successful. Collaboration is a profoundly human endeavor. The success of collaboration depends primarily on the actual ways people work together. The human and cultural behavior between the collaborators will drive, dictate, and ultimately determine the success of your collaboration projects. If you ignore or downplay the human factors, you are setting up your project for failure.

A Closer Look at Collaboration

Collaboration takes place at the intersection where the individual efforts of the people involved meet. At the same intersection will be a number of different cultures, depending on the particular individuals. The cultures may mesh well with each other, or they may react poorly and refuse to mix at all. In most cases, the collaborators end up somewhere in between the two streams.

Collaboration tool implementation will be most successful when it takes place in a culture that already accepts collaboration, when the tool is introduced with respect for the existing culture. If a spirit of collaboration does not already thrive in the culture of an organization or between organizations, more work will be necessary to encourage collaboration. If the tools

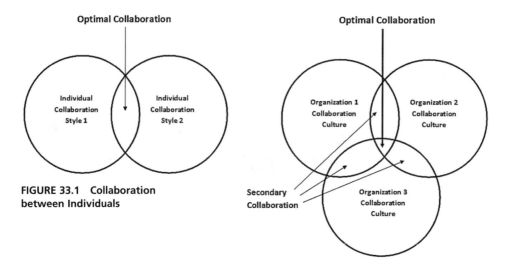

FIGURE 33.1 Collaboration between Individuals

FIGURE 33.2 Collaboration between Organizations

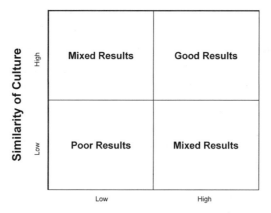

FIGURE 33.3 Likelihood of Successful Collaboration

you introduce do not reflect and respect the existing collaboration patterns of a firm or company, you may run into resistance. Most important, if collaboration is not already a part of a firm's culture, you should expect to spend at least as much time on human and cultural issues as you do on tool selection and technology issues. Even if a thriving collaboration culture is in place at your firm, you will want to make sure it is not taken for granted and continue to monitor and nurture it.

While collaboration technologies are still relatively new for many lawyers, the legal profession does have a history with collaboration tools over the years. The biggest example is in the area of knowledge management. Knowledge management is the idea that the institutional experience and know-how of an organization can be captured and maintained in such a way that all firm or company employees can benefit from the collective wisdom of others. The expertise and experience that constitute "knowledge" tend to stay with the individual who has that knowledge, and they are usually transferred only by happenstance or in a one-on-one conversation. Knowledge management projects strive to systematically collect knowledge and make it available to others in a way that it can be acted upon. Especially for large organizations, knowledge management projects have for many years taken on the aspect of a holy grail.

Unfortunately, knowledge management efforts in the legal profession do not have a record of resounding success, and their history is largely one of disappointment. There are many stories of failed projects, dashed expectations, and minor successes, sometimes attributable to overly optimistic promises and lack of a mature technology. The primary reason for this lack of success has more to do with the cultures of the organizations attempting to implement the knowledge management tools.

Even within departments of firms, lawyers tend to have highly individual practices, or at least perceive that they do. Lawyers often work autonomously, without much supervision. Indeed, this is because law firms do not have the same degree of hierarchal management that most businesses have. Lawyers are notoriously slow adopters of technology, and some lawyers proudly and stubbornly resist using it in their practices. The billable hour structure and compensation systems tied to billable hours also reduce incentives for lawyers to collect or contribute the information necessary for a robust knowledge management system.

In the face of these barriers, knowledge management efforts are often large-scale projects designed to capture and utilize great amounts of knowledge for broadly defined purposes. These projects may also promise to find needle-in-a-haystack results or locate documents that can be instantly reused. However, an overly mechanical approach to knowledge management simply does not appreciate or respect the fundamental creativity at the core of a lawyer's working processes, as so often seen in the best lawyers. In short, knowledge management efforts tend to create new silos outside the scope of a lawyer's work, rather than create a convenient tool that enhances a lawyer's ability to work productively and efficiently. Thus, lawyers lack incentive to contribute to such a system. Unless the firm culture is one that encourages participation in such collaboration projects, it is likely to fail—or at best, be of marginal value.

▼▼▼▼▼
A Simple 15-Minute Exercise

Think about your last few group projects where things really worked well. Jot down a few notes on how you and your team communicated and worked together. What factors or people were responsible for the success of these projects? What types of projects were they, and what lessons might you draw from them?

Next, complete a similar exercise for group projects that did not go so well. What didn't work? What might have made them work better?

Take a look at your notes, and see if you can find common threads and patterns. Dig into the meanings of phrases like "poor management," "fun," or "dropped the ball."

What does this exercise tell you about your culture and how it affects your use of collaboration tools?

Collaboration: Addressing Cultural Issues

What techniques can help you address the cultural issues in your collaboration projects? Here are a few rules of thumb to follow when examining how your firm or company culture might affect the success or failure of your next collaboration project.

Know Thyself

Consider well the famous pronouncement attributed to the Oracle at Delphi: "Know thyself." In plainer English, try to gain a good understanding of your work, how you prefer to work, and what methods have been successful in the past—for you and your organization. Condense the key factors into a short list, and keep that list close at hand when considering your collaboration strategy.

Know Thy Collaborators

No, the Oracle of Delphi did not say this; but we will. Collaboration is a team sport. You must learn the skills, strengths, weaknesses, and preferences of the people you work with. Other firms or companies have different cultures, and it is important that you discover enough about those cultures to help you select the tools and processes that will mesh well. In our increasingly global business world, calculating for these differences will become even more important—and perhaps more difficult.

Stay out of People's Way While They Are Working

Think back to the first time you got to work with a parent on a project at home. Although you were just trying to help, inevitably you would stand too close, block the light, grab the wrong tool, or do something else not quite right. You may have realized, even at a young age, that you probably were not much help. Your parent may have had an easier time working alone, but they also were pleased that you wanted to help. Once you learned to relax, stay put, and start watching, things got much better.

It's the same with collaboration tools. Completing the task at hand is the overriding goal. The tools are not the thing; what you can accomplish with the tools is the thing. Like a nurse who has the scalpel ready when the surgeon asks for it, you want to understand the process and how people work within it, and have the collaboration tool ready when and where it is needed. The great paradox here is that the more effective the collaboration tool, the less you tend to notice it.

Top-Down versus Bottom-Up

People are stubborn, independent, and often unpredictable creatures. It should be no surprise, then, that the history of failed knowledge management projects calls into question the processes that are imposed from the highest levels of management and then filtered down to the levels where the work is actually done. Even the United States military, that most hierarchal of institutions, is experimenting with shifting certain types of authority down to its lowest level, to soldiers who are directly involved in the action. The rise of blogs, wikis, social networking tools, and other public collaboration projects suggests that the balance needs to tip farther toward the bottom-up approach than it has in the past.

Build on What Works

People respond to success. If something works, they want more of it and are more receptive if new features are added or changes made. One secret of a successful collaboration project is simply to implement it in phases. A phased approach reduces the expectations that come with Big Projects, and you prepare your collaborators for future, incremental improvements. In the world of Web 2.0, tools seem to be in a perpetual state of "beta testing." As a result, we are tolerant of shortcomings and receptive to changes and improvements because we expect them to occur. Because they are also small adjustments that build on what we already have, they are easy to learn and assimilate.

Try to Achieve Critical Mass

People also respond to positive momentum. Malcolm Gladwell has written extensively about the notion of a tipping point, which he defined as that point where adoption of a tool reaches the stage where everyone must have it and suddenly the rate of adoption significantly increases. For example, a single fax machine had no value until someone else had a fax machine to receive the fax. The adoption of fax machines grew at a slow pace until businesspeople understood that joining the network of those with fax machines had great value. Shortly thereafter, the number of people with fax machines exploded, and fax machines became ubiquitous. This notion is sometimes referred to as gaining critical mass. Can you identify enough people in your firm or organization who are ready and willing to adopt a collaboration tool so that its usage will reach critical mass and drive the adoption by other users?

Invest in Team Building

If you do not have a collaborative culture, can you build one? While the idea of lawyers participating in Outward Bound, ropes courses, or other team-building activities might bring a few chuckles, law firms with many offices in different geographic locations recognize that to be successful, they must create a common culture. If they do not, one of two things will happen: either the individual offices will become isolated and insular, or a common culture will arise that no one expects or particularly wants. After analyzing your firm culture, consider investing in ways to build teamwork and create a culture of collaboration. Even minor improvements might pay off over the long run.

Learn about Collaboration

The Internet is teeming with information and studies about collaboration, corporate culture, teamwork, social networking, and other aspects of collaboration technology, and new materials are appearing regularly. There are books, audios, videos, blogs, and other resources on these topics, and we've included some of our favorite collaboration resources in Appendix 2. Take advantage of these rich sources of information as you develop and maintain your collaboration strategy.

Consider Using Incentives or Penalties

To our knowledge, there are no authoritative studies on the positive impact of free food for improving lawyer participation in projects. However, there is sufficient anecdotal information to suggest that many projects originally thought to be impossible were successfully implemented with simple incentives and/or penalties. One example we've heard involves lawyers who protested that filling out daily time sheets was impossible; however, those same lawyers converted to the practice when the firm imposed a $20 penalty on those who failed to submit their billing on time. The point here is that small efforts can change behavior in surprising ways. We prefer the use of incentives over penalties, but you will understand your culture best.

Remember That Culture Is a Moving Target

As lawyers come and go, as a new generation of lawyers raised on computers and the Internet joins the practice, and as the practice becomes more diverse, the culture of your organization will change. The ways that people work together also shift over time, which can affect your culture of collaboration. More important, the introduction of collaboration technologies can also change the collaborative environment. If handled properly, the tools and the culture will coevolve. It is vital to monitor your workplace continually and adjust your collaboration strategies as the culture changes.

We believe successful collaboration technologies evolve from an understanding of the ways people actually work well together. Culturally attuned collaboration technologies also increase your chances for other benefits—improved recruiting and hiring, better retention of personnel and clients, and better knowledge transfer than a formal knowledge management initiative might otherwise accomplish. If you match the collaboration tools to your firm or company culture, your chances over the long run are indeed good.

The Future of Collaboration in the Practice of Law

34

Before starting this book, we had a general sense of how lawyers collaborate—with their clients, colleagues, and others. As we worked our way through writing the book, however, we were struck by how collaboration permeates literally every aspect of the practice of law, affecting lawyers and everyone who works with them. In fact, lawyers are *constantly* collaborating, internally and externally, with those on the same side as well as on the other side. Understanding this reality—that collaboration is *not* an option—is the first step in making smart choices about collaboration tools and technologies.

Hopefully, as you read this book you realized that you already use a wide variety of tools for collaboration. Many of these tools do not involve technology—sticky notes, comments scrawled on documents, a chance meeting in the hallway, or a planning meeting with the client. But some of the tools you use do involve technology, and you've probably been using them for years—a modified spreadsheet for project management, a docket in a word processor, or an outliner tool.

We had three goals in this book. First, we wanted you to consider the existing methods and systems you use to collaborate today, and we suggested ways to bring those thoughts to the surface. Our second goal was to discuss and show you a new generation of collaboration technologies and point out how they can help you improve your current systems in ways you might never have expected. Finally, and most importantly, we wanted to help move you from what you're doing now to a better way to collaborate, using technology that is surprisingly affordable and can make a significant impact on your practice and in your life. Now, it's your turn.

When you consider the technologies we discuss in the book, we remind you of our main message—that collaboration tools are evolutionary, rather than revolutionary, in their effect on the actual work that lawyers do. However, when collaboration technologies are well chosen for the project or client at hand, they have the potential to completely revolutionize the way legal services are delivered. The most interesting aspect of technology is not that it makes us more productive or efficient, but that it helps us to work better with others in the practice of law. With the rise of the Internet as a communications and collaboration medium, we will increasingly see our work carry us across time zones, beyond state and national borders, and into working relationships with a variety of people outside the walls of law firms and legal departments. These changes are happening at a relentless and quickening pace—a pace that may quicken further as lawyers and other workers become increasingly mobile and begin working from places other than their office.

For reasons that will be clear to most lawyers, law firms and other legal professionals are naturally slow to adopt legal technology, and technology in general. Legal technology evolved over the years as technology began to play a larger part in the practice of law and the budgets of law firms. In the first generation, technology efforts focused on the staff; most lawyers certainly weren't using technology at that time. Firms implemented word processing programs and computers to improve staff efficiency and productivity, often reducing the number of secretaries needed by the firm. The second generation of legal technology saw the rise of computer networks, where the stability of the network took priority, along with the standardization of hardware and software. The firm's IT department was typically the driver of technology during this generation. During the third generation, the focus shifted to the lawyer and getting tools that lawyers needed into their hands. Electronic discovery, practice-specific applications, BlackBerrys, and broadband Internet access symbolize this era. It was during the third generation that we began to see lawyers driving the demand for new and better technologies. Finally, in the coming fourth generation, we expect to see technologies that are client focused as well as client driven, with an emphasis on finding convenient, efficient ways to deliver legal services. If you have been paying attention, you'll know that we believe collaboration tools and technologies will be at the core of the fourth generation of legal technology. Most legal professionals are probably still stuck in the second generation or moving toward the third. A few pioneers are moving toward the fourth generation. Where do you fall?

The dizzying pace of technology has created, for better or worse, a real gap between the technology haves and have-nots. The divide between lawyers who use technology well (third–fourth generation) and those who do not (second generation) continues to grow. The convergence of collaboration technologies, the Internet, notions like Web 2.0 and Enterprise 2.0, and the expectations for delivery of services these phenomena have engendered will only increase the gap between those who are moving forward and those who are not. We need only look to the encyclopedia, travel agency, and music industries to understand that new technologies literally can change the face of your business overnight. And it's happening in the legal profession too; e-lawyering, the growth of companies like LegalZoom, and trends such as the outsourcing of legal services are changing the fabric of the legal practice. If you're standing still today, it really means that you're moving backward.

If you find yourself in that position, you're in luck. This is a time of enormous opportunity in using collaboration technologies because, as we have emphasized throughout the book, the low cost and broad availability of these tools allows you to easily catch up and bridge the gap. We are constantly impressed with what startup solos and small firms, both newly minted lawyers and breakaways from large firms, are doing with simple, inexpensive tools like Basecamp, Google Docs, or wikis, with a strong focus on customer service and typically very small technology budgets. A single lawyer with a notebook computer and an Internet connection really can take on the world today.

We end with two very important questions as we look at the future of collaboration tools in the legal profession. What is the practice of law? What does it mean to be a law firm? In Appendix 2 we point you to resources to help you think about these questions, but here we leave you with a few thoughts of our own. We hope to provide a vehicle for continuing that discussion on the companion website for this book at http://www.lawyersguidetocollaboration.com.

Thinking about collaboration tools challenges our assumptions about the practice of law and delivery of legal services in general. Over the past few years, pundits have started using terms like "Law 2.0" and "Electronic Discovery 2.0" as a play on the "Web 2.0" phenomenon, but more importantly to denote new ways of delivering legal services in a world where new generations grow up not knowing what it was like not to have a computer or the Internet. Our clients' expectations are changing, and the roles of lawyers as gatekeepers of information and intermediaries for transactions are increasingly called into question.

The idea of Law 2.0 involves greater collaboration between lawyers and clients. It also involves a sense of self-service (whether it be creating legal documents online or researching for legal information), expanded access, and changing notions of deliverables. The lines between lawyer, client, and what actually constitutes the practice of law have begun to blur, and fundamental assumptions about law firm practice and economics are increasingly the subject of scrutiny. When it comes to technology, the debate between hourly billing and value billing is just the entry point to the discussion. How does hourly billing work when you use extranets, knowledge management, or other collaborative content-creation tools in representing your client? Collaboration technologies allow lawyers to create reusable content or special tools for their practice. Will a new business model evolve that handles licensing or other nontraditional products and services? For example, a series of specialty extranets that train clients or their employees on workplace issues might provide a significant new income stream, with lawyers becoming content producers through the collaborative medium of the extranet. Indeed, many law firms are already doing this, as well as considering other income models and new forms of services. The pioneers of e-lawyering efforts, including the ABA Law Practice Management Section's e-Lawyering Task Force, have explored the implications of these trends.

The Internet acts to eliminate or disintermediate middlemen. Lawyers are classic middlemen. The key to business survival for service industries in the Internet era is finding a way to re-intermediate, or maintain that middleman status. To do this, lawyers must find new ways to provide a higher value as a middleman. Do collaboration tools offer a path to re-intermediation for lawyers?

The very idea of the law firm is now facing its most serious challenge. By using collaboration tools, lawyers can work together with the best legal professionals available for their projects. Clients can assemble the best lawyers for their cases or transactions. Geographic and other barriers are eliminated. What happens when the best lawyer to represent you is not the law firm down the street, but someone in another firm in another part of the country who is even easier to work with because of technology? Doesn't the logic of collaboration technologies lead us toward what many have called virtual law firms?

As we said at the beginning of this book, lawyers are at a crossroads with their collaboration tools. What worked well before likely will not work in the future. New tools and technologies make it possible for lawyers to work together in better ways. Hopefully, we've given you some ideas to help you make solid choices about the directions you want to take and the right tools to use. Whichever path you take to using collaboration technologies, we encourage you to get on a path and move forward. Collaboration tools and technologies really do offer lawyers and those who work with lawyers better ways to work together—especially if we make smart decisions and keep the client's needs in mind at all times.

Appendix 1: Glossary*

adware—Software that has advertising integrated into or bundled with it, often displaying automatically. Sometimes referred to as "pop-up ads."

AJAX (Asynchronous JavaScript and XML)—A web development technique associated with Web 2.0 that refreshes only the portion of a web page being changed, allowing for a user experience similar to that of a desktop program.

applet—A software component with limited functionality that does not run independently of another program; often installed and running in a web browser.

asynchronous—Not occurring at the same time; the opposite of synchronous.

authentication—A process for confirming a user's identity.

authorization—A process that protects computer resources by limiting their use to only those who have been granted specific permission.

blog—A frequently updated website based on a template produced by easy-to-use content management or "blogging" software and characterized by certain common elements, including the display of content in the form of individual "posts," reverse chronological entries, RSS feeds, archives, and comments.

click-wrap agreement—An online contract accepted without negotiation by clicking an Accept button or taking a similar action. *Also called* click-through agreement.

conference calls—A telephone call with more than two separate participants calling from more than two phones. Sometimes refers to a traditional one-to-one call where one or both sides have several people participating via a speakerphone in the same room.

---

*Wikipedia (http://www.wikipedia.org) and What Is (http://whatis.techtarget.com) were used as resources in compiling this glossary.

cookies—Small text files sent by a web server to the web browser of a visitor on each visit to provide authentication, tracking, and/or personalization.

cracking—A process for breaking passwords or otherwise defeating computer security systems.

dashboard—A management tool that creates visual displays of data pulled from a variety of underlying sources and presents them in unified fashion, commonly as a box that appears on a home page or portal page.

deal rooms—Extranets used for transactions.

document management system—A computer program for managing, identifying, tracking, and searching documents and files.

ECM (enterprise content management)—Broadly refers to all technologies used to capture, manage, store, preserve, and deliver content and documents related to organizational processes, including document management, records management, and knowledge management.

electronic discovery—The discovery process in a litigation matter or case that deals with electronically stored information.

email blast—A form of email sent to many recipients at the same time for a specific purpose, often to announce an event.

emoticon—A symbol consisting of a typed character or combination of characters designed to express emotion in a text-based message. The best-known emoticon is the smiley face (colon, hyphen, right parenthesis). :-)

Enterprise 2.0—A general term applying to the use of Web 2.0 services and concepts in the enterprise setting.

extranet—A private, secure website, often designed for a specific purpose, that is the basis for many online collaboration tools. Extranets can also be thought of as external versions of intranets.

fob—A small hardware device that is synchronized with a network's password on a minute-by-minute basis.

freeware—Computer software made available at no charge, generally subject to click-wrap license terms similar to commercial software licenses.

FWIW (For What It's Worth)—A commonly used term in instant messaging and online message boards.

Gartner's Magic Quadrant—Gartner Inc.'s well-known system for evaluating vendors in industry segments to identify leaders, challengers, niche players, and visionaries and plotting those vendors on a quadrant to help organizations choose vendors.

hacking—Can mean either the work of a computer enthusiast to understand a technology or system, or the act of trespassing into a system beyond the permitted authorization.

HTML (HyperText Markup Language)—The predominant language in which web pages are written.

identity theft—Criminal or other activity relating to the use of another person's identification materials.

IM (instant messaging)—A form of real-time text-based communication by means of computer or telephone.

IMHO (In My Humble Opinion)—A commonly used term in instant messaging and message boards.

intranet—A private, secure, internal website used to share information within an organization.

JavaScript—A scripting language commonly used in web development; a key component of AJAX and Web 2.0 development.

keystroke logger—A small program that records a user's keystrokes. Often installed secretly and maliciously to steal passwords and other sensitive information.

knowledge management system—A system that identifies, stores, distributes, and makes shareable a firm's institutional knowledge.

license—An agreement in which the owner of intellectual property rights permits the licensee to exercise certain of these rights.

malware—A general term used to describe viruses, spyware, Trojan horses, keystroke loggers, and other programs that can harm computers, networks, and/or data.

metadata—Data about data, including hidden data about documents from creation dates and author names to revisions and comments.

milestone—Something assigned to a particular person and due on a specified date. It can be a deadline for a filing, a meeting with the client, or a date for a first draft of a contract agreement.

mind map—A brainstorming or thinking tool in the form of a diagram in which a central keyword or idea is linked to other words or images arranged radially around the central keyword or idea. Mind maps help generate, visualize, structure, classify, and organize ideas.

Open Source software—Computer software under one of a limited number of standard, permissive licenses allowing modification of the program in exchange for limitations on liability. Often available at no cost and developed by a loose community of developers rather than a single software vendor. Open Source software is widely used in the infrastructure of the Internet.

P2P (peer-to-peer) network—An ad hoc or temporary computer network comprised of computers connecting directly over the Internet rather than using the traditional web servers hosting websites.

packet sniffer—A software tool for capturing, intercepting, and logging data traffic over a network.

Pareto principle (80/20 rule)—A rule of thumb that says that 80 percent of the effects come from 20 percent of the causes. The 80/20 rule also includes many variations, each based on the 80/20 proportion.

password cracker—A computer program that automates the process of guessing or breaking passwords.

PBX (Private Branch Exchange)—A private telephone exchange that serves a particular business or office and connects to the telephone system.

PDF (Portable Document Format)—A file format created by Adobe Systems to simplify document exchange by representing documents in a descriptive manner that is device-independent. PDF includes text, fonts, and images so that the document looks like the original printout.

phishing—A method of attempting to fraudulently acquire identity or other sensitive information—including passwords, bank account, or credit card information—by posing as a trustworthy entity in an email or other electronic communication.

platform—A software framework on which other specialized applications or tools can operate.

plug-in—A small program required to be added to a host application, such as a browser, to seamlessly provide limited, specific functionality for a service.

portal—A web page that serves as a single point of access to external or internal information.

project management—Organizing and managing resources so projects are completed within defined scope, quality, time, and cost specifications.

redlining—A method for marking up a version of documents to show revisions from another version of the document. Sometimes called "blacklining."

RSS (Really Simple Syndication)—A family of XML formats for web feeds used to automatically publish frequently updated content such as blog entries, news headlines, or podcasts. RSS feeds are usually read in a program or online service known as an RSS reader, newsreader, or news aggregator. The term "RSS" is often used generically to include other feed formats, such as Atom and RDF.

RTF (Rich Text Format)—A proprietary document file format developed by Microsoft for exchanging documents that is simpler and more universal than the Word (.doc) format is. Most word processors can read and write RTF documents.

SaaS (Software as a Service)—A method of making software applications available over the Internet for a monthly or other periodic fee. In SaaS, the software is not installed on individual computers or networks; it is installed on the vendor's servers and accessed through a web browser. Other similar terms are hosted services and application service providers (ASPs).

screen sharing—A process generally defined as the ability to transmit the contents of your computer screen to the computers of one or more individuals.

silos (of information)—A reference to information stored in a separate program or space where it is not integrated with or accessible from other programs or sources.

SLA (Service-Level Agreement)—The portion of a technology service, usually a separate exhibit or attachment, in which the detailed support and service requirements are spelled out.

SMS (Short Message Service)—A communications protocol for exchanging short text messages between mobile phones that serves as the basis for text messaging. SMS is also used colloquially to describe text messages and text messaging of any kind.

social engineering—Using human interaction rather than technological operations to obtain confidential information, including passwords, by manipulating users so that they "volunteer" the information.

social networking—Websites and services that allow users to create, build, and manage online communities or networks of people who share similar interests and activities. Facebook (www.facebook.com) and LinkedIn (www.linkedin.com) are well-known and popular examples of social networking platforms.

spoofing—A security attack in which the attacker poses as another, trusted actor using falsified data to obtain sensitive information.

spyware—Software automatically installed on a user's computer without the user's knowledge or informed consent for the purpose of obtaining sensitive information or taking partial control of the user's computer.

SQL (Structured Query Language)—A widely used standard interactive and programming language for querying and modifying data and managing databases. Many collaboration tools are built on SQL relational databases.

SSL (Secure Sockets Layer)—A cryptographic protocol used to provide secure communications over the Internet for data transfers as part of web browsing and other Internet activities. SSL has been succeeded by TLS (Transport Layer Security), although the term "SSL" is still commonly used generically in referring to these types of protocols.

strong password—A hard-to-crack password generally consisting of a combination of eight or more characters including uppercase and lowercase letters, numbers, and symbols.

SWOT analysis—a strategic planning tool for evaluating a project or in a business venture by focusing on the internal and external strengths, weaknesses, opportunities, and threats associated with the project or business.

synchronous—Happening simultaneously or in real time; the opposite of asynchronous.

Track Changes—A document reviewing feature of Microsoft Office applications that allows users to identify and mark revisions to a document. Similar to "redlining."

Trojan horse—A form of spyware that allows an attacker to later take control of a user's computer without the user's knowledge.

VNC (Virtual Network Computing)—A graphical desktop-sharing system for remotely controlling another computer over the Internet or another network. VNC transmits only the keyboard and mouse activities of one computer to the other and relays screen updates back to the other computer.

VoIP (Voice over Internet Protocol)—The protocol optimized for transmission of voice over the Internet that enables Internet telephony.

Web 2.0—Commonly refers to a perceived second generation of websites and Internet usage, including hosted services and community sites designed for collaboration, sharing, and similar purposes. Another definition of Web 2.0 emphasizes using the Internet itself as an application platform through the use of AJAX and similar technologies. Web 2.0 is often characterized by the presence of user-generated content. Wikis and social networking sites are often given as examples of Web 2.0 sites.

web browser—A software program (most commonly Internet Explorer or Firefox) that lets a user view and interact with web pages and other information on the Internet.

webinar (or teleseminar)—A live meeting or seminar presented over the Internet (or by conference call).

web parts—Modules that implement a specified function, such as a task list, discussion board, calendar, or shared document area.

widget—A small piece of third-party code that can be incorporated into a web page to produce specific results. For example, a weather widget could be placed on a web page so visitors to the page would see current weather information.

wiki—A simple database program, often hosted on the Internet, that allows users to view and easily create, edit, and link web pages.

Wikitext—A simplified markup language used as an alternative to HTML in connection with wikis.

XHTML (Extensible HyperText Markup Language)—A markup language similar to HTML, but with stricter requirements so that it also conforms to XML syntax.

XML (Extensible Markup Language)—A general-purpose markup language in which users can define their own tags. XML is used to structure data and separates content from its display, making it a flexible medium for delivering information.

Appendix 2:
Collaboration Resources

To learn more about the collaboration strategies and tools we mention in this book, we recommend the following books, websites, and other resources.

Recommended Books on Collaboration

The Collaboration Challenge, by James E. Austin (Jossey-Bass, 2000)

Creative Collaboration: Simple Tools for Inspired Teamwork (Fifty-Minute Series), by Bruce Honig (Crisp Learning, 2003)

The Culture of Collaboration, by Evan Rosen (Red Ape Publishing, 2007)

How to Make Collaboration Work: Powerful Ways to Build Consensus, Solve Problems, and Make Decisions, by David Straus and Thomas C. Layton (Berrett-Koehler Publishers, 2002)

Managing Virtual Teams: Getting the Most from Wikis, Blogs, and Other Collaborative Tools (Wordware Applications Library), by Brenda Huettner, M. Katherine Brown, and Char James-Tanny (Worldware Publishing, Inc., 2007)

Managing Without Walls: Maximize Success with Virtual, Global, and Cross-cultural Teams, by Colleen Garton and Kevin Wegryn (Mc Press, 2006)

Mastering Virtual Teams: Strategies, Tools, and Techniques That Succeed (Jossey Bass Business and Management Series), by Deborah L. Duarte and Nancy Tennant Snyder (Jossey-Bass, 2000)

Radical Collaboration: Five Essential Skills to Overcome Defensiveness and Build Successful Relationships, by James W. Tamm and Ronald J. Luyet (Collins, 2004)

Teaching an Anthill to Fetch: Developing Collaborative Intelligence @ Work, by Stephen James Joyce (Mighty Small Books, 2007)

Virtual Teams: People Working Across Boundaries with Technology, Second Edition, by Jessica Lipnack and Jeffrey Stamps (Wiley, 2000)

Virtual Teams That Work: Creating Conditions for Virtual Team Effectiveness, by Cristina B. Gibson and Susan G. Cohen (Jossey-Bass, 2003)

Wikinomics: How Mass Collaboration Changes Everything, by Don Tapscott and Anthony D. Williams (Portfolio Hardcover, 2006)

Resources by Part and Chapter

Part II: Getting Started

Chapter 2: Collaboration at the Crossroads

"The Collaboration Continuum," Optimize, November 2001, by C.K. Prahalad and Dr. Venkatram Ramaswamy (http://www.providersedge.com/docs/km_articles/ The_Collaboration_Continuum.pdf)

"Enabling an Efficient, Collaborative Law Firm with an Intelligent Information Network," Cisco Systems, Inc., October 2003 (http://www.cisco.com/web/ strategy/legal/law_firm.html)

"The Future Law Office: Going Virtual," Law Practice, January/February 2004, by Ron Friedmann (http://www.prismlegal.com/index.php?option=content&task= view&id=62)

Wikipedia on "Collaboration," Wikipedia (http://en.wikipedia.org/wiki/ Collaboration)

Chapter 3: Collaboration Inside the Firm

"Promoting Internal Collaboration with an Enterprise Wiki," *Peer to Peer,* August 2007, by Monroe Horn (http://www.iltanet.org/communications/article.aspx?nvl D=000000010805&snvID=000000010805&h4ID=000001003305)

"Social Networks and Partners' Desks," Adam Smith, Esq., October 12, 2007, by Bruce MacEwen (http://www.bmacewen.com/blog/archives/2007/10/partners_ desks_and_the_im.html)

"Social Space and Social Networks Inside a Law Firm," KM Space, October 22, 2007, by Doug Cornelius (http://kmspace.blogspot.com/2007/10/social-space -and-social-networks-inside.html)

Chapter 4: Collaboration Outside the Firm

DuPont Legal Model (http://www.dupontlegalmodel.com)

Chapter 5: First Steps

Being Effective with Collaboration Blog, by Michael Sampson (http://www .michaelsampson.net/)

Cisco Collaboration Blog, Cisco Systems, Inc. (http://blogs.cisco.com/ collaboration/)

The Collaboration Blog, Collaborative Strategies (http://collaborate.com/cs_evl/ collab.php)

Collaboration Blog, The Gilbane Group (http://gilbane.com/collaboration/)

"Elements of Collaboration," Mindquarry, by Lars Treiloff (http://www
.mindquarry.com/community/articles/elements-collaboration)

MetaCollab (A collaborative resource on collaboration) (http://collaboration.wikia
.com/wiki/Main_Page)

"Spotlight on Collaboration Technologies (Theme Issue)," *Peer to Peer,* August
2007 (http://www.iltanet.org/communications/archive.aspx?nvID=000000010805
&snvID=000000011005)

"Work Together: 60+ Collaborative Tools for Groups," Mashable, July 22, 2007, by
Sean P. Aune (http://mashable.com/2007/07/22/online-collaboration/)

Brainstorming Resources

Brainstorming: Creative Problem Solving from MindTools.com, http://www
.mindtools.com/brainstm.html

Brainstorming Techniques Resource Center, http://www.innovationtools.com/
Resources/brainstorming.asp

Instant Creativity: Simple Techniques to Ignite Innovation & Problem Solving, by
Brian Clegg and Paul Birch (Kogan Page, 2007)

*The Mind Map Book: How to Use Radiant Thinking to Maximize Your Brain's
Untapped Potential,* Tony and Barry Buzan (Plume, 1996)

ThinkerToys: A Handbook of Creative-Thinking Techniques, by Michael Michalko
(Ten Speed Press, 2006)

Wikipedia: Mind Map, http://en.wikipedia.org/wiki/Mind_map

Part III: Collaborating on Documents, Online and Off

Chapter 6: The Benefits of Improved Document Collaboration and Using Document Collaboration Tools

"Spotlight on Collaboration Technologies (Theme Issue)," *Peer to Peer,* August
2007 (http://www.iltanet.org/communications/archive.aspx?nvID=000000010805
&snvID=000000011005)

"Time for Lawyers to Collaborate in Real Time," *Law Technology News,* June 8,
2007, by Brett Burney (http://www.law.com/jsp/legaltechnology/pubArticleLT
.jsp?id=1181207138704)

Chapter 7: Basic Collaboration on Documents

A special thank you to Dan Woodruff, Vice President and Managing Counsel at
MasterCard International, Inc. for sharing his ideas on using the table approach
to collaborate on documents.

Special Edition Using Microsoft® Office Word 2007, by Faithe Wempen (Que Publishing, 2007)

"Staying on Track with Track Changes," *Law Practice Today,* March 2007, by Dennis Kennedy and Tom Mighell (http://www.abanet.org/lpm/lpt/articles/slc03071
.shtml)

"Track Changes While You Edit," Microsoft Office Online (http://office.microsoft
.com/en-us/word/HA012186901033.aspx)

Word 2003 for Law Firms, by Donna Payne (Payne Consulting Group, Inc., 2004)

Word 2007: The Missing Manual, by Chris Grover (Pogue Press, 2007)

Chapter 8: Creating a Document Online—Getting Started with the Major Players

Google Powered: Productivity with Online Tools, by Jerri L. Ledford (Wiley, 2007)

How to Do Everything with Google Tools, by Donna Baker (McGraw-Hill Osborne
Media, 2007)

"My Office 2.0 Setup," Office 2.0 Database (http://o20db.com/db/setup/)

"Online Office Suites," Wikipedia (http://en.wikipedia.org/wiki/List_of_office_
suites#Online_office_suites)

"Web Office Suites: Who's Leading the Pack," ReadWriteWeb, June 19, 2007, by
Richard MacManus (http://www.readwriteweb.com/archives/web_office_suite_
comparison.php)

"Video: Google Docs in Plain English," Common Craft, LLC, September 17, 2007
(http://www.commoncraft.com/video-googledocs)

Chapter 9: Working Simultaneously on a Document

Google Apps Administrator Guide: A Private-Label Web Workspace, by David W.
Boles (Course Technology PTR, 2007)

"Google Docs Tour," Google Docs (http://www.google.com/google-d-s/tour1.html)

Google Powered: Productivity with Online Tools, by Jerri L. Ledford (Wiley, 2007)

"Video: Google Docs in Plain English," Common Craft, LLC, September 17, 2007
(http://www.commoncraft.com/video-googledocs)

Chapter 10: Hidden Dangers, Security and Metadata

"Beyond Data About Data: The Litigator's Guide to Metadata," CraigBall.com, 2005,
by Craig Ball (http://www.craigball.com/metadata.pdf)

Beyond Fear, by Bruce Schneier (Springer, 2006)

Computer Security Basics, by Rick Lehtinen (O'Reilly Media, Inc., 2006)

*Essential Computer Security: Everyone's Guide to Email, Internet, and Wireless Secu-
rity,* by Tony Bradley (Syngress, 2006)

Information Security for Lawyers and Law Firms, by Sharon D. Nelson, David K.
Isom, and John W. Simek, editors (American Bar Association, 2006)

"Mining the Value from Metadata," Discovery Resources, January 2006, by Dennis
Kennedy, Tom Mighell and Evan Schaeffer (http://www.discoveryresources
.org/04_om_thinkingED_0601.html)

"The Mysterious World of Metadata," DennisKennedy.com, January 2005, by Dennis Kennedy (http://www.denniskennedy.com/blog/2005/10/the_mysterious_
world_of_metada.html)

Secrets and Lies: Digital Security in a Networked World, by Bruce Schneier (Wiley,
2004)

Part IV: Collaboration on Cases, Transactions, and Projects

Chapter 11: The Benefits of Collaboration in Lawsuits and Transactions

"Enabling an Efficient, Collaborative Law Firm with an Intelligent Information Network," Cisco Systems, Inc. (http://www.cisco.com/web/strategy/legal/law_firm .html)

"Spotlight on Collaboration Technologies (Theme Issue)," *Peer to Peer,* August 2007 (http://www.iltanet.org/communications/archive.aspx?nvID=000000010805 &snvID=000000011005)

Chapter 12: Instant Collaboration—From Conference Calls to IM

"Communication Tools: Make Them Simple and Ubiquitous or They Won't Be Used," How to Save the World, May 29, 2007, by David Pollard (http://blogs .salon.com/0002007/2007/05/29.html#a1879)

"Conference Call Etiquette," Management for the Rest of Us, by Lindsay Swinton (http://www.mftrou.com/conference-call-etiquette.html)

"Guide to Collaborationg Online," The Cochrane Collaboration (http://www .cochrane.org/resources/guide_to_online_collaboration.htm)

Moms' Survival Guide to Instant Messaging, by Mary B. Braun (Sun Prairie Moms, LLC, 2004)

"The Strongest Links: Instant Messaging Resources," *Law Practice Today,* September 2005, by Dennis Kennedy and Tom Mighell (http://www.abanet.org/lpm/lpt/ articles/slc09051.html)

Chapter 13: How to Hold a Meeting on the Internet

Challenges in Virtual Collaboration: Videoconferencing, Audioconferencing and Computer—Mediated Communications, by Lynne Wainfan (RAND Corporation, 2005)

"Remote PC Access Tools: A Mini-Guide," Master New Media, March 18, 2007, by Robin Good and Livia Iacolare (http://www.masternewmedia.org/ news/2007/03/18/remote_pc_access_tools_a.htm)

Smart Videoconferencing: New Habits for Virtual Meetings, by Janelle Barlow (Berett-Koehler Publishers, 2002)

The Web Conferencing Book: Understand the Technology, Choose the Right Vendors, Software, and Equipment, Start Saving Time and Money Today, by Sue Spielman and Liz Winfeld (AMACOM/American Management Association, 2003)

The Web Conferencing Imperative for Collaboration, Productivity, and Training, by Henry E. Liebling and Ruth Ann Forrester (Strategic Business and Technology Alliances, Inc., 2007)

Voice and Video Conferencing Fundamentals, by Scott Firestone, Thiya Ramalingam and Steve Fry (Cisco Press, 2007)

Chapter 14: Simple Project Management—Basecamp

Absolute Beginner's Guide to Project Management, by Greg Horine (Que Publishing, 2005)

"Basecamp Tour," Basecamp (http://www.basecamphq.com/tour)

"Basecamp," Wikipedia (http://en.wikipedia.org/wiki/Basecamp_%28software%29)

"Lawyers as Accidental Project Managers," Legal Project Management System, by Grant Collingsworth (http://www.mmmlaw.com/articles/article_318.pdf)

Rule the Web: How to Do Anything and Everything on the Internet—Better, Faster, Easier, by Mark Frauenfelder (St. Martin's Griffin, 2007)

The Fast Forward MBA in Project Management, by Eric Verzuh (Wiley, 1999)

Chapter 15: Setting Up a Simple Extranet or Deal Room

"Extranet Basics," DennisKennedy.com, October 30, 2005, by Dennis Kennedy (http://www.denniskennedy.com/blog/2005/10/extranet_basics_taking_a_step.html)

"Online Storage: 80+ File Hosting and Storage Sites," Mashable, July 28, 2007, by Sean P. Aune (http://mashable.com/2007/07/28/online-storage/)

The Lawyer's Guide to Extranets: Breaking Down Walls, Building Client Connections, by Douglas Simpson and Mark Tamminga (American Bar Association, 2003)

Part V: Commonly Used Collaboration Platforms

Chapter 16: Email as a Collaboration Platform

E-Mail: A Write It Well Guide—How to Write and Manage E-Mail in the Workplace, by Janis Fisher Chan (Write It Well, 2005)

The Hamster Revolution: How to Manage Your Email Before It Manages You, by Mike Song, Vicki Halsey, Tim Burress and Ken Blanchard (Berett-Koehler Publishers, 2007)

Send: The Essential Guide to Email for Office and Home, by David Shipley and Will Schwalbe (Knopf, 2007)

"Taming the Email Tiger," DennisKennedy.com, October 14, 2005, by Dennis Kennedy (http://www.denniskennedy.com/blog/2005/10/taming_the_email_tiger_article.html)

"Ten Habits of Highly Effective Emailers," DennisKennedy.com, October 13, 2005, by Dennis Kennedy (http://www.denniskennedy.com/blog/2005/10/ten_habits_of_highly_effective.html)

Chapter 17: Sharepoint

Beginning SharePoint 2007: Building Team Solutions with MOSS, by Amanda Murphy and Shane Perran (Wrox, 2007)

Creating Client Extranets with SharePoint 2003, by Mark Gerow (Apress, 2006)

Microsoft SharePoint 2007 Unleashed, by Michael Noel and Colin Spence

SharePoint 2007 and Office Development Expert Solutions, by Randy Holloway, Andrej Kyselica and Steve Caravajal (Wrox, 2007)

"SharePoint 2007 at Sheppard Mullin," Caselines, August 23, 2007, by David Hobbie (http://caselines.blogspot.com/2007/08/last-ilta-session-sharepoint-2007-at.html)

SharePoint 2007: The Definitive Guide, by James Pyles, Christopher Buechler, Bob Fox, and Murray Gordon (O'Reilly Media, Inc., 2007)

SharePoint 2007 User's Guide: Learning Microsoft's Collaboration and Productivity Platform, by Seth Bates and Tony Smith (Apress, 2007)

"SharePointPedia," Microsoft (http://sharepoint.microsoft.com/pedia/Pages/Home.aspx)

Chapter 18: Collaborating Inside and Outside the Office: Intranets and Extranets

Corporate Portals: Revolutionizing Information Access to Increase Productivity and Drive the Bottom Line, by Heidi Collins (AMACOM/American Management Association, 2000)

eCave (http://www.ecave.net/)

"Extranets 2.0: Using Extranets to Build Client Relationships," *Law Technology Today,* May 2007, by John C. Tredennick, Jr. (http://www.abanet.org/lpm/ltt/articles/vol1/is3/Using_Extranets_to_Build_Client_Relationships.shtml)

"Implementing Large-scale Extranets," Law.com, November 19, 2007, by Mark Gerow (http://www.law.com/jsp/legaltechnology/pubArticleLT.jsp?id=1195207452210)

Intranets for Info Pros, by Mary Lee Kennedy and Jane Dysart (Information Today, Inc., 2007)

"Law Firm Collaboration Via Extranets," LLRX, April 1, 2002, by Mila Bartos (http://www.llrx.com/features/lextranet.htm)

The Law Firm Intranet Blog (http://lawfirmintranet.wordpress.com/)

The Lawyer's Guide to Extranets: Breaking Down Walls, Building Client Connections, by Douglas Simpson and Mark Tamminga (American Bar Association, 2003)

The Lawyer's Guide to Marketing on the Internet, Third Edition, by Gregory H. Siskind, Deborah McMurray and Rick Klau (American Bar Association, 2007)

Chapter 19: Adobe Acrobat

Acrobat for Legal Professionals Blog, Adobe (http://blogs.adobe.com/acrolaw/)

"Acrobat Solutions for Legal Professionals," Adobe (http://www.adobe.com/products/acrobat/solutions/legal/)

Adobe Acrobat 8 Classroom in a Book, by Adobe Creative Team (Adobe Press, 2007)

Adobe Acrobat 8 PDF Bible, by Ted Padova (Wiley, 2007)

How to Do Everything with Adobe Acrobat 8, by Doug Sahlin (McGraw-Hill Osborne Media, 2007)

The Lawyer's Guide to Adobe Acrobat, Third Edition, by David L. Masters (American Bar Association, 2008)

PDF for Lawyers Blog (http://www.pdfforlawyers.com/)

Chapter 20: Wikis—Web Collaboration

"Legal Wikis Are Bound to Wow You," *Legal Technology News,* May 7, 2007, by Robert Ambrogi (http://www.law.com/jsp/ihc/PubArticleIHC.jsp?id=1178541412778)

Professional Wikis, by Mark S. Choate (Wrox, 2007)

"Promoting Internal Collaboration with an Enterprise Wiki," *Peer to Peer,* August 2007, by Monroe Horn (http://www.iltanet.org/communications/article.aspx?nvID=000000010805&snvID=000000010805&h4ID=000001003305)

"The Strongest Links: Wikis in the Legal Profession," *Law Practice Today,* February 2007, by Dennis Kennedy and Tom Mighell (http://www.abanet.org/lpm/lpt/articles/slc02071.shtml)

"Video: Wikis in Plain English," Common Craft LLC, May 29, 2007 (http://www.commoncraft.com/video-wikis-plain-english)

Wikinomics: How Mass Collaboration Changes Everything, by Don Tapscott and
   Anthony D. Williams (Portfolio Hardcover, 2006)
WikiMatrix (http://www.wikimatrix.org)
Wikipatterns, by Stewart Mader (Wiley, 2007)
WikiPatterns (http://www.wikipatterns.com)

Chapter 21: Other Web 2.0 Collaboration Tools

Dion Hinchcliffe's Web 2.0 Blog (http://web2.socialcomputingmagazine.com/)
"Does Web 2.0 Point Us Toward Law 2.0?" *Law Practice Today,* January 2006
   (http://www.abanet.org/lpm/lpt/articles/tch01061.html)
ReadWriteWeb Blog (http://www.readwriteweb.com/)
Real Lawyers Have Blogs, by Kevin O'Keefe (http://kevin.lexblog.com/)
"The Strongest Links: Web 2.0," *Law Practice Today,* January 2006, by Dennis Ken-
   nedy and Tom Mighell (http://www.abanet.org/lpm/lpt/articles/slc01061.html)
"Web 2.0 collection," by Ed Yourdon and collaborators worldwide (http://docs
   .google.com/TeamPresent?docid=dd2trp3s_0tj8txc)
Web 2.0 Patterns: What entrepreneurs and information architects need to know, by
   Duane Nickull, Dion Hinchcliffe and James Governor (Adobe Dev Library, 2008)
Unleashing Web 2.0: From Concepts to Creativity, by Gottfried Vossen and Stephan
   Hagemann (Morgan Kaufmann, 2007)

Chapter 22: Specialized and High-End Collaboration Platforms

"The Best Collaboration Tools," *TechMagazine,* October 1, 2007 (http://
   techmagazine.ws/the-best-collaboration-tools/)
Collaboration Loop (http://www.collaborationloop.com/index.php)
"Collaboration Software: Best Directories," The Bumble Bee, August 12, 2007, by
   Ken Thompson (http://www.bioteams.com/2007/08/12/collaboration_software_
   best.html#more)
"Collaboration Tools Category," Download.com (http://www.download.com/3150
   -2654_4-0.html?tag=catat.8)
Effective Knowledge Management for Law Firms, by Matthew Parsons (Oxford Uni-
   versity Press, USA, 2004)
"Elements of Collaboration," Mindquarry, by Lars Trieloff (http://www.mindquarry
   .com/community/articles/elements-collaboration)
"Enterprise 2.0," Wikipedia (http://en.wikipedia.org/wiki/Enterprise_2.0)
"The Great Software List," Access Foundation (http://www.anova.org/software/
   index.html)
"LifeHacker: Collaboration Tools," LifeHacker (http://lifehacker.com/software/
   collaboration-tools/)
"List of Collaborative Software," Wikipedia (http://en.wikipedia.org/wiki/List_of_
   collaborative_software)
Microsoft Office Project 2007 Step by Step, by Carl Chatfield and Timothy Johnson
   (Microsoft Press, 2007)
"Revolutionizing Client Relations with CaseMap's New Reportbooks Feature,"
   DennisKennedy.com, October 17, 2005, by Dennis Kennedy (http://www
   .denniskennedy.com/blog/2005/10/revolutionizing_client_relatio.html)

"Spotlight on Collaboration Technologies (Theme Issue)," *Peer to Peer,* August 2007 (http://www.iltanet.org/communications/archive.aspx?nvlD=000000010805 &snvlD=000000011005)

"Social and Enterprise Groupware Primer," ReadWriteWeb, November 12, 2006, by Ebrahim Ezzy (http://www.readwriteweb.com/archives/groupware_primer.php)

Part VI: Developing a Collaboration Strategy

Chapter 23: Must-Have Features for Your Collaboration Tools

"Checklist: What to Look for When Choosing Collaboration Software," Aconex (http://www.aconex.com/Media/docs/CollaborationChecklist-d00b3a03-5204 -44d8-8901-acf21f56b662.pdf)

Chapter 24: Free vs. Pay

"Collaboration Tools Category," Download.com (http://www.download.com/ 3150-2654_4-0.html?tag=catat.8)

DVD: Revolution OS, by J. T. S. Moore (Wonderview Productions, 2003)

Open Source Initiative (http://www.opensource.org/)

Open Sources 2.0: The Continuing Evolution, by Chris DiBona, Mark Stone, and Danese Cooper (O'Reilly Media, Inc., 2005)

SourceForge (http://www.sourceforge.net)

The Success of Open Source, by Steven Weber (Harvard University Press, 2005)

Chapter 25: Involving Clients in Your Decisions and Choices

DuPont Legal Model (http://www.dupontlegalmodel.com/)

Law Partnering Institute (http://www.lawpartnering.com/index.tmpl)

"Placing Your Bet on Client-Driven Technologies," DennisKennedy.com, October 14, 2005, by Dennis Kennedy (http://www.denniskennedy.com/archives/000883 .html)

Chapter 26: Determining Which Factors Will Drive Your Strategic Planning

Creating Dominance: Winning Strategies for Law Firms, by H. Edward Wesemann (AuthorHouse, 2005)

The Lawyer's Guide to Strategic Planning, by Thomas C. Grella and Michael L. Hudkins (American Bar Association, 2004)

60 Minute Strategic Plan, by John E. Johnson and Anne-Marie Smith (60 Minute Strategic Plan, 2006)

Part VII: Practical Issues, Tips, and Techniques

Chapter 27: Getting the Word Out to Your Collaborators

How to Do Everything with Google Tools, by Donna Baker (McGraw-Hill Osborne Media, 2007)

RSS and Atom: Understanding and Implementing Content Feeds and Syndication, by Heinz Wittenbrink (Packt Publishing 2005)

"RSS Resources You Can Use," *Law Practice Today,* November 2006, by Dennis Kennedy and Tom Mighell (http://www.abanet.org/lpm/lpt/articles/slc11061.shtml)

Syndicating Web Sites with RSS Feeds For Dummies, by Ellen Finkelstein (For Dummies, 2005)

"Top Ten Uses for RSS in Law Firms," Vancouver Law Librarian Blog, September 26, 2006, by Steve Matthews (http://vancouverlawlib.blogspot.com/2006/09/top-10-uses-for-rss-in-law-firms.html)

"Video: RSS in Plain English," Common Craft LLC, April 23, 2007 (http://www.commoncraft.com/rss_plain_english)

Chapter 28: Ethics, Metadata, and Other Practical Issues

"ABA Formal Opinion 99-413," Standing Committee on Ethics and Professional Responsibility, American Bar Association, March 10, 1999 (http://www.abanet.org/cpr/fo99-413.html)

Legal Ethics in a Nutshell, by Ronald D. Rotunda (Thomson West, 2006)

"More Data on Metadata," *YourABA,* January 2006, by Peter Geraghty (http://www.abanet.org/media/youraba/200612/article11.html)

"The Strongest Links: Ethics," *Law Practice Today,* December 2005, by Dennis Kennedy and Tom Mighell (http://www.abanet.org/lpm/lpt/articles/slc12051.html)

Chapter 29: Ownership, Control, and Other Legal Issues

Edison in the Boardroom: How Leading Companies Realize Value from Their Intellectual Assets, by Julie L. Davis and Suzanne S. Harrison (Wiley, 2001)

Einstein in the Boardroom: Moving Beyond Intellectual Capital to I-Stuff, by Suzanne S. Harrison and Patrick H. Sullivan (Wiley, 2006)

Law Firm Partnership Agreements, by Leslie D. Corwin and Arthur J. Ciampi (Law Journal Press, 1998)

Mind Over Matter: Why Intellectual Capital Is the Chief Source of Wealth, by Ronald J. Baker (Wiley, 2007)

Chapter 30: Potential Pitfalls of Collaboration— Where to Be Wary

Information Security for Lawyers and Law Firms, by Sharon D. Nelson, David K. Isom, and John W. Simek, editors (American Bar Association, 2006)

Chapter 31: Implementing Collaboration Tools

Being Effective with Collaboration Blog, by Michael Sampson (http://www.michaelsampson.net/)

"Communication Tools: Make Them Simple and Ubiquitous or They Won't Be Used," How to Save the World, May 29, 2007, by David Pollard (http://blogs.salon.com/0002007/2007/05/29.html#a1879)

"Elements of Collaboration," Mindquarry, by Lars Trieloff (http://www.mindquarry.com/community/articles/elements-collaboration)

The First Great Myth of Legal Management Is that It Exists: Tough Issues for Law Firm Managing Partners and Administrators, by H. Edward Wesemann (AuthorHouse, 2004)

Implementing Your Strategic Plan: How to Turn "Intent" into Effective Action for Sustainable Change, by C. Davis Fogg (BookSurge Publishing, 2006)

"Selecting and Implementing the Best Collaboration Tools for Your Practice," *Law Practice Today,* October 2007, by Stewart Levin (http://www.abanet.org/lpm/lpt/articles/mba10071.shtml)

"The Strongest Links: Outsourcing," *Law Practice Today,* April 2006, by Dennis Kennedy and Tom Mighell (http://www.abanet.org/lpm/lpt/articles/slc04061.shtml)

The Successful Lawyer: Powerful Strategies for Transforming Your Practice, by Gerald A. Riskin (American Bar Association, 2005)

Part VIII: Conclusion

Chapter 32: Recommended Choices for Common Scenarios— From Solos to Large Firms

"Selecting and Implementing the Best Collaboration Tools for your Practice," *Law Practice Today,* October 2007, by Stewart Levin (http://www.abanet.org/lpm/lpt/articles/mba10071.shtml)

Chapter 33: Creating a Culture of Collaboration

Being Effective with Collaboration Blog, by Michael Sampson (http://www.michaelsampson.net/)

The Bumble Bee Blog, by Ken Thompson (http://www.bioteams.com/)

"Collaboration Is about People," CM Briefing, December 13, 2007, by James Robertson (http://www.steptwo.com.au/papers/cmb_collabpeople/index.html)

Collaborative Thinking Blog (http://mikeg.typepad.com/perceptions/)

Common Knowledge: How Companies Thrive by Sharing What They Know, by Nancy M. Dixon (Harvard Business School Press, 2000)

"Communication Tools: Make Them Simple and Ubiquitous or They Won't Be Used," How to Save the World, May 29, 2007, by David Pollard (http://blogs.salon.com/0002007/2007/05/29.html#a1879)

The Culture of Collaboration, by Evan Rosen (Red Ape Publishing, 2007)

First Among Equals: How to Manage a Group of Professionals, by Patrick J. McKenna and David H. Maister (Free Press, 2002)

Managing Interactively: Executing Business Strategy, Improving Communication, and Creating a Knowledge-Sharing Culture, by Mary E. Boone (McGraw-Hill, 2000)

Chapter 34: The Future of Collaboration in the Practice of Law

"The Clementi Report," Department for Constitutional Affairs, December 2004, by Sir David Clementi (http://www.dca.gov.uk/legalsys/lsreform.htm)

Creating Dominance: Winning Strategies for Law Firms, by H. Edward Wesemann (AuthorHouse, 2005)

"Does Web 2.0 Point Us Toward Law 2.0?" *Law Practice Today,* January 2006 (http://www.abanet.org/lpm/lpt/articles/tch01061.html)

DuPont Legal Model (http://www.dupontlegalmodel.com/)

eCave (http://www.ecave.net/)

"The End of Lawyers?" *The Times,* October 23, 2007, by Richard Susskind (http://www.timesonline.co.uk/tol/system/topicRoot/The_End_of_Lawyers/)

The Firm of the Future: A Guide for Accountants, Lawyers, and Other Professional Services, by Paul Dunn and Ronald J. Baker (Wiley, 2003)

"The Fully Connected Law Firm," DennisKennedy.com, December 13, 2005, by Dennis Kennedy (http://www.denniskennedy.com/blog/2005/12/the_fully_connected_law_firm_a.html)

The Future of Law: Facing the Challenges of Information Technology, by Richard Susskind (Oxford University Press, USA, 1998)

Managing the Modern Law Firm: New Challenges, New Perspectives, by Laura Empson (Oxford University Press, 2007)

"Outside Counsel Inside Counsel Partnering: Through Technology to the Virtual Law Firm," LLRX, February 17, 2003, by Dennis Kennedy (http://www.llrx.com/features/counseltech.htm)

Transforming the Law: Essays on Technology, Justice, and the Legal Marketplace, by Richard Susskind (Oxford University Press, USA, 2001)

Appendix 3:
Tools by Category

Conference Calls

AccuConference (http://www.accuconference.com)
AT Conference (http://www.atconference.com)
Budget Conferencing (http://www.budgetconferencing.com)
Conference Calls Unlimited (http://www.conferencecallsunlimited.com)
ConferenceCall.com (http://www.conferencecall.com)
ECI Conferencing (http://www.calleci.com)
FreeConference.com (http://www.freeconference.com)
Global Conference (http://www.globalconference.com)
Raindance (http://www.raindance.com)
Star Conferencing (http://www.starconferencing.com)
Teleconference.com (http://www.teleconference.com)

Email

9cays (http://9cays.com)
Google Groups (http://groups.google.com)
MailMan (http://www.list.org/)
Majordomo (http://www.greatcircle.com/majordomo/)
Prolify (http://www.prolify.com)
Sperry Email Add-In Tools (http://www.sperrysoftware.com/Outlook)
Yahoo! Groups (http://groups.yahoo.com)

Extranets

AMS Legal (http://ams-legal.com/)
Basecamp (http://www.basecamp.com)
Hosted SharePoint Services (check your ISP; multiple providers)

Merrill Lextranet (http://www.legalintranet.com/)
Microsoft Windows SharePoint Services (http://office.microsoft.com/en-us/
   sharepointtechnology/FX100503841033.aspx)
NetDocuments from LexisNexis (http://law.lexisnexis.com/net-documents)
TrialNet (http://www.trialnet.com)
Xerdict Technologies (http://www.xerdict.com/)

Instant Messaging

Personal IM Clients

AOL Instant Messenger (http://aimpro.premiumservices.aol.com/)
Apple iChat (http://www.apple.com/macosx/features/ichat/)—Mac only
Gizmo Project (http://www.gizmoproject.com)
Google Talk (http://www.google.com/talk)
ICQ (http://www.icq.com)
ineen (http://www.ineen.com/)
Jabbin (http://www.jabbin.com/)
KoolIM (http://koolim.com/)
Meebo (http://www.meebo.com)
Miranda IM (http://www.miranda-im.org/)
Trillian (http://www.trillian.com)
Windows Live Messenger (http://get.live.com/messenger/overview)
Yahoo! Messenger (http://messenger.yahoo.com/webmessengerpromo.php)
Skype (http://www.skype.com)

Enterprise Instant Messaging Clients

Akeni (http://www.akeni.com)
Jabber (http://www.jabber.com)
Lotus SameTime (http://www.ibm.com/developerworks/lotus/products/
   instantmessaging/)
Microsoft Windows Live (http://get.live.com/messenger/overview)
Openfire, by Jive Software (http://www.jivesoftware.com/products/openfire/)
Sonork (http://www.sonork.com/)

Metadata Removal Tools

iScrub (http://www.esqinc.com)
Payne's Metadata Assistant (http://www.payneconsulting.com)
WorkShare Protect (http://www.workshare.com)

Online Meeting Tools

Aspen Conferencing (http://www.aspenconferencing.com)
Convoq (http://www.convoq.com/)
eBLVD (http://eblvd.com/)

GatherPlace (http://www.gatherplace.net)
Glance (http://www.glance.net)
GoMeetNow (http://www.gomeetnow.com/)
GoToMeeting (http://www.gotomeeting.com)
HelpMeeting Presenter (http://www.hostpresentation.com/)
InstantPresenter (http://www.instantpresenter.com/)
LiveConference (http://www.liveconferencepro.com/)
MeetMeNow (http://www.meetmenow.com)
Microsoft LiveMeeting (http://office.microsoft.com/livemeeting)
Persony (http://www.persony.com)
PresenterNet (http://www.presenternet.com/)
Spreed (http://spreed.com/)
Vyew (http://vyew.com)
WebEx (http://www.webex.com)
Yugma (http://www.yugma.com)

Online Office Tools—Documents, Spreadsheets, and Presentations

Ajax13 (http://us.ajax13.com)
CuteFlow (http://www.cuteflow.org)
Google Apps (http://www.google.com)
Google Docs (http://docs.google.com)
Sheetster (http://www.sheetster.com)
Solodox (http://www.solodox.com)
SynchroEdit (http://www.synchroedit.com/)
ThinkFree (http://www.thinkfree.com)
Zoho Office (http://www.zoho.com)
Zoho Business (http://business.zoho.com)

Open Source Software

Firefox (http://www.mozilla.com/firefox/)
Thunderbird (http://www.mozilla.com/thunderbird)

PDF Creation and Management

Adobe Acrobat (http://www.adobe.com)

Project Management

ActiveCollab (http://www.activecollab.com)
Basecamp (http://www.basecamphq.com)

Central Desktop (http://www.centraldesktop.com)
GoPlan (http://goplan.info/)
Huddle (http://www.huddle.net/)
Microsoft Project (http://office.microsoft.com/en-us/project/)
Project360 (http://www.project360.com)
Project2Manage (http://www.project2manage.com/)
Solodox (http://www.solodox.com/)
Sosius (http://www.sosius.com)
Zoho Project (http://projects.zoho.com)

Redlining Tools

ChangePro (http://www.change-pro.com)
DiffDoc (http://www.softinterface.com)
DocuComp (http://www.docucomp.com)
WorkShare Professional (http://www.workshare.com)

Screen-Sharing Meeting Tools

Adobe Connect (http://www.adobe.com/products/connect)
BeamYourScreen (http://www.beamyourscreen.com)
BLive (http://www.blive.com/)
Bomgar (http://www.bomgar.com/)
Bosco's Screen Share (http://www.componentx.com/ScreenShare/)
CrossLoop (http://www.crossloop.com)
GoToAssist (http://www.gotoassist.com/)
Invitt (http://invitt.com/)
ISL Light (http://www.isllight.com)
NCH Software (http://www.nchsoftware.com)
Netviewer (http://www.netviewer.net/)
RealVNC (http://www.realvnc.com/)
ShareItNow (http://www.shareitnow.com/)

SharePoint Tools

eSentio Technologies (http://www.esentio.com/)
Handshake Software (http://www.handshakesoftware.com/)
Hubbard One (http://www.hubbardone.com/)
MindJet (http://www.mindjet.com)
SocialText (http://www.socialtext.com)
SV Technology (http://www.svtechnology.com/)
XMLaw (http://www.xmlaw.com/)

Specialized, High-End, and Alternative Collaboration Platforms

Amicus Attorney (http://www.amicusattorney.com)
CaseMap (http://www.casesoft.com)
Catalyst Secure (http://www.catalystsecure.com/)
Litera (http://www.litera.com)
Microsoft Office 2007 (http://office.microsoft.com)
Microsoft OneNote (http://office.microsoft.com/en-us/onenote/)
Microsoft Project (http://office.microsoft.com/en-us/project/)
PracticeMaster (http://www.practicemaster.com)
Time Matters (http://www.timematters.com)
WorkShare (http://www.workshare.com)

Wikis

Web Based

ClearWiki (http://www.clearwiki.com/)
EditMe (http://www.editme.com/)
Netcipia (http://www.netcipia.com)
Nexdo (http://www.nexdo.com/)
PBwiki (http://pbwiki.com/)
StikiPad (http://www.stikipad.com/)
ServerSideWiki (http://www.serversidewiki.com/)
tiddlyspot (http://tiddlyspot.com/)
TiddlyWiki (http://www.tiddlywiki.com/)
Wikia (http://www.wikia.com/)
Wikispaces (http://www.wikispaces.com/)

Enterprise

BrainKeeper (http://www.brainkeeper.com/)
Confluence (http://www.atlassian.com/software/confluence/)
eTouch Systems (http://www.etouch.net/home/)
instiki (http://instiki.org)
MindTouch (http://mindtouch.com)
Near-Time (http://www.near-time.net/)
Socialtext (http://www.socialtext.com)
TWiki (http://twiki.org/)

Web 2.0

Bookmarking

Del.icio.us (http://del.icio.us)
Yahoo MyWeb (http://myweb.yahoo.com)

Calendars

30 Boxes (http://30boxes.com/)
Airset (http://www.airset.com)
CalendarHub (http://www.calendarhub.com/)
Google Calendar (http://www.google.com/calendar)
Kiko (http://www.kiko.com/)
Now Software (http://www.nowsoftware.com/)
Planzo (http://www.planzo.com/)
Yahoo Calendar (http://www.yahoo.com/calendar)

File Sharing and Online Storage

Adobe Share (http://share.adobe.com)
Box.net (http://www.box.net)
Driveway (http://www.driveway.com/)
EatLime (http://www.eatlime.com)
.Mac (http://www.apple.com/dotmac/storage.html)
MailBigFile (http://www.mailbigfile.com)
MediaMax (http://www.mediamax.com/)
MegaUpload (http://www.megaupload.com/)
Microsoft Live Spaces (http://home.services.spaces.live.com/)
OmniDrive (http://www.omnidrive.com)
SendSpace (http://www.sendspace.com/)
TransferBigFiles (http://transferbigfiles.com/)
xDrive (http://www.xdrive.com)
YouSendIt (http://www.yousendit.com)

Mind Mapping

bubbl.us (http://bubbl.us/)
GroupSystems (http://www.groupsystems.com/)
Mind42 (http://www.mind42.com)
Mind Manager (http://www.mindjet.com)
MindMeister (http://www.mindmeister.com/)
Mindomo (http://www.mindomo.com/)
Wridea (http://www.wridea.com/)

Miscellaneous Web 2.0 Tools

GoogleDocDownload (http://1st-soft.net/gdd/googledocdownload.user.js)
Twitter (http://www.twitter.com)

RSS Tools and Newsreaders

FeedDemon (http://www.feeddemon.com)
Google Reader (http://www.google.com/reader)

Social Networking

CollectiveX (http://www.groupsites.com)
Facebook (http://www.facebook.com)
LinkedIn (http://www.linkedin.com)
Texas Bar Circle (https://texasbar.affinitycircles.com/)

Index

Selected Books from . . .
THE ABA LAW PRACTICE MANAGEMENT SECTION

The Essential Little Book of Great Lawyering
By James A. Durham
In a convenient, pocket-sized handbook, veteran marketer Jim Durham shares his secret on how to be a great lawyer. His core thesis is simple: being a great lawyer IS the best business development plan. You'll benefit from his wisdom and guidance as he communicates how to set the stage for greatness, the essence of great lawyering, the common characteristics of great lawyers, and more. He explains that being a great lawyer means that you truly understand your client's business. It's a classic pocketbook to share with your colleagues and members of your firm.

The Lawyer's Guide to Marketing on the Internet, Third Edition
By Gregory H. Siskind, Deborah McMurray, and Richard P. Klau
In today's competitive environment, it is critical to have a comprehensive online marketing strategy that uses all the tools possible to differentiate your firm and gain new clients. The Lawyer's Guide to Marketing on the Internet, in a completely updated and revised third edition, showcases practical online strategies and the latest innovations so that you can immediately participate in decisions about your firm's Web marketing effort. With advice that can be implemented by established and young practices alike, this comprehensive guide will be a crucial component to streamlining your marketing efforts.

The Lawyer's Field Guide to Effective Business Development
By William J. Flannery, Jr.
"In this wonderful book, Bill Flannery, who changed the legal marketplace forever, does what he's been doing so effectively throughout his extraordinary career—he teaches lawyers how to sell. How can you build your firm's business without it?"
—Richard S. Levick, Esq., President and CEO, Levick Strategic Communications

Long-term, profitable client relationships form the foundation for the enduring success of any law firm. Winning and retaining long-term, attractive clients doesn't happen by accident. In his new book, The Lawyer's Field Guide to Effective Business Development, renowned legal marketer Bill Flannery shares his practical approach to acquiring and refining the face-to-face skills necessary for winning and keeping valuable clients.

In a handy, pocket-sized format, this unique guidebook is designed so you can take it with you as you travel in search of new business. The chapters are organized chronologically to take you step by step from your initial search for clients through the process of building and maintaining long-term profitable client relationships.

The Electronic Evidence and Discovery Handbook: Forms, Checklists, and Guidelines
By Sharon D. Nelson, Bruce A. Olson, and John W. Simek
The use of electronic evidence has increased dramatically over the past few years, but many lawyers still struggle with the complexities of electronic discovery. This substantial book provides lawyers with the templates they need to frame their discovery requests and provides helpful advice on what they can subpoena. In addition to the ready-made forms, the authors also supply explanations to bring you up to speed on the electronic discovery field. The accompanying CD-ROM features over 70 forms, including, Motions for Protective Orders, Preservation and Spoliation Documents, Motions to Compel, Electronic Evidence Protocol Agreements, Requests for Production, Internet Services Agreements, and more. Also included is a full electronic evidence case digest with over 300 cases detailed!

The Lawyer's Guide to Extranets: Breaking Down Walls, Building Client Connections
By Douglas Simpson and Mark Tamminga
An extranet can be a powerful tool that allows law firms to exchange information and build relationships with clients. This new book shows you why extranets are the next step in client interaction and communications, and how you can effectively implement an extranet in any type of firm. This book will take you step-by-step through the issues of implementing an extranet, and how to plan and build one. You'll get real-world extranet case studies, and learn from the successes and failures of those who have gone before. Help your firm get ahead of the emerging technologies curve and discover the benefits of adopting this new information tool.

The Law Firm Associate's Guide to Personal Marketing and Selling Skills
By Catherine Alman MacDonagh and Beth Marie Cuzzone
This is the first volume in ABA's new groundbreaking Law Firm Associates Development Series, created to teach important skills that associates and other lawyers need to succeed at their firms, but that they may have not learned in law school. This volume focuses on personal marketing and sales skills. It covers creating a personal marketing plan, finding people within your target market, preparing for client meetings, "asking" for business, realizing marketing opportunities, keeping your clients, staying in touch with your network inside and outside the firm, and more. An accompanying trainer's manual illustrating how to best structure the sessions and use the book is available to firms to facilitate group training sessions.

Many law firms expect their new associates to hit the ground running when they are hired on. Although firms often take the time to bring these associates up to speed on client matters, they can be reluctant to invest the time needed to train them how to improve personal skills such as marketing. This book will serve as a brief, easy-to-digest primer for associates on how to develop and use marketing and selling techniques.

LawPracticeManagementSection
MARKETING • MANAGEMENT • TECHNOLOGY • FINANCE

The Lawyer's Guide to Marketing Your Practice, Second Edition

Edited by James A. Durham and Deborah McMurray

This book is packed with practical ideas, innovative strategies, useful checklists, and sample marketing and action plans to help you implement a successful, multi-faceted, and profit-enhancing marketing plan for your firm. Organized into four sections, this illuminating resource covers: Developing Your Approach; Enhancing Your Image; Implementing Marketing Strategies and Maintaining Your Program. Appendix materials include an instructive primer on market research to inform you on research methodologies that support the marketing of legal services. The accompanying CD-ROM contains a wealth of checklists, plans, and other sample reports, questionnaires, and templates—all designed to make implementing your marketing strategy as easy as possible!

The Lawyer's Guide to Increasing Revenue: Unlocking the Profit Potential in Your Firm

By Arthur G. Greene

Are you ready to look beyond cost-cutting and toward new revenue opportunities? Learn how you can achieve growth using the resources you already have at your firm. Discover the factors that affect your law firm's revenue production, how to evaluate them, and how to take specific action steps designed to increase your returns. You'll learn how to best improve performance and profitability in each of the key areas of your law firm, such as billable hours and rates, client relations and intake, collections and accounts receivable, technology, marketing, and others. Included with the book is a CD-ROM featuring sample policies, worksheets, plans, and documents designed to aid implementation of the ideas presented in the book. Let this resource guide you toward a profitable and sustainable future!

The Lawyer's Guide to Strategic Planning: Defining, Setting, and Achieving Your Firm's Goals

By Thomas C. Grella and Michael L. Hudkins

This practice-building resource is your guide to planning dynamic strategic plans and implementing them at your firm. You'll learn about the actual planning process and how to establish goals in key planning areas such as law firm governance, competition, opening a new office, financial management, technology, marketing and competitive intelligence, client development and retention, and more. The accompanying CD-ROM contains a wealth of policies, statements, and other sample documents. If you're serious about improving the way your firm works, increasing productivity, making better decisions, and setting your firm on the right course, this book is the resource you need.

The Successful Lawyer: Powerful Strategies for Transforming Your Practice

By Gerald A. Riskin

Available as a Book, Audio-CD Set, or Combination Package.

Global management consultant and trusted advisor to many of the world's largest law firms, Gerry Riskin goes beyond simple concept or theory and delivers a book packed with practical advice that you can implement right away. By using the principles found in this book, you can live out your dreams, embrace success, and awaken your firm to its full potential. Large law firm or small, managing partners and associates in every area of practice—all can benefit from the information contained in this book. With this book, you can attract what you need and desire into your life, get more satisfaction from your practice and your clients, and do so in a systematic, achievable way.

How to Start and Build a Law Practice, Platinum Fifth Edition

By Jay G Foonberg

This classic ABA bestseller has been used by tens of thousands of lawyers as the comprehensive guide to planning, launching, and growing a successful practice. It's packed with over 600 pages of guidance on identifying the right location, finding clients, setting fees, managing your office, maintaining an ethical and responsible practice, maximizing available resources, upholding your standards, and much more. You'll find the information you need to successfully launch your practice, run it at maximum efficiency, and avoid potential pitfalls along the way. If you're committed to starting—and growing—your own practice, this one book will give you the expert advice you need to make it succeed for years to come.

Flying Solo: A Survival Guide for Solo and Small Firm Lawyers, Fourth Edition

Edited by K. William Gibson

This fourth edition of this comprehensive guide includes practical information gathered from a wide range of contributors, including successful solo practitioners, law firm consultants, state and local bar practice management advisors, and law school professors. This classic ABA book first walks you through a step-by-step analysis of the decision to start a solo practice, including choosing a practice focus. It then provides tools to help you with financial issues including banking and billing; operations issues such as staffing and office location and design decisions; technology for the small law office; and marketing and client relations. Whether you're thinking of going solo, new to the solo life, or a seasoned practitioner, *Flying Solo* provides time-tested answers to real-life questions.

30-Day Risk-Free Order Form
Call Today! 1-800-285-2221
Monday–Friday, 7:30 AM – 5:30 PM, Central Time

Qty	Title	LPM Price	Regular Price	Total
_____	The Essential Little Book of Great Lawyering (5110579)	$ 9.95	$ 11.95	$_____
_____	The Lawyer's Guide to Marketing on the Internet, Third Edition (5110585)	74.95	84.95	$_____
_____	The Lawyer's Field Guide to Effective Business Development (5110578)	49.95	59.95	$_____
_____	The Electronic Evidence and Discovery Handbook: Forms, Checklists, and Guidelines (5110569)	99.95	129.95	$_____
_____	The Lawyer's Guide to Extranets: Breaking Down Walls, Building Client Connections (5110494)	59.95	69.95	$_____
_____	The Law Firm Associate's Guide to Personal Marketing and Selling Skills (5110582)	39.95	49.95	$_____
_____	Trainer's Manual for the Law Firm Associate's Guide to Personal Marketing and Selling Skills (5110581)	49.95	59.95	$_____
_____	The Lawyer's Guide to Marketing Your Practice, Second Edition (5110500)	79.95	89.95	$_____
_____	The Lawyer's Guide to Increasing Revenue (5110521)	59.95	79.95	$_____
_____	The Lawyer's Guide to Strategic Planning (5110520)	59.95	79.95	$_____
_____	The Successful Lawyer: Powerful Strategies for Transforming Your Practice (5110531)	64.95	84.95	$_____
_____	How to Start and Build a Law Practice, Platinum Fifth Edition (5110508)	57.95	69.95	$_____
_____	Flying Solo: A Survival Guide for Solo and Small Firm Lawyers, Fourth Edition (5110527)	79.95	99.95	$_____

*Postage and Handling	
$10.00 to $24.99	$5.95
$25.00 to $49.99	$9.95
$50.00 to $99.99	$12.95
$100.00 to $349.99	$17.95
$350 to $499.99	$24.95

**Tax
DC residents add 5.75%
IL residents add 9.00%

*Postage and Handling	$_____
**Tax	$_____
TOTAL	$_____

PAYMENT

❏ Check enclosed (to the ABA)

❏ Visa   ❏ MasterCard   ❏ American Express

_____
Account Number   Exp. Date   Signature

Name _____ Firm _____

Address _____

City _____ State _____ Zip _____

Phone Number _____ E-Mail Address _____

Guarantee
If—for any reason—you are not satisfied with your purchase, you may
return it within 30 days of receipt for a complete refund of the price of the
book(s). No questions asked!

Mail: ABA Publication Orders, P.O. Box 10892, Chicago, Illinois 60610-0892
♦ **Phone: 1-800-285-2221** ♦ **FAX: 312-988-5568**

E-Mail: abasvcctr@abanet.org ♦ **Internet: http://www.lawpractice.org/catalog**